INSPIRE / PLAN / DISCOVER / EXPERIENCE

PERU

DK EYEWITNESS

PERU

CONTENTS

DISCOVER PERU 6

Welcome to Peru........................ 8
Reasons to Love Peru 10
Explore Peru 14
Getting to Know Peru............... 16

Peru Itineraries.......................... 22
Peru Your Way........................... 36
A Year in Peru 66
A Brief History........................... 68

EXPERIENCE LIMA 76

3 Days in Lima 80

Lima Your Way 82

Central Lima............................ 88

Miraflores and San Isidro............ 104

Barranco................................... 116

Beyond the Center.................... 126

EXPERIENCE PERU 134

The Southern Coast 136

Arequipa, Canyons,
and Lake Titicaca................... 150

Cusco and the Sacred Valley 170

Central Sierra 196

Cordillera Blanca.............................206

The Northern Desert.................... 222

The Northern Highlands..............236

The Amazon Basin......................... 248

NEED TO KNOW 266

Before You Go........................... 268
Getting Around........................ 270
Practical Information................ 274

Index 276
Phrase Book.............................. 284
Acknowledgments..................... 287

Left: Hand-woven textiles in Písac market
Previous page: Turquoise lake in the Andes
Front cover: Ruins of the Inca Empire city on Huaynapicchu Mountain, Cusco

DISCOVER

Cusco and the Andes mountains

Welcome to Peru.............................8

Reasons to Love Peru..................10

Explore Peru...................................14

Getting to Know Peru..................16

Peru Itineraries............................22

Peru Your Way...............................36

A Year in Peru................................66

A Brief History...............................68

WELCOME TO
PERU

Peru overflows with riches: steaming Amazon jungle, scorched coastal desert, fascinating ancient cultures, a fabulous array of wildlife, and the legendary Inca ruins of Machu Picchu. Whatever your dream trip to Peru entails, this DK Eyewitness travel guide will prove the perfect companion.

1 Surfer riding a wave at Punta Hermosa, Lima.

2 Arequipa's Monasterio de Santa Catalina.

3 Dancers at a Candelaria folk parade in Lima.

4 Cobbled road at sunset in Ollantaytambo, Cusco.

Stretching from the western to the central part of South America, Peru is known worldwide for its extensive coastline and archeological wonders. The capital city, Lima, presides over the coast with its Spanish colonial center and hip neighborhoods buzzing with pisco bars, live music, and some of the finest restaurants in the world. Heading north, a fun-loving surfing paradise beckons round Máncora, while to the south, the desert-etched Nazca Lines have puzzled and enthralled visitors for decades.

The magnificent Andes are justifiably the country's main draw, delivering history, culture, and adventure by the bucketload. Omnipresent is the enduring legacy of the Inca Empire – and even earlier cultures – from imposing ruined citadels to joyous traditional festivals. While the beauty of Cusco's elegant squares and cobbled streets is renowned, the resplendent plazas of Arequipa, Ayacucho, and Cajamarca ooze plenty of old-world charm. Lose yourself in the cloud-forested eastern flank of Peru's mountainous spine, brimming with dazzling birds, orchids, and butterflies, as it plunges into the lowland rainforest and majestic Amazon River. However you choose to experience Peru's natural beauty, its snow-crusted peaks, glacial lakes, and yawning canyons will not disappoint.

Peru's vastness and diversity can feel over-whelming, but this guidebook breaks the country down into easily navigable chapters, full of expert knowledge and insider tips. We've created detailed itineraries and colorful maps to help you plan the perfect trip, whether you're on a short break or an extended adventure. Enjoy the book, and enjoy Peru.

REASONS TO LOVE
PERU

From Andean peaks to Amazon rainforest, Peru promises variety. With its stunning ancient ruins, lively entertainment, and fascinating wildlife, there are so many reasons to love Peru. Here, we pick some of our favorites.

1 **MACHU PICCHU**
On many a bucket list, this iconic Inca citadel, set atop a forest-cloaked mountain, is one of the world's most wondrous sights *(p184)*.

AMAZON RIVER ADVENTURES *2*
Whether dolphin-spotting from the deck of a luxury riverboat or fishing for piranha from a motorized dugout, adventure is guaranteed in the Amazon *(p248)*.

3 **BIRDWATCHING PARADISE**
Peru is one of the world's bird-watching hot spots, with over 1,800 species, including the cock-of-the-rock, hummingbirds, and the Andean condor *(p56)*.

PERUVIAN FOOD 4

Lima hosts several of the world's top restaurants, but toasted sweetcorn from a street grill in Ayacucho or a tangy ceviche in Máncora will excite foodies just as much.

WILD HIGHLAND FESTIVALS 5

A fusion of colonial Catholic and ancient Andean beliefs, traditional festivals are a riot of dancers and musicians, colorful costumes, and paraded saints (p40).

PRE-COLUMBIAN CIVILIZATIONS 6

Peru harbors impressive remains of ancient cultures: from the adobe walls of the Chimú citadel of Chan Chan (p232) to Nazca's puzzling geoglyphs (p140).

HIKING IN THE ANDES *7*
Many spectacular hikes across the Andes afford breathtaking views, punctuated by encounters with alpacas, traditional communities, and crumbling ruins *(p38)*.

PISCO SOUR *8*
The tangy taste of fresh lime juice on ice, a spirit with a kick, and a whisked egg white on top together make up Peru's delicious national drink: pisco sour *(p50)*.

9 DIVERSE CULTURES
Indigenous people make up around 20 per cent of the Peruvian population, representing a rich diversity of languages and cultures. The vast majority are Quechua *(p74)*.

10 JUNGLE LODGES

Whether you're being lulled to sleep by chirping crickets or awakened by squawking parrots, a stay in a lodge in the heart of the rainforest is an unmissable experience.

THE WORLD'S DEEPEST CANYONS 11

Over twice the depth of the Grand Canyon, the Cañón del Colca *(p166)* and the more remote Cotahuasi *(p168)* feature excellent hiking terrain and relaxing thermal pools.

PEÑAS 12

An essential part of Lima's nightlife and popular in other cities, these informal and intimate bars are the place to go to soak up live folk music *(p84)*.

EXPLORE
PERU

This guide divides Peru into nine color-coded sightseeing areas, as shown on this map. Find out more about each area on the following pages.

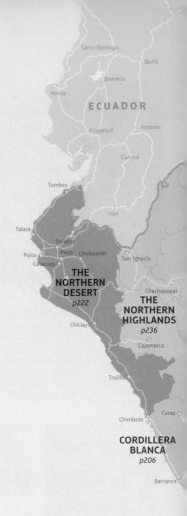

Santo Domingo

Quito

Quevedo

Manta

ECUADOR

Guayaquil

Ambato

Cuenca

Tumbes

Loja

Talara

Sullana

Piura   Chulucanas

Paita

Catacaos

San Ignacio

THE NORTHERN DESERT
p222

Chachapoyas

THE NORTHERN HIGHLANDS
p236

Cajamarca

Chiclayo

Trujillo

Caraz

Chimbote

CORDILLERA BLANCA
p206

Barranca

Pacific Ocean

SOUTH AMERICA

MEXICO

GUATEMALA   HONDURAS

COSTA RICA   VENEZUELA

PANAMA   GUYANA

COLOMBIA   FRENCH GUIANA

ECUADOR

BRAZIL

Lima

PERU   BOLIVIA

Pacific Ocean

CHILE   PARAGUAY

URUGUAY

ARGENTINA

Atlantic Ocean

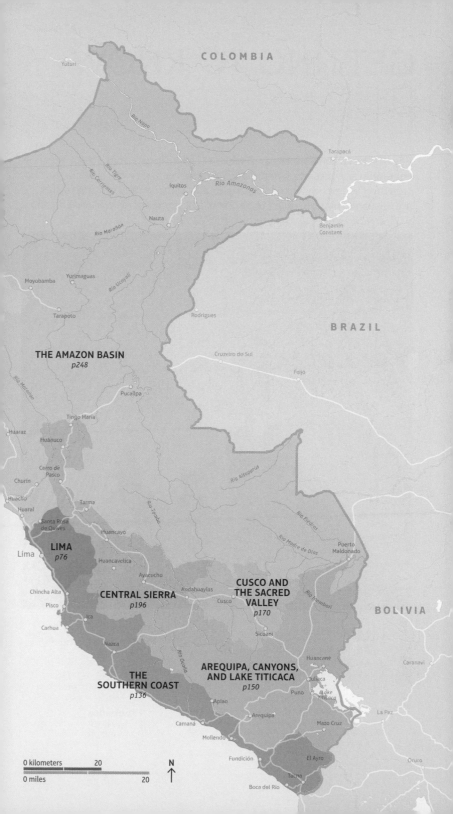

GETTING TO KNOW
PERU

Beyond the landmark fortress of Machu Picchu, Peru is a country of extreme geographical contrasts, comprising dry desert coast, sweltering jungle, and snow-frosted peaks. Nestled throughout is a biodiversity of wildlife plus pre-Hispanic ruins proving it to be one of the cradles of American civilization.

PAGE 76

LIMA

Situated on the steep, cliffside edges of the barren Pacific coast, Peru's capital city is a clash of the old and new. Here, Inca temples lead to trendy boulevards, while 16th- to 19th-century architecture plays host to priceless, millennial-old artifacts. With an internationally renowned dining scene and a mix of sophisticated and traditional nightlife, Lima offers its own take on what defines a modern Latin American city.

Best for
Museums, colonial architecture, and fine dining

Home to
San Francisco, Huaca Pucllana, Museo Nacional de Arqueología, Antropología e Historia del Perú

Experience
Peña-hopping in the bohemian Barranco neighborhood

PAGE 136

THE SOUTHERN COAST

Home to one of Peru's most famous archeological sites, the Southern Coast is a long stretch of desert scattered with coastal towns reaching as far as the Chilean frontier. Despite its aridity, its biggest attraction is the wildlife reserve of Islas Ballestas. This is a region of surprising fertility, and, further inland, centuries-old vines cultivated on river plains play an important role in the production of the nation's favorite spirit, pisco.

Best for
Desert landscapes and vast pre-Columbian sites

Home to
Nazca Lines, Reserva Nacional de Paracas

Experience
An early morning flight over the Nazca Lines

PAGE 150

AREQUIPA, CANYONS, AND LAKE TITICACA

This Andean territory is home to a volcano-speckled cordillera that meets two of the world's deepest canyons and the dazzling glare of Lake Titicaca. With proximity to colonial and Indigenous cultures, the dramatic white city of Arequipa is a standout attraction. It also grants access to remote communities steeped in tradition and encounters with the soaring, sacred bird of the Inca, the Andean condor.

Best for
Breathtaking landscapes, hiking, and traditional Andean culture

Home to
Monasterio de Santa Catalina, Lake Titicaca, Cañón del Colca

Experience
The views of El Misti volcano from a rooftop café in Arequipa

→

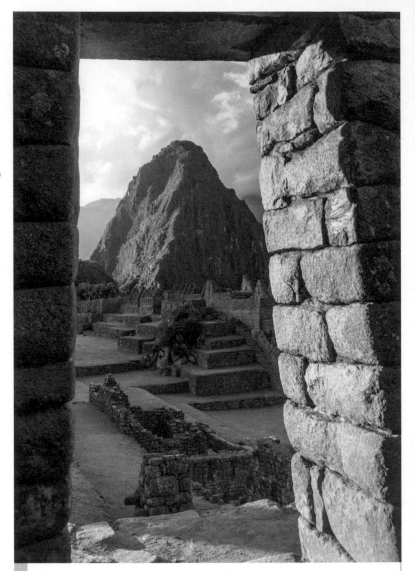

PAGE 170

CUSCO AND THE SACRED VALLEY

Extravagant colonial mansions and religious buildings crowd the old center of Cusco, but it's the mountainside remains of expertly built temples that loom most tangibly over the city. The extraordinary Inca ruins of Machu Picchu are inescapable and the region's ultimate drawcard, but the photogenic villages scattered across the Sacred Valley offer a compelling glimpse into the robust connection between ancient and modern Indigenous life.

Best for
Andean textiles and discovering Inca culture

Home to
La Catedral, the Inca Trail, Machu Picchu

Experience
Strolling around an Andean market in Pisac

PAGE 196

CENTRAL SIERRA

The Andes are the back-bone of the Central Sierra, a region of surprisingly lush valleys and attractive remote towns, where mountain traditions hold fast. Ayacucho is the most photogenic of these, rivaling even Cusco with its 17th- and 18th-century architecture and hordes of churches. It is here, and in villages near Huancayo, where the country's finest handicrafts are produced.

Best for
Stark Andean scenery, handicrafts, and traditional festivals

Home to
Ayacucho, Mantaro Valley

Experience
One of the world's highest train journeys from Huancayo to Huancavelica

PAGE 206

CORDILLERA BLANCA

Stretching north and inland of Lima, the Cordillera Blanca is Peru on a superlative scale. Its angular landscapes are crowned by frosted 20,000-ft (6,000-m) peaks, attracting mountaineers and hikers in their droves. But the most wonderful sights in this region are found at lower altitudes: the ancient archeological sites of Chavín de Huántar, the remains of a feline worshipping cult, and Caral, the oldest urban center in the Americas, rank among the most important in Peru.

Best for
Spectacular snowcapped peaks, trekking, and mountaineering

Home to
Parque Nacional Huascarán, Chavín de Huántar, Caral

Experience
A hike to a remote, glacial lake in the Cordillera

$\rightarrow$

PAGE 222

THE NORTHERN DESERT

This long, thin slice of desert reaches to the border with Ecuador. Its powdery, white-sand beaches are among the most stunning in Peru, and are home to some of the freshest ceviche it's possible to find. Yet the Northern Desert is more than just sand and sea; the weathered, dusty remains of ancient, pre-Inca cultures and fine archeological museums are among the continent's best.

Best for
Beaches, pre-Inca archeological sites, and museums

Home to
Trujillo, Museo Tumbas Reales de Sipán

Experience
The beach at the lively resort and surfer's paradise, Máncora

PAGE 236

THE NORTHERN HIGHLANDS

Peru's typically wild blend of deep river valleys and soaring mountain peaks characterizes the Northern Highlands. This was once the stronghold of the Chachapoya culture, who left their mark with Kuélap, a fortress that rivals Machu Picchu in magnificence. Nonetheless, the human impact on these landscapes pales in comparison with the drama of the natural world, with hiking being just one way of appreciating waterfalls that pound the earth from colossal heights and lush cloud forest that blooms with orchids.

Best for
Getting off the beaten path and the Chachapoya culture

Home to
Cajamarca, Kuélap

Experience
Sampling traditional cheese dishes in Peru's dairy heartland, Cajamarca

PAGE 248

THE AMAZON BASIN

Just under two-thirds of the country is covered by the dense, damp foliage of the Amazon jungle, a place where nature is wholly in charge. As the most biodiverse corner of the planet, the rainforest provides the perfect cover for myriad species, where vibrantly colored macaws flit through the canopy above and capybaras slink into muddy waterways. Gateway towns – Iquitos in the north and Puerto Maldonado further south – offer unforgettable jungle adventures by languid riverboat.

Best for
Jungle wildlife, Amazonian cultures, and riverboat trips

Home to
Iquitos, Reserva Nacional Pacaya Samiria, Reserva de la Biosfera de Manu

Experience
A stay in a cosy lodge deep in the Amazon jungle

2 WEEKS

across Peru

Peru brims with travel possibilities, from four-day tours around the big cities to grand odysseys across the entire region. These itineraries will help you to chart your own course through this vibrant and varied country.

Day 1

Spend a day soaking up Lima's rich cultural history, colonial architecture, and live entertainment *(p80)*.

Day 2

Catch a three-hour early morning bus south to the town of Paracas *(p144)*, a scenic coastal resort once popular among wealthy Limeños. After lunch at the sea-facing patio of La Negra y El Blanca *(www.lanegrayelblanco.pe)*, tour the Islas Ballestas *(p144)*, home to a squawking, swarming mass of Humboldt penguins and sea lions. Back on dry land, rent a bike and explore the Reserva Nacional de Paracas *(p142)*. For an unbeatable fresh fish dinner in the town of Paracas, scout out a simple restaurant near the jetty.

Day 3

The sunny city of Ica *(p144)*, an hour south, is surrounded by a fertile valley dotted with Peru's oldest vineyards. Begin your day getting to grips with the local spirit by hopping between artisanal pisco *bodegas* and lunching at a winery restaurant. Back in Ica, tour the Museo Regional Adolfo Bermúdez Jenkins *(p145)* with its textiles from the Paracas culture. Travel to Nazca in the evening by a two-hour bus and dine on criollo-style food at Los Angeles *(p146)* on arrival.

Day 4

Board an early flight for the clearest conditions for observing the mysterious geoglyphs that are the Nazca Lines *(p140)*. Despite numerous theories for

① Lima's stunning cathedral.
② Humboldt penguins on
   Islas Ballestas.
③ Volcano behind Arequipa.
④ Passage in Monasterio de
   Santa Catalina.
⑤ Boats on Lake Titcaca.

why they were etched into the desert some 2,000 years ago, there's still no consensus. After your flight, catch an afternoon bus for the nine-hour journey to Arequipa (p154), a volcano-ringed city prized for its colonial architecture. Upon arrival, wind down after the journey in the easygoing pisco bar, Museo del Pisco (p169).

Day 5

Start the day by exploring Arequipa's historic and elegant UNESCO World Heritage center, constructed mostly from white, volcanic sillar stone, giving it the label the "white city". To further appreciate Arequipa's singular architectural style, amble through the pretty cloisters of the Monasterio de Santa Catalina (p158). Continue on a self-guided tour of Arequipa's finest churches, including the lavishly carved facade of the Iglesia de la Compañía (p156). As the evening approaches, sample local cuisine, such as rocoto relleno (stuffed, spicy pepper) at one of the city's typical picantería restaurants.

Day 6

Leave Arequipa on a 3am bus, taking just over three hours, for the Cañón del Colca (p166), the world's second deepest canyon. Have your camera at the ready at the Mirador Cruz del Cóndor (p166), where, if you're lucky, you may see Andean condors floating gracefully in the skies between 7am and 9am. Back on the eastern rim of the canyon, relax in Chivay, home to the iron-rich La Calera thermal baths (p166). After dinner at Maray (Avenida Salaverry N-103, Chivay), catch the six-hour long overnight bus to Puno (p164).

Day 7

From the port, sail across the sparkling waters of Lake Titicaca (p162) in the morning, considered by the Inca to be the birthplace of the sun. Spend an hour on the Islas Uros (p163) – islands constructed entirely from buoyant reeds. In the afternoon, arrive at Isla Amantaní (p164), an island admired for its colorful textiles. Stay overnight in a snug homestay with a Quechua-speaking family.

→

Day 8

As you land the next morning on the smaller Isla Taquile *(p164)*, take the 500-or-so steps up to the square slowly to avoid feeling the altitude. At the top, do not miss the expertly crafted garments for sale in a community-run shop. Dine on simple food at a restaurant overlooking the lake, before hiking back to the boat. Return to Puno and catch a six-hour night bus to Cusco *(p174)*.

Day 9

Spend your first morning touring the Plaza de Armas *(p174)*, home to La Catedral *(p178)* with its painting of the *Last Supper* featuring a roasted guinea pig as the table's centerpiece. Later, marvel at the paintings from the Cusco school *(p179)* in the Museo de Arte Religioso *(p177)* and find the famous 12-sided Inca stone that forms part of the museum's exterior wall. Take a taxi up to Sacsayhuamán *(p175)* and spend the afternoon exploring this Inca fortress. For dinner, dive into Andean food at Greens Organic *(Santa Catalina Angosta 135)*.

Day 10

Begin the day by seeing fleeting evidence of the Inca at Koricancha *(p176)*, a once golden-walled temple worshiping the Sun God, which was sacked of its priceless treasures by the Spanish and rebuilt as the beautiful church and convent of Santo Domingo *(p176)*. In the afternoon, admire the prettiest part of the city, the San Blas *(p176)* neighborhood. If visiting at the weekend, its craft fair presents opportunities for buying traditional Andean textiles and other souvenirs. Go on the hunt for alpaca steaks for dinner in one of the tiny restaurants in the San Blas district.

Day 11

Hop on a *colectivo* (shared minibus) north west to reach Písac *(p194)* for its famed artisans' market, held daily but liveliest on Sundays. Continue along the valley to Ollantaytambo *(p195)*, considered the last living Inca town. Here, cobbled streets lead to Araqama Ayllu *(p195)*, a fortress used successfully by Manco Inca against the Spanish. For dinner, try inventive,

1 Stone archway on
Isla Taquile.

2 Cusco's San Blas district.

3 Ruins of Machu Picchu.

4 Textiles in Písac market.

5 Family of capybaras.

organic Andean cuisine at El Albergue (*www.elalbergue.com/restaurant*) before an early night in preparation for your train ride to Machu Picchu the next day.

Day 12

Wake at first light to make a pilgrimage to the spectacular Inca citadel of Machu Picchu (*p184*), but be sure to reserve at least six months in advance. This UNESCO World Heritage Site is perched between two mountains, with agricultural terraces carved into the hillsides and flawless Inca stonework visible at the Templo del Sol (*p188*). Board the train back to Ollantaytambo and then on to Cusco and wind down back at your lodgings.

Day 13

Take a 30-minute flight from Cusco to Puerto Maldonado (*p258*), and the Amazon Rainforest. Travel up the Río Tambopata (*p258*) and stay at the wilderness lodge Refugio Amazonas (*www.rainforestexpeditions.com*), on the right side of the river. As part of your tour,

visit a nutritious clay lick (*p259*) for the perfect opportunity to spot and photograph bright-colored parrots and trek to a nearby lake for sightings of rare giant otters. Take a jungle night walk for a chance to see a poison dart frog before falling asleep to the sounds of the jungle.

Day 14

Take a four-hour boat journey from your lodge through rainforest on a sight-seeing hunt to spot colorful macaws, capybaras, howler monkeys, river otters, and even piranha. Return downriver by boat to Puerto Maldonado. To end your two weeks, catch a flight back to Lima.

To extend your trip:

Spend four days and three nights hiking the Inca Trail (*p180*) from Cusco to Machu Picchu, but it is essential to reserve at least six months in advance as tickets are limited. The alternative five- to seven-day Salkantay to Machu Picchu trail is an option only for acclimatized, experienced hikers due to its high altitude passes.

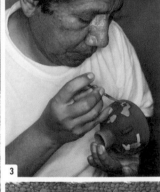

→

1. Stunning facade of the Hacienda San José.
2. Reserva Nacional de Paracas.
3. Painting a clay pot.
4. Impressive Acueducto de Cantalloc.

4 DAYS
on the Southern Coast

Day 1

Morning Start your tour in Chincha Alta, the hub of Afro-Peruvian culture. Take in the Hacienda San José *(www.casa haciendasanjose.com/en)*, a former sugar plantation built in the 17th century.

Afternoon Heading southbound, stop at Tambo Colorado *(p145)*, one of the best-preserved adobe cities in Peru. From there, it's an hour's bus journey to reach Pisco *(p145)*. Unfortunately, many of the city's buildings were destroyed by the 2007 earthquake; visit the main square to see the remaining monuments.

Evening Take a bus to Paracas *(p144)* for a stroll along the harborside. Keep an eye out for pelicans as you indulge in a sundowner at an oceanside bar.

Day 2

Morning Board a motor boat for a spin around the Islas Ballestas *(p144)*, home to Humboldt penguins and sea lions. Back in Paracas, rent a bike to explore the Reserva Nacional de Paracas *(p142)*, a protected area where desert cliffs meet Pacific waters. Stop for lunch at the ramshackle fishing community of Lagunillas *(p142)*.

Afternoon A one-hour bus journey south-east brings you to Ica *(p144)*, a taxi ride from the oasis of Huacachina *(p145)*. Here, ramp it up a notch with an adrenaline-fueled dune buggy ride up and down the surrounding sand dunes.

Evening Back in Huacachina, grab an outside table for dinner at a restaurant overlooking the oasis.

Day 3

Morning Reserve a tour around Destilería La Caravedo *(www.piscoporton.com)*, one of the top pisco *bodegas* in the country-side surrounding Ica. Take a horseback ride around their vineyards – some of the oldest in Peru – before enjoying a gourmet lunch.

Afternoon Explore the town of Nazca *(p146)* and its intriguing Museo Didáctico Antonini *(p146)* with its collection of mummies uncovered from the nearby pyramids of Cahuachi *(p146)*. Next, dive into the ceramic workshops in San Carlos, where local artisans create high-quality replicas of Nazca pottery.

Evening To learn more about the town's most famous archeological site – the Nazca Lines *(p140)* – stay overnight at the Hotel Nazca Lines *(p145)*. Their 45-minute lecture introduces the theories regarding the geoglyphs' origins and uses.

Day 4

Morning Take a flight over the Nazca Lines, the giant collection of geoglyphs etched into the desert floor around 2,000 years ago. The nearby Acueducto de Cantalloc *(p146)*, a series of spiraled aqueducts built by the Nazca, are also worth a visit.

Afternoon Tour La Reserva Nacional Pampa Galeras Barbara D'Achille *(p146)*, home to several thousand wild vicuña.

Evening To finish off the day, spend a final evening in Nazca browsing the restaurants along Jirón Bolognesi for a bite of traditional food.

←

① Arequipa's cathedral.

② Weaving textiles at Mundo Alpaca.

③ Entrance to Chivay.

④ Souvenirs from the Islas Uros, Lake Titicaca.

5 DAYS
in Canyon Country

Day 1

Morning Start on Arequipa's Plaza de Armas *(p154)* to appreciate one of Peru's most majestic squares. Cross the square to the Iglesia de la Campañía *(p156)* and wander next door for souvenir shopping.

Afternoon Stop for a savory crepe on the patio of Crepísimo *(p155)* and then head to the Convento de la Recoleta *(p155)* to admire Arequipa's architectural style.

Evening Indulge at Zig Zag *(www.zigzag restaurant.com)*, which serves alpaca steaks on sizzling slabs of volcanic rock.

Day 2

Morning Go behind the scenes of Inca sacrifice at the Museo Santuarios Andinos *(p157)*, home to Juanita, the mummified girl found frozen on a nearby volcano.

Afternoon For a look at Peru's weaving traditions, trot along to Mundo Alpaca *(p156)*, where alpacas graze on the lawns as you learn about turning wool into textiles; you can even buy some samples.

Evening Take in a contemporary art exhibition at Casona Iriberry *(p154)*, before heading to Chicha *(p155)* for the ultimate fine-dining experience.

Day 3

Morning Catch a bus for Chivay (taking three and a half hours) *(p166)* but get off to see the vicuñas on the high-altitude plateaus of the magnificent Reserva Nacional de Salinas y Aguada Blanca, found 73 miles (117 km) north of Arequipa.

Afternoon Stop in Chivay for a quick lunch before relaxing at one of the five pools at La Calera hot springs *(p166)*.

Evening Travel west for 15 minutes by bus to Yanque *(p166)*, a traditional farming village and a good base for a tour of the rim of the Cañón del Colca *(p166)*.

Day 4

Morning Rise early to admire the snow-white Iglesia de la Inmaculada Concepción *(Plaza de Armas, Yanque)* built from *sillar*. Next up is Mirador Cruz del Cóndor *(p166)*, a viewpoint over the canyon where Andean condors glide on thermal currents.

Afternoon Continue to the trailhead for the hike into the canyon. Along the 4,000-ft- (1,300-m)- descent, admire the Collagua terraces *(p166)* on the hills.

Evening At the Valle de Sangalle, an oasis deep within the valley, relax overnight in rustic accommodation.

Day 5

Morning Start the steep, four-hour hike back out of the canyon early to avoid the height of the day's heat. At Cabanaconde *(p166)*, travel back to Chivay to connect with a six-hour bus to Puno *(p164)*, passing dazzling, high-altitude scenery.

Afternoon From the jetty, join a tour of the Islas Uros *(p163)*, a group of islands constructed from buoyant totora reeds, before landing on Isla Taquile *(p164)*.

Evening Stay overnight in a homestay *(p163)* with one of the island's families.

1

2

3

4

←

1 Tambomachay ruins and platforms in Cusco.

2 Selection of fruit and vegetable at Písac market.

3 Impressive Moray terraces.

4 Salinas de Maras salt pans.

5 DAYS

in Cusco and the Sacred Valley

Day 1

Morning Start your tour of Cusco at the Museo Inka (*p174*), a must for Inca-philes. Once you've had your fill of Inca history, wander along Calle Hatunrumiyoc (*p177*), where the famous 12-angled stone built into a wall evidences the culture's skill.

Afternoon The cacao bean originates from the Amazon Jungle, so there's no better place to try your hand at chocolate making than in a workshop at the Choco Museo (*p176*).

Evening Stop in at the Museo de Arte Precolombino (*p174*) for Moche pottery masterpieces before settling in next door in MAP Café (*p177*) for Peruvian fine-dining.

Day 2

Morning Hail a cab to Tambomachay above Cusco, with its ruins of niches. Hike down and follow the road back to Cusco, stopping at Sacsayhuamán (*p175*) on the way, a former Inca fortress.

Afternoon Back in the city, visit the Iglesia de Santo Domingo (*p176*) atop the Koricancha ruins. Cross the gardens behind to buy handwoven gifts at the Centro de Textiles Tradicionales de Cusco (*p176*).

Evening As night falls, enjoy a pisco sour overlooking the square from the balcony of Calle del Medio (*p177*).

Day 3

Morning Start early for a trip to the gates at Rumicolca (*p192*), used by the Inca to control entry into Cusco. Finish your morning at San Pedro de Andahuaylillas (*p192*), a church known as the "Sistine Chapel of the Americas" for its interior.

Afternoon Returning in the direction of Cusco, stop in Tipón (*p193*) for an Andean lunch: roasted guinea-pig. Afterwards, marvel at the water canals of Tipón.

Evening Sink into a soundtrack of criolla music in the lively Museo del Pisco (*Santa Catalina Ancha 398, Cusco*).

Day 4

Morning Catch an early *colectivo* to Písac (*p194*), followed by a taxi up to the hill-side ruins here. Back in the village, spend a few hours wandering around the artisans' market, one of the region's largest.

Afternoon Settle into the K'uychi Rumi mountain lodge (*www.urubamba.com*) near Urubamba and join a horseback ride or bike ride of the valley's fertile river plains.

Evening Enjoy a mouthwatering dinner at the cosy Tres Keros (*p193*).

Day 5

Morning Hire a taxi up to the circular Moray terraces (*p194*) and take the path to the Salinas de Maras (*p194*), pans where local people have been extracting salt for centuries.

Afternoon A *colectivo* back into the valley brings you to Ollantaytambo (*p195*), a village with excellent ice cream parlors.

Evening Settle down in front of a fire back in your lodge and prepare for an early morning train to Machu Picchu (*p184*).

1 Trujillo's pretty cathedral.

2 A traditional reed boat on Huanchaco beach.

3 Fresh ceviche dish topped with chili.

4 Ceramic at the Museo de las Tumbes Reales de Sipán.

10 DAYS
in Northern Peru

Day 1

Morning Start by touring the colorfully painted mansions of Trujillo's colonial center. Stop at the mustard-yellow facade of the restored, 17th-century cathedral *(p226)* on the Plaza de Armas *(p226)*, the largest central square in Peru.

Afternoon To better understand the region's pre-Inca history, take a bus to Chan Chan *(p232)*, the biggest adobe city in the world and the former capital of the Chimú Empire. Elaborate friezes decorated with marine motifs that have been painstakingly restored evidence its former grandeur.

Evening End your day at El Mochica *(www.elmochica.com.pe)* to sample the local dish, *cabrito con frijoles* (goat and bean stew), and to catch a performance of Trujillo's typical dance, the *marinera (p52)*.

Day 2

Morning Take a bus south of the city and spend a few hours touring Huaca de la Luna and Huaca del Sol *(p232)*, two adobe temples constructed by the Moche culture. Look out for the fascinating and somewhat grizzly multicolored friezes that narrate religious sacrifice rituals.

Afternoon Plan a route north as far as Huanchaco *(p233)*, a laid-back beach town with a fishing village ambience just outside of Trujillo. Choose from one of the seafront restaurants to enjoy a lazy, languid lunch of fresh fish or ceviche *(p49)*.

Evening Catch a ride out on the waves aboard a traditional *caballito de totora* ("reed horse" sea raft) and appreciate a picturesque sunset from Huanchaco's fine golden sands.

Day 3

Morning Slip on a wetsuit and wake up with a dip in the chilly waters of the Humboldt current – a hired surfboard let's you dive right into the action. Finish with a well-needed stint soaking up the sunshine on the beach.

Afternoon Join a tour to the unparalleled Complejo Arqueológico El Brujo *(p233)*, a Moche complex where the 1,500-year-old mummified body of a female shamanic leader was discovered in 2006 – the only ancient female ruler ever found in Peru. You can view her tattoo-covered body in the on-site museum.

Evening Continue back to Trujillo and grab a spot for dinner at El Celler de Cler *(Jirón Independencia 588)* on their atmospheric, 18th-century balcony with views of the pretty Iglesia San Francisco nearby.

Day 4

Morning Take the three-hour bus journey north to reach Chiclayo *(p233)*, once a small colonial town and now the second-largest city in northern Peru.

Afternoon A local *colectivo* brings you to Lambayeque and the unique pyramid structure of the Museo de las Tumbas Reales de Sipán *(p230)*, crammed with over 1,400 precious artifacts. Many belonged to the Lord of Sipán's burial chamber *(p230)*, a site that now ranks among Peru's most important archeological discoveries.

Evening Reserve a table at Fiesta Chiclayo Gourmet *(p235)* and indulge in a night of fine traditional Peruvian dining at the original restaurant of celebrity chef Hester Solís.

→

Day 5

Morning Fields clustered with sugar cane line the roads to Túcume *(p235)*, a group of 26 adobe pyramids that acted as the capital of the Lambayeque culture. As part of a circuit of the site, climb to the top of the 646-ft (197-m) El Purgatorio hill for all-encompassing views of the complex.

Afternoon Continue east to the nearby temples of Batán Grande *(p234)*, tucked within a forest of algarrobo trees and where 80 per cent of all pre-Columbian gold artifacts now on display in Peru are thought to have originated.

Evening Return to Chiclayo and spend the evening in Cuatro Once *(Calle Juan Cuglievan 411, Chiclayo)*, a restobar serving Peruvian craft beer and typical local specialties such as ceviche.

Day 6

Morning Take a six-hour bus to the lovely colonial city of Cajamarca *(p240)*.

Afternoon Few cities can compete with the historic atmosphere of Cajamarca's pretty cobblestone streets, which played witness to the Spanish conquistadores' capture and later execution of Inca emperor Atahualpa *(p69)* in the early 16th century. To learn more about this event, El Cuarto del Rescate (the Ransom Chamber) *(p241)* is worth a visit. Later, explore the Museo Arqueológico y Etnográfico in Belén *(p241)*, with its engaging displays of ceramics, weavings, everyday utensils, and other artifacts from diverse pre-Inca cultures.

Evening Drop in on one of Cajamarca's typical *peñas*, Peña Usha Usha *(Amalia Puga 320)*. In one of these intimate and often hidden local bars, live music and friendly company are on the cards.

Day 7

Morning Catch an early bus to the striking Ventanillas de Otuzco *(p244)*, ancient cemeteries carved into a cliff of volcanic rock, located 5 miles (8 km) outside of Cajamarca.

Afternoon From the Ventanillas, a pleasant path follows the river south to join up with Los Baños del Inca *(p244)*,

① Túcume site.

② Cajamarca's cathedral.

③ Ventanillas de Otuzco.

④ Main square in Chachapoyas.

⑤ Kuélap ruins.

⑥ Stunning Cataratas Gocta.

thermal baths used for relaxation by Atahualpa and ideal for a few hours' soaking in a private pool.

Evening Try the regional delicacy, *caldo verde* (green soup filled with chunks of soft cheese), at the classic Cajamarca restaurant, Salas *(Jr Amalia Puga 637)*.

Day 8

Morning Embark on the 12-hour journey to Chachapoyas *(p245)* via Celendín and Leymebamba *(p244)*. Skirting plunging valleys and chugging up to 13,000-ft- (4,000m-) passes, the road is hair-raising.

Evening Upon arrival in Chachapoyas, stretch your legs with a walk along the pedestrianized street, Jirón Amazonas, heading east of the Plaza de Armas, and dine at one of its cosy restaurants.

Day 9

Morning Rise early to catch the cable car up to the mountaintop citadel of Kuélap *(p242)*, a huge stone fortress built by the Chachapoya people some 1,500 years ago.

Study the ground inside the 400 circular houses on the site and look out for the stone runs used for keeping guinea pigs.

Afternoon Back in Chachapoyas, wander over to the municipal-run Museo el Reino de las Nubes *(p245)* on the main square. This small museum houses excellent exhibitions on most of the ancient sites surrounding the city and their cultures.

Evening Wind down over a glass of *macerado* (a fermented fruit liquor) made on the premises at lively locale, Licores la Reina *(Jr Jirón Ayacucho 544)*.

Day 10

Morning Bus out to the trailhead for the 4-mile (6-km) hike through cloud forest to the base of the Cataratas Gocta *(p247)*, one of the tallest waterfalls in the world. It dramatically cascades down over 2,525 ft (770 m) in two tiers.

Afternoon Post-hike, pop into Café Fusiones *(p245)* for heavenly, organic meals and coffee cultivated in nearby farms.

Evening Catch a flight back to Lima.

Food Markets

Bustling Andean markets are a patchwork of smells and textures, and sell much the same vegetables as they did in Inca times. Browse the sacks of quinoa, kiwicha, and potatoes – some of the 3,000 plus varieties of spud that originated from around Lake Titicaca can even be sampled in the food stalls of Puno's markets *(p164)*.

↓ Mounds of multi-colored fruit and vegetables at Písac market

EXPERIENCE
INCA PERU

The Inca Empire left behind a trail of magnificent ancient treasures throughout the Andes, stretching beyond the renowned Machu Picchu. A host of lesser known, little-visited remains and experiences beckon, allowing you to follow in the footsteps of, and even eat, like the Incas.

Q'eswachaka Rope Bridge

This is the last surviving example of an Inca Rope bridge. Spanning the raging Río Apurimac, you can take a tour from Cusco *(p174)* to Q'eswachaka to marvel at this imposing structure. Every June a replacement bridge is woven and hung with much skill in a joyous community festival.

← Crossing the famous Q'eswachaka Rope Bridge and *(above)* replacing the bridge in June

Machu Picchu

Top of any visitor's list, and often their reason for traveling to Peru, Machu Picchu *(p184)* does not disappoint. The remarkably restored ruins of this iconic Inca citadel are impressive, but the stunning natural setting is what makes it truly magical. Clinging onto a precipitous ridge, and surrounded by forested mountains, Machu Picchu's majesty is best appreciated from Intipunku ("Gateway of the Sun") *(p183)*, which affords the classic view of the site, and an irresistible photo opportunity.

↑ Dramatic scenery around the impressive Machu Picchu ruins

TOP 3 MUSEUMS FOR INCA HISTORY

Museo Inka, Cusco
Displays a wide collection of Inca mummies, textiles, and more *(p174)*.

Museo Machu Picchu, Cusco
Tells the history of the Inca citadel *(p177)*.

Museo Arqueológico Rafael Larco Herrera, Lima
Features excellent collections of Inca gold and silver *(p131)*.

The Capaq Ñan

The world-famous Inca Trail *(p180)* comprises a mere fraction of the Capaq Ñan (Royal Highway), a 25,000-mile (40,000-km) network of stone roads that crisscrossed the Inca Empire. Travel up stone stairways, through glorious scenery, and get your fill of ancient ruins by trekking the wonderfully preserved 37-miles (60-km) section from Castillo to Huánuco Pampa in the Central Sierra *(p196)*.

←

Hiking along the Inca Trail

Gaze at Glaciers on the Salkantay Trek

The favorite alternative to the Inca Trail centers on snowcapped Nevado Salkantay - the jewel in the crown of the Cordillera Vilcabamba in Cusco. Whether taking the high road that skirts the sacred mountain's glittering glacier, or opting for the classic trek, the mountain vistas are breathtaking. Soften the five-day challenge by swapping your tent and sleeping bag for the comfort of a rustic lodge, complete with gourmet food and muscle-soothing hot tubs.

→

Rock-strewn path leading to the snow-topped Nevado Salkantay

SPECTACULAR
INCA TREKS

There's no need to feel disappointment if the oversubscribed Inca Trail is fully reserved. Other equally exciting treks await, with the lure of stunning scenery, memorable cultural encounters, and impressive Inca ruins – all without the crowds and easily organized in Cusco at the last minute.

Encounter Ancient Traditions

The top choice for the less experienced hiker is the three-day Lares Trek. At 20.5 miles (33 km) long, this glorious trek passes through traditional Andean villages, providing a precious glimpse of everyday life in Andean weaving communities. It also offers fabulous hot springs and scenic highland valleys dotted with picturesque lakes and waterfalls.

←

Carrying a heavy load down Calle Lares, Ollantaytambo

GREAT VIEW
Casa Andina Observatory

The Casa Andina hotel *(www.casa-andina. com)* in the Sacred Valley *(p171)* offers a great planetarium and observatory. At this magical spot you can marvel at the Milky Way and appreciate the importance of the night sky to Inca cosmology.

Did You Know?

The best time to hike is during May–September, when the days are usually dry and sunny.

Keep Your Adrenaline Count High

A blend of thrilling activities and hiking on the three-day Jungle Trek calls out to all adventure-lovers. A daring descent by mountain bike precedes a trek along a flourishing sub-tropical valley, with rafting and ziplining as optional extras. Before setting off on the final day's hike along the railway tracks to Machu Picchu Pueblo (Aguas Calientes) *(p183)*, a dip in the thermal baths at Cocalmayo is the perfect pick-me-up. To find out more visit *www.iperu.org/aguas-termales-de-cocalmayo-santa-teresa.*

↑ Ziplining over the top of the Peruvian jungle

Challenge Yourself Toward Choquequirao

Perched on an isolated hilltop, Machu Picchu's sister citadel, Choquequirao, has ruins and a panorama to match. Since much of the site remains buried beneath tropical forest, it retains an atmospheric air reminiscent of when Hiram Bingham stumbled across Machu Picchu over a century ago. Since the ruins lie at the end of a tough seven-day hike, you'll likely have the place to yourself.

←

Choquequirao, nestled within mountains covered with stunning Amazonian flora

PERU FOR
FANTASTIC
FESTIVALS

Peru's 3,000 annual festivals are a dazzling fusion of Indigenous cultures and colonial Spanish Catholicism. From the spiritual to the musical, traditional festivals are laden with symbolism, and energetic visitors can be sure to dance for days regardless of the time of year.

Carnaval in Cajamarca

Though the riotous pre-Lenten festivities are celebrated countrywide, the highland city of Cajamarca *(p240)* throws one of the best parties. Expect water-balloon fights, allegorical floats, and the ceremony of the "yunza" – a large decorated tree covered in gifts, symbolizing abundance – which is cut down in a ritual dance to mark the end of the fun. The Queen Carnival and the comical Rey Momo (or Ño Carnavalón) preside over events, with an effigy of the king burned on Ash Wednesday.

→

One of the colorful masked parades in Cajamarca's Plaza de Armas

Fiesta de la Virgen de la Candelaria

Head and shoulders above all Peruvian folkloric festivities is this annual sixteen-day cultural extravaganza. Taking place in February, it fuses veneration of the Virgin with ancient Andean rituals related to harvesting and fertility. Though celebrated in other parts of Peru, nowhere are the costumes as dazzling as in Puno *(p164)*, where some 40,000 dancers flock. Once an effigy of the Virgin has been paraded around town, the dance troupes compete for prizes before spilling into the streets in a riot of technicolor and sound. The La Diablada, which symbolizes the victory of good over evil, is the festival's most famous dance, featuring armies of devils in elaborate costumes pursued by angels.

↑ Dancers performing choreographed routines in their glittering finery

TOP
4 **FUN FESTIVALS**

Inti Raymi
Held on June 24 in Sacsayhuaman, Cusco, to celebrate the winter solstice, it features a dramatic reenactment of the Inca festival in honor of the Sun God.

Virgen del Carmen
Three days in July of outlandish masked costume parades in Paucartambo in honor of the town's patron saint.

Mistura
Latin America's biggest food festival, held in Lima, is a culinary feast and lasts ten days in early September.

Selvámonos
This fun music festival and culture week in the small Tyrolean-Peruvian town of Oxapampa is held at the end of June.

← Acting out the scene of Christ on the cross during Semana Santa

Semana Santa

Known as Holy Week, Easter is the most important week in Peru's religious calendar. Ayacucho *(p200)* stages the most elaborate devotions, with fabulous carpets of flowers depicting iconic Easter scenes and many candlelit processions. On Good Friday the Señor de Santo Sepulcro and the Virgen Dolorosa are carried on towering litters adorned with white roses and illuminated with thousands of white candles.

→ Carrying sculptures of Mary Magdalene to Lima's Catedral

Sunrise at Tres Cruces
The anticipation is tangible at this mountain-top vigil east of Cusco (p174). As the sun rises above the mist, a dazzling ray of light leaks color into the clouds, tingeing them pink, then gold, unveiling the vastness of the Peruvian Amazon below. It's a stunning photo opportunity at any time, but round the June solstice an otherworldly optical illusion can produce three suns that appear as crosses (hence the name, Tres Cruces).

↑ Spectacular golden hues round the winter solstice at Tres Cruces

PERU FOR
NATURAL
WONDERS

From snow-frosted summits to sweltering jungle, vast canyons to desert sand dunes, Peru has a plethora of diverse and awe-inspiring landscapes. Some can be marveled at from afar; others require persistence to reach: either way, the rewards are truly spectacular.

💬 INSIDER TIP
Sorting the Seasons in Peru

The coastal desert strip is dry year-round but hotter in summer (Dec–Mar/Apr). In the Andes and the Amazon the rainy season (Oct–Apr) is called winter, but it does rain in the Amazon to some extent all year.

Catarata de Yumbilla
Peru has many waterfalls, from Cataratas Gocta (p247) to the Catarata Bayoz (p264), but the most spectacular is the Catarata de Yumbilla in Chachapoyas (p245). Plunging 2,952 ft (900 m) over a cliff into cloud forest, these breathtaking falls in northern Peru are one of the world's highest.

→

Stunning Catarata de Yumbilla, falling over a sheer cliff

Amazon Rainforest

Few places capture the imagination as much as the jungle *(p249)*. Covering well over half the country, and teeming with wildlife, Peru's surprisingly varied rainforest is a vast emerald patchwork quilt of towering trees, swamps, mangroves, and floodplains, united by its life-force, the majestic Amazon River.

← Splendid Amazon River, and visitors exploring the rainforest *(above)*

Ausangate and Vinicunca

At over 19,700 ft (6,000 m), this sparkling snowcapped peak, and revered *Apu* (mountain deity), soars skywards, feeding into a necklace of crystalline lakes. A five-day loop trek circumnavigates the massif, providing endless vistas of glistening glaciers, rugged cliffs, and strangely hued rocks. The most striking colorful striations lie a day's detour from the circuit on Vinicunca (Rainbow Mountain) *(p192)*, whose kaleidoscopic glory was revealed around 2013 by the retreating glacier.

→ Astonishing colors of Vinicunca (Rainbow Mountain), located in Cusco

Hands-On Experience

Textiles are integral to Quechua culture, with ancestral narratives literally woven into the fabric. Specialist tour operators working with local communities in and around the Sacred Valley *(p170)* offer workshops on the highly skilled ancient art of weaving on a backstrap loom. Serious would-be practitioners can opt for an immersion programme.

Where to go: Ollantaytambo *(www.awamaki.org)*; Cusco *(www. textilescusco.org)*; Huancayo *(www.incasdelperu.org)*.

→

Learning from experts in the Centro de Textiles Tradicionales de Cusco

PERU FOR
CRAFTS

From pots and ponchos to masks and miniatures, Peru's traditions of handmade, high-quality crafts have evolved with its various cultures over thousands of years. Whether you're looking to pick up an original souvenir or learn from the masters, Peru's craft scene offers something for everyone.

US$1,700
—
Is the price of a vicuña scarf, made from the world's finest and rarest animal fibre.

Picking Up a Bargain

Browsing bustling Highland markets and bartering is half the fun of shopping in Peru, though it's worth remembering when negotiating that profit margins are already slight. Prices are lower than in the smart stores of Lima – especially if you get a reduction by buying several items from the same vendor – but the choice can be overwhelming and the quality variable.

Where to go: For textiles, Písac *(p194)* and Chinchero *(p194)*; for Mantaro Valley crafts, Feria Dominical in Huancayo *(p202)*; for filigree jewelry and Chulucana ceramics, Catacaos in northern Peru; for last-minute shopping, Calle Petit Thouars in Miraflores *(p105)*.

Colorful souvenirs adorning a shop in Ollantaytambo

←

Intricately patterned ceramic pots at Písac market

Learning From the Experts

Peru's artisans possess immense skill and patience, handed down through generations, to create stunning works of art. A large, intricately carved gourd or a finely woven shawl can take months to complete, but many artisans are keen to demonstrate their techniques to visitors and answer questions, especially if they secure a sale at the end.

Where to go: For workshops, Ayacucho *(p200)*; for weaving cooperatives, Isla Taquile *(p164)*; for on-site artisans working on backstrap looms, Mundo Alpaca *(p156)*.

↑ Backstrap loom weaving at Mundo Alpaca in Arequipa

TOP 5 PERUVIAN CRAFTS

Textiles
Weavings and knitwear from the Sacred Valley, Arequipa, and Taquile are highly prized.

Ceramics
Pottery ranges from Nazca reproductions to delicate Shipibo pots.

Jewelry
Natural Amazonian seed-based necklaces sold in Iquitos are particularly popular.

Woodwork
Ayacucho's painted folk-scene *retablos* (portable altarpieces) are highly sought-after.

Painted Gourds
Exquisitely produced and engraved in the Mantaro Valley.

Flying High in the Sky

Whether ziplining in the Sacred Valley or paragliding amid the Cordillera Blanca, you're guaranteed incredible mountain vistas. Yet paragliding over Lima offers an altogether different view of the capital's dramatic clifftop skyline. For those wanting an even bigger rush of adrenaline, South America's highest bungee jump is located just outside of Cusco (www.actionvalley.com.pe).

←

Paragliding over Lima's extensive coast, with a great view over the capital

PERU FOR
ADVENTURERS

With the world's highest tropical mountain range, the Andes, giving rise to the world's mightiest river, the Amazon, thrill-seekers have plenty to enjoy in Peru. What's more, local tour operators are constantly dreaming up new ways to keep the pulse racing.

Explorations on Foot and by Wheel

One of the world's brilliant trekking destinations, Peru has plenty of routes to choose from around the Cordillera Blanca (p206), the Cañón del Colca (p166), or the Sacred Valley (p170), each offering lovely wilderness dotted with Indigenous hamlets. Thankfully, several have hot springs. Give mountain-biking a try for an exhilarating experience, where operators drive you to the top of the mountain before you begin whizzing downhill. The hairpin bends of the Abra Málaga route (www.amazon-explorer.com) – part of the Machu Picchu Jungle Trail – produce the greatest buzz.

→

Hiking trail with the sun setting over beautiful mountain scenery

STAY

Sky Lodge

Clinging to the rock face, hanging 1,312-ft (400-m) high above the Sacred Valley, are the transparent pods of the unique Sky Lodge. Just reaching your bed entails a rock-climbing challenge, and is only the start of the adventure. This one-of-a-kind experience offers impressive views of the valley below and the twinkling night sky above for those who are brave enough.

🅰 F6 🏠 Valle Sagrado, Pista 224 km
🌐 naturavive.com

S/ S/ S/

Fishing for piranhas at Tambopata National Reserve ↑

Deep in the Jungle

Taking a cargo boat from Pucallpa to Iquitos *(p252)* may be enough adventure for some, but serious explorers should consider taking part in an exciting jungle survival training course. Check out Amazonia Expeditions *(www.perujungle.com)* and hone your bush skills by constructing shelters and balsa rafts while seeking out fresh water and fishing for piranha.

Did You Know?

Many of Peru's classic trails and ancient sites can be visited on horseback.

On the Water

With raging torrents and a beach-laden northern coast, Peru has plenty to offer for water thrillseekers. The Cañón de Cotahuasi *(p168)* offers exhilarating multi-day rafting thrills, while kayaking on Lake Titicaca *(p162)* offers a more sedate foray. The weeklong Andes-to-Amazon rafting and camping trip also promises an unforgettable adventure.

→

Scenic white-water rafting trip on Río Urubamba

PERU FOR
FOODIES

Renowned for its succulent seafood, home to super grain quinoa, and having over 3,000 varieties of potato, Peru's culinary landscape is as diverse as its scenery. Whether dining off damask in Arequipa or snacking on ceviche on a beach in Máncora, your taste buds are in for a treat.

Lima's Food Scene

Thanks to Gastón Acurio, the superstar chef who brought Novoandina cuisine (traditional Andean ingredients given a modern twist) to international attention, Lima is synonymous with culinary innovation. If you can't get a reservation at the legendary Central Restaurante (*www.centralrestaurante.com. pe*), you can give a culinary tour or cooking class a go, offered by Lima Gourmet Company (*www.limagourmetcompany. com.pe*) and Sky Kitchen (*www. skykitchen.com.pe*).

→

Peruvian chef Virgilio Martínez Véliz at Central Restaurante, offering exquisite fine-dining

Fabulous Fruits

Peruvian markets offer a colorful abundance of fruits, equally delicious as freshly squeezed juices or in cocktails. Alongside tropical favorites such as mango, papaya, and pineapple, you'll find heavenly chirimoya, camu-camu, and lúcuma. Known as Inca Gold and associated with fertility, lúcuma's creamy, caramel texture makes it Peru's favorite ice-cream flavor.

←

Pitahaya – a fruit native to the Americas – on sale at a Peruvian market

CEVICHE

With its origins in colonial Peru, ceviche is the country's national dish and the number one meal to try when visiting. The classic seafood recipe comprises chunks of raw fish marinated in lime juice, onions and chilies, served with toasted corn and sweet potato. The Northern Desert *(p222)* is where you'll find some of the best ceviche in the country.

Mistura

Attracting chefs, farmers, and hundreds of thousands of eager visitors to Lima every year, Mistura is Latin America's biggest food fair, usually held for 10 days in September. Started by Gastón Acurio to showcase the best in Peruvian cuisine, it's a chance to sample gourmet fusion delights alongside regular street-food favorites, plus cookery demonstrations, competitions, tastings, and the ever popular pisco tent.

←

Promoting the popular Peruvian quinoa grains at Mistura

TOP 3 MUST-TRY PERUVIAN DISHES

Lomo Saltado
Sautéed strips of beef with onions, chilies, tomatoes, spices, fries, and rice.

Rocoto Relleno
Spicy roasted red peppers stuffed with meat, topped with melted cheese.

Suspiro a la Limeña
For the seriously sweet tooth, a blend of egg yolks, condensed milk, cinnamon, and port, topped with meringue.

↑ Dining at the Mercado Central in downtown Cusco

Dine Like a Local

Offering a chance to interact with the locals, hole-in-the-wall traditional *picanterías* or market stalls often serve an inexpensive *menú* (lunchtime set menu). Generally including a soup, main course, and a drink, it is as agreeable to the wallet as it is to the stomach, but get there early for the freshest fare.

From Chicha to Craft Beer

Most often sold during highland festivals, *chicha de jora* (fermented maize beer) is a potent homebrew that has been in existence since Inca times. *Chica* may still be the tipple of choice for the rural populations, but downing the popular bottled Pilsen Callao, Cristal, and Cusqueña is infinitely more refreshing after a long day. To sample the burgeoning craft beer scene, head for the Cervecería del Valle Sagrado in Urubamba *(www.cerveceriadelvalle. com)*, the Barranco Beer Company in Lima *(www.barrancobeercompany. pe)*, Nuevo Mundo in Cusco *(Portal de Confituria 233)*, or Sierra Andina in Huaraz *(www.sierraandina.com)*.

Draft beer available to sample at Cervecería del Valle Sagrado

PERU FOR
HOME BREWS

Crossing desert, clambering up mountains, and traipsing through the jungle can easily leave you parched. Thankfully, Peru possesses a wealth of alcoholic and non-alcoholic beverages that hit the spot, from its world-renowned pisco to a cornucopia of delicious fruit and vegetable-based drinks.

TOP 3 PISCO COCKTAILS

Pisco Sour
One of the most popular choices, a classic mix of pisco, lime, sugar syrup, and bitters, topped with whisked egg white.

Pisco Chilcano
A refreshing combination of pisco with lime, ginger ale, and bitters.

El Capitán
Resembling a Manhattan cocktail, comprising a blend of pisco, sweet vermouth, and bitters.

Pisco Reigns Supreme

When it comes to alcohol, pisco is king in Peru. Popular all year, it is particularly consumed with much pomp and partying twice a year: on its national day, the fourth Sunday in July, and on the first Saturday in February, when pisco sour – the renowned cocktail – is also celebrated. Expect fun tastings, food stalls, and music in the major pisco-producing regions, particularly Ica *(p144)* and Lima. Year-round you can learn all about this emblematic *aguardiente* (grape brandy) on a fascinating tour of Ica's major *bodegas* (wineries), accompanied by a tipple or two.

Classic pisco sour cocktail with bitters and fresh lime

Staving Off the Highland Chill

Visitors to the Andean highlands are likely to be offered *maté de coca* (coca leaf tea), an ancient Indigenous remedy believed to counteract altitude sickness. Tastier *matés* (herbal teas) include *manzanilla* (camomile), *canela* (cinnamon), and *anis* (aniseed). Coffee-addicts may need to manage their expectations. As Peru's reputation for coffee continues to grow, Peruvians are increasingly leaving behind the traditional *café pasado* (percolated coffee mixed with hot water) and developing a taste for Americano, espresso, and cappuccino.

←

Dried coca leaves for coca leaf tea, great for counteracting altitude sickness symptoms

Quenching the Thirst

Though the fluorescent-yellow and bubble-gum flavor of Inca Kola, Peru's top-selling soft drink, is not to everyone's taste, *chicha morada*, concocted from boiled purple corn/maize, pineapple, apple, lime and cloves, is always gaining new fans. In Peru's many markets, juice stalls flourish. Ask for the "jugo especial" to sample the house special blend.

↑ Wine-colored *chicha morada*, said to have medicinal properties

> ⊙ INSIDER TIP
> **Ley Seca (Dry Law)**
>
> During national elections and in Semana Santa (Holy Week) the sale of alcohol is prohibited in Peru. Yet in the rural district of Tuti, in the Valle del Colca, *ley seca* prevails year-round, except on two days of riotous local celebrations: May 12 and December 12.

Andean Huayno

The panpipe is the archetypal Andean instrument, which together with flutes, harps, and *charangos* (small lutes) form the core of *huayno* bands, whose decibel count is often bolstered by drums, brass, and other wind instruments. A central feature of any Andean festival, you can hear them accompanying joyful dance troupes as they sashay through the streets.

→
Playing the panpipe at the market in Písac

PERU FOR
MUSIC AND DANCE

Music and dance are integral to Peruvian life, reflecting the fusion of Hispanic, African, and Andean roots. While folk traditions are still thriving in the highlands, the infectious rhythms of *criolla* and salsa, alongside the throbbing beats of local rock, hold sway in the clubs of lowland cities.

Do the Marinera

With regional variations, Peru's national dance is a flirtatious courtship ritual of waving white handkerchiefs. The woman performs barefoot, swishing her voluminous skirt while the man seduces with his sombrero. One of the best chances of seeing this dance is at the Festival Nacional de la Marinera *(p66)*.

→
Dancing the *marinera*, performed countrywide

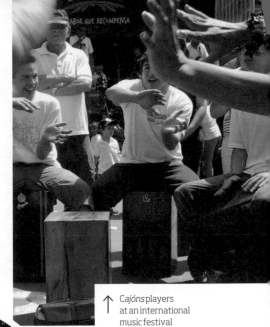

Afro-Peruvian and Criolla

With its origins in the enslaved communities on the central coastal strip, the infectious rhythm of Afro-Peruvian music and *criolla* is a favorite in Lima's *peñas (p84)*. Powered by *cajóns*, rectangular wooden box-drums, in tandem with a grating *quijada de burro*, an instrument made from a donkey's jawbone, the pulsating beat of *festejo* incites dancers.

↑ *Cajóns* players at an international music festival

Modern Sounds

Hit any club in Lima and you'll find proof that Peru's urban youth are into a host of modern music. Electronica, Latin hip-hop, rap, rock, and the insistent beat of reggaeton (rapping and singing, typically in Spanish) all have their fans. You can also find this music blaring out of any beach bar in Máncora *(p234)*.

←

Olaya Sound System, a Peruvian indie band, performing at a festival

Supaypa Wasin Tusuq (Scissors Dance)

The all-male scissors dance is a spectacle. In this historical symbol of resistance against Spanish colonialism, dancers perform eye-popping cart-wheels, somersaults, and aerial jumps, all the while clicking giant scissors in time to the music. See this dance performed at any festival round Ayacucho *(p200)*, but especially during Yaku Raymi *(p67)*, the Big Water Festival, at Andamarca.

→

Vibrant costumes and towering headdresses of the scissors dance

TOP 3 SECLUDED PARADISES

Arennas, Las Pocitas
🅰 B2 🆆 arennas
mancora.com
Stylish boutique
oceanfront hotel that
includes villas with a
private pool.

Kichic, Las Pocitas
🅰 B2 🆆 kichic.com
Rustic luxury in nine
uniquely styled rooms
made from natural
materials.

Yemaya, Punta Sal
🅰 B2 🆆 yemayaperu.com
Thai-style stone-and-
thatch accommodation
possessing all mod cons.

↑ Beautiful night sky above
the bustling party town
of Máncora

THE NORTHERN DESERT'S
BEAUTIFUL BEACHES

Peru's desert coastline provides endless stretches of sand and year-round sun, but the best beaches and warmest waters lie in the north. From Trujillo to Tumbes, there are beach scenes to suit all tastes, be it surfing, fishing, snorkelling, partying, or simply kicking back and watching the waves.

Play in the Waters of Punta Sal

The shallow rippling waters of Punta Sal, near Zorritos (p234), are perfect for safe swimming or trying out a new watersport. Sea-kayaks, windsurfers, and stand-up-paddle boards are all available for rent, with instruction on hand. You may even glimpse migrating hump-back whales, visible from the shore between July and October.

←

The broad belt of flat sand on Punta Sal, arguably Peru's most attractive beach

Party on the Shores of Máncora

Surf-and-party central, Máncora (p234) is one of South America's best-known holiday resorts. Packed with beach bars and fun-seeking Limeños who fly up for the festive season between December and March, this is the spot to dance and drink the night away. Bask on the soft sands during the day, hit the waves surfing, or learn to dive at Peru's first PADI-affiliated school.

 INSIDER TIP
Whale Watching

Responsible whale-watching trips led by marine biologists set out from Los Órganos, south of Máncora, in search of humpbacks in the migration season. Visit www.pacifico adventures.com for more details.

Unwind on the Sands of Las Pocitas

Máncora's palm-fringed satellite strand is distinctly more luxurious and tranquil than the raucous resorts - the only night-time rhythms to reach your oceanside cabaña are those of breaking waves. Las Pocitas is a heavenly spot to relax: feast on succulent seafood, laze in a hammock, or stroll along the beach at sunset.

→

Rows of palm trees along the blissful beach of Las Pocitas

Surf on the Waves of Chicama

On the bucket list for all serious surfers, Chicama claims to have the longest left-breaking wave in the world, providing over two miles of surfing heaven. For non-surfers, the splendid Chicama Surf Resort (www. waterwaystravel.com) nonetheless offers plenty of entertainment, from the swimming pool to ping-pong or table football, as well as day-trips to Trujillo (p226) and the surrounding ancient sites.

↑ Riding a wave at the splendid Chicama beach

Colorful Displays at Madre de Dios

The dawn spectacle of macaws descending on an Amazon clay lick to eat the mineral-rich clay is truly breathtaking. Although they depart as quickly as they arrive, it is not difficult to seek out other impressive birds: bright-billed toucans or the extraordinary hoatzin spend much of their time here. Lodges and camps in Manu (p256) organize visits to clay licks, though they are a lot more accessible from Tambopata (p258).

→

A moving kaleidoscope of macaws on a clay lick at Madre de Dios

PERU FOR
BIRDWATCHING

Peru is home to over 1,800 bird species, making it a magnet for wildlife enthusiasts. The jungle offers some fantastic areas to exhibit the dazzling colors and extraordinary behaviours of Peru's tropical birdlife, so make sure to pack some binoculars.

 HIDDEN GEM
Chaparrí Lodge

Peru's first privately owned reserve, the splendid Chaparrí Reserva Ecológica is home to 70 endemic bird species. Experience the reserve with a stay in rustic cabins at Chaparrí Ecolodge (www.chaparrilodge.com).

Close Encounters on a Canopy Walkway

Since most animal activity occurs in the rainforest canopy, it pays to join them up in the treetops. You can find a number of canopy towers or walkways in several places, but for something spectacular, check out Explorama Lodges (www.explorama.com) near Iquitos or Rainforest Expeditions in Tambopata (www.rainforestexpeditions.com).

→

Birdwatching from a canopy walkway deep in the rainforest

Seabird Central on Islas Ballestas

In a deafening cacophony, millions of squabbling and squawking seabirds jostle for position on these crowded rocky islets. Visitor favorites include the comical Humboldt penguins and the smart grey Inca terns, sporting white whiskery moustaches and scarlet beaks. Boats to Islas Ballestas (p144) leave Paracas daily.

→

Cormorants gathering on rock formations on the Islas Ballestas

Giant Condors at the Cruz del Cóndor

A close encounter with a condor will surely amaze. Usually a distant black speck soaring high over a remote Andean valley, at the Cruz del Cóndor – a viewpoint overhanging the Cañón del Colca (p166) – these avian giants rise up majestically from the canyon floor, mesmerizing crowds.

←

Condor flying over the Cañón del Colca

↑ Peru's national bird, a male cock-of-the-rock, perching on a tree

Star Attractions at Cloud Forest Gems

Two private patches of cloud forest safeguard rare Andean treasures. Owlet Lodge in the Reserva Abra Patricia protects its long-whiskered namesake – absolutely tiny, it was for many years thought to be extinct. Nearby Reserva Huembo's star resident is the marvelous spatuletail hummingbird, dazzling visitors with its shimmering racket-tail feathers in a magical acrobatic display. Visit their shared website (www.owlet lodge.org) for more details on both spectacular spots.

Hiking Off the Beaten Path

While the dramatic peaks of the Cordillera Blanca *(p206)* are a magnet for both casual and experienced hikers, the undeniably challenging 12-day circuit of the neighboring Cordillera Huayhuash *(p221)* promises equally magnificent Andean scenery without the tourists. High mountain passes afford breathtaking panoramas across snow-frosted peaks and sheer rock faces that plunge into glacial lakes. Meanwhile, a break at the hot springs near the midway point provides welcome relief and a massage for your sore muscles. Sign up with a tour operator in Huaraz *(p220)*, or hire a guide locally.

$\rightarrow$

Camping near the picture-perfect landscapes in Cordillera Huayhuash

PERU FOR
HIDDEN GEMS

The vast, varied, and challenging terrain in Peru makes it easy to escape the tourist track without too much effort. There are bountiful treasures to be discovered, from crashing waves in secluded coves to stunning mountain-top vistas that are all yours.

Homestay with an Indigenous Family

Rich in ancient traditions, the majestic Lake Titicaca offers a host of homestay options. With a smattering of Spanish, visitors can delve deeper into the culture by staying with a local family. Learn about medicinal plants, turn your hand at fishing, or help prepare a tasty *pachamanca* (meal cooked in an earth oven). Eschewing the more visited islands of Taquile and Amantaní *(p164)*, a warm welcome is guaranteed in the mainland communities of Chucuito *(p165)* or Llachón.

$\rightarrow$

Gathering beside a reed boat on one of the Islas Uros on Lake Titicaca

The Dirt Road Less Traveled

Impassable at times during the rainy season, which lasts from October to March or April, the unpaved road north from Oxapampa *(p264)* provides a spectacular, hair-raising ride as it plunges down to charming sub-tropical Pozuzo *(p265)* – a small Tyrolean-Peruvian settlement. Skirting the edge of a ravine for much of the way, the road spans countless streams, offering tantalizing glimpses of cascading falls, lush forested slopes, and the raging river below.

To experience an even greater adrenaline rush, rent a mountain bike.

← The Oxapampa-Ashaninka-Yanesha Biosphere Reserve

TOP 3 **REMOTE RETREATS**

Tapiche Jungle Reserve
⌂ 249 miles (400 km) S of Iquitos ⓦ tapichejunglereserve.com
Rustic accommodations in a private reserve brimming with wildlife deep in the rainforest.

Llanganuco Lodge
⌂ 22 miles (36 km) N of Carhuaz ⓦ llanganucolodge.com
Luxurious mountain hiking lodge with stunning views in the Cordillera Blanca.

Wayqecha Lodge
⌂ 26 miles (42 km) N of Paucartambo ⓦ birding.amazonconservation.org
Simple wooden cabins for birdwatchers set in dreamy cloud forest.

Dining Afloat in the Amazon

For a unique culinary experience, take a ferry from Iquitos *(p252)* out to Al Frio y Al Fuego *(www.alfrioyalfuego.com)* – a floating upscale restaurant. Sip a jungle-juice cocktail, soak up a glorious Amazonian sunset if dining in the evening, and sample the local mouth-watering gourmet cuisine.

↑ The picturesque location of Al Frio y Al Fuego, complete with a pool and sun deck

→ Treasures inside the Museo de las Tumbas Reales de Sipán, and a spider necklace *(inset)*

Gazing at Gold

All that glitters really is gold in the Museo de las Tumbas Reales de Sipán *(p230)* at Lambayeque, home to some of Peru's most notable treasures, which were unearthed in an imperial Mochica tomb. Gold and silver breastplates, goblets, and exquisite jewelry inlaid with semi-precious stone are superbly displayed in a darkened pyramid, reminiscent of the period, alongside an impressive reconstruction of the grave site.

PERU FOR
ARCHEOLOGY ENTHUSIASTS

Machu Picchu and the Incas may hog the headlines, but a host of earlier cultures have left a monumental mark on the Peruvian landscape. From the impressive northern citadel of Kuélap to the enigmatic Nazca Lines in the southern desert, there's no shortage of fascinating archeological wonders.

Peering at Mummies

A common practice among pre-Columbian cultures, mummification has always held a macabre fascination. In the Cementerio de Chauchilla *(p147)*, seated skeletons well over a thousand years old stare back at you eerily. Remarkably preserved in elaborate shrouds, their hair and even fragments of skin remain intact due to the arid desert climate. The Museo Regional Adolfo Bermúdez Jenkins in Ica *(p144)* also houses a fascinating collection of mummies.

Mummies on display at the Cementerio de Chauchilla, near Nazca ↓

Exploring Ancient Ruins

Looming out of the northern desert, the vast adobe Huaca del Sol (Temple of the Sun) (p232), center of the ancient Mochica Empire, is an imposing sight. Yet the real thrill is examining the lavishly painted friezes of the sibling Huaca de la Luna (Temple of the Moon), depicting an array of natural spirits and the fierce face of ruling deity Ai-Apaec. A visit to one of Peru's best-preserved adobe ruins, Tambo Colorado (p145) is extraordinary.

TOP 3 ARCHEOLOGY MUSEUMS

Museo Arqueológico Rafael Larco Herrera
Private collection in Lima laden with gold, silver, and Mochica erotic art (p131).

Museo de Arte Precolombino
Superb wide-ranging set of ancient artifacts in Cusco (p174).

Museo Nacional de Arqueología, Antropología e Historía del Perú
Comprehensive trawl through all of Peru's ancient cultures (p128).

←
Evocative painted frieze at Huaca de la Luna in Trujillo

SEÑOR DE WARI

The discovery of the Lord of Wari's tomb in 2011 in Espiritú Pampa was proof that it had been occupied by the Wari before the Incas made their last stand there against the Spanish. Objects found are held in the museum at Pikillacta (p192).

↑ Familia Real, Palpa Lines, featuring the eye-boggling *dios oculado*

Deciphering Desert Etchings

Peering out of the plane window as you sweep over the mysterious Nazca Lines (p140) – including the giant monkey, hummingbird, and spider – is an exhilarating experience. Now the thrill can be extended to include the more recently unearthed Palpa Lines (p140), even older geoglyphs etched into hillsides by the Paracas culture. The best known, Familia Real (Royal Family), features the *dios oculado* deity.

Charming Spectacled Bear

The inspiration for children's favorite Paddington, the spectacled bear gets its name from the rings around its eyes. South America's only species of bear is a shy, mild-mannered creature that prefers chewing bamboo to eating meat. The best chance of spotting one is the Reserva Nacional Chaparrí *(www.chaparrilodge.com)*, which also runs a rehabilitation center.

←

Spectacled bear, named after the disinctive rings around its eyes

PERU FOR
ASTOUNDING WILDLIFE

One of the top spots in the world for wildlife, Peru is home to an array of species. Many can be found on the coastal deserts and in the mountains, but most inhabit the eastern slopes of the Andes and the lush Amazon.

Majestic Jaguar

Much revered by Peru's population, this powerful cat is the Amazon's supreme predator, equally at home on land, up a tree, or in water. Staying at a remote lodge or camp in Tambopata *(p258)* or Manu *(p256)*, accompanied by a naturalist guide, increases your chances of catching a rare glimpse of this magnificent beast.

→

The jaguar's spotted coat provides the perfect camouflage

Comical Camelids

Llamas and alpacas are synonymous with the Andes, their faintly humorous appearance – long necks and camel-like faces – making them the stars of many a photo. Llamas are larger, with longer ears and coarser coats, while alpacas are smaller and fluffier. Their threatened wild relative, the vicuña, can be seen grazing the plains in Pampa Galeras *(p146)*.

↑ Herd of wild and elegant vicuña in the Andes in Arequipa

Beautiful Butterflies

Flitting around Peru's tropical forests are stunning butterflies adding splashes of color and ethereal elegance. The spectacular blue morpho is especially dazzling, its iridescent wings shimmering in the sunlight. Lepidoptera enthusiasts tend to head for the Pakitza region of the Manu National Reserve *(p256)*, which has the richest butterfly environment of anywhere on the planet.

←
Morpho peleides, or blue morpho butterfly

↑ Beautiful spider monkey perched on a tree branch

Marvelous Monkeys

Fabulous treetop entertainers, monkeys top the must-see list of most visitors to the rainforest. Over 30 species cavort in the canopy, from the rare scarlet-faced uakari, to the more commonly spotted acrobatic troupes of spider monkeys and mischievous capuchins. At almost any jungle camp or lodge, you'll be woken by the pre-dawn chorus of bellowing howler monkeys, who may oblige with an encore before dusk.

AMAZON
ADVENTURES

The enticing prospect of a boat trip is guaranteed in the rainforest. Whether in a motorized dugout bound for a jungle lodge, or on a converted steamship cruising up the Amazon, the possibilities for adventure along the splendid waters in Peru are endless.

Great Views by Riverboat Cruises

Riverboat cruises are a wonderful way to unwind on the Amazon. For those craving action, land excursions promise forays into the undergrowth while explorations by dugout involve close encounters with aquatic life. Most vessels head out of Iquitos to explore the Reserva Nacional Pacaya Samiria *(p254)*, but consult Rainforest Cruises *(www.rainforest cruises.com)* for options.

→

Deck of riverboat Ayapua, perfect for lounging on or watching the sunset

Explorations by Dugout

It's much easier to navigate narrow tributaries and shallow lagoons by dugout. What's more, it enables closer encounters with wildlife, drifting right up to dazzling kingfishers ready to plunge after prey, basking caimans, or even a family of watchful giant river otters. Most lodges organize trips by dugout as part of their package; otherwise, simply turn up at your chosen dock to begin the adventure.

←

Boat gliding through the Madre de Dios River tributary of the Amazon River

💬 INSIDER TIP
Wildlife Photography

The best time to photograph wildlife is at dusk or dawn, when light is just above the horizon. If shooting in cloudy conditions, the light will be more even and provide the perfect atmospheric shot. Remember not to shoot with flash, as this may frighten the wildlife.

↑ A passenger ferry crossing the Amazon river near the Port of Iquitos

Lazy Journeys by Lancha

Swinging in a hammock on a *lancha* (chugging cargo boat) is a no-frills way to travel downriver and experience river life first-hand. Timetables can be vague, and it's best to bring your own food. The main routes lie between Yurimaguas *(p260)* or Pucallpa *(p262)* and Iquitos *(p252)*; just roll up at the dock the day before.

↑ Hammocks on a *lancha*, a unique way to engage with traveling Peruvians

A YEAR IN
PERU

JANUARY

△ **Festival de la Marinera** *(Jan/Feb)*. Couples of all ages compete in Trujillo to be named Peru's best *marinera* dancers.

Aniversario de Lima *(Jan 18)*. Celebrations for Lima's anniversary involve fireworks and music.

FEBRUARY

△ **Fiesta de la Virgen de la Candelaria** *(Feb 2–mid-Feb)*. Religious parades, folkloric music, and dancing honor the patron of Puno, the Virgin of Candelaria.

Festival del Verano Negro *(Feb/Mar)*. A celebration of Afro-Peruvian culture takes place in Chincha and El Carmen.

MAY

Corpus Christi *(May/Jun)*. Statues of 16 saints are carried to the cathedral in Cusco in this religious celebration.

△ **Qoyllur Rit'i** *(late May/early Jun)*. During this religious festival, people hike overnight to a shrine at Nevado Ausangate in Cusco.

JUNE

△ **Inti Raymi** *(Jun 24)*. The Festival of the Sun celebrates the Inca Sun God, Inti, with a procession up to Sacsayhuaman in Cusco.

Festival del Andinismo Cordillera Blanca *(end Jun)*. Expect weekends of sports competitions, films, and even rock concerts at this mountain-climbing festival in Huaraz.

SEPTEMBER

△ **Mistura** *(second week of Sep)*. Celebrity chefs and restaurants from across Peru converge in Lima for this culinary festival.

Fiesta de la Primavera *(Sep/Oct)*. Spring is marked across the country with houses decked with flowers and the procession of the city's new beauty queen in Trujillo.

OCTOBER

△ **Fiesta del Señor de los Milagros** *(Oct 18–28)*. Tens of thousands of penitents follow an image of the Lord of Miracles on its 24-hour journey across Lima.

Día de la Canción Criolla *(Oct 31)*. Creole music is honored with concerts in Lima.

MARCH

Festival de la Vendimia *(early Mar)*. Expect to see live grape-stomping from the Harvest Queen and her handmaidens in Ica.

△ **Domingo de Ramos** *(Mar/Apr)*. A donkey is led by children dressed as angels at this Palm Sunday festival in Cruces de Porcón, mixing Andean and Catholic traditions.

APRIL

△ **Semana Santa** *(Mar/Apr)*. The week leading up to Easter ushers in religious processions countrywide.

Concurso Nacional del Caballo Peruano de Paso *(mid-Apr)*. Celebrated in Lima, more than 700 animals and horse breeds are presented at the National Peruvian Paso Horse Contest.

JULY

Fiesta de la Virgen del Carmen *(Jul 15–18)*. Virgin del Carmen, patroness of the mestizo people, is paid tribute to in Paucartambo.

Fiestas Patrias *(Jul 28–29)*. Independence Day is celebrated across the country.

△ **Día Nacional del Pisco** *(last Sun)*. Bars and restaurants throw pisco-themed parties in Lima, Arequipa, and in vineyards around Ica to celebrate the national drink.

AUGUST

Selvámonos *(end Jun–Aug)*. Celebrate national and international bands and DJs at Peru's largest alternative music and art festival in Oxapampa.

△ **Aniversario de Arequipa** *(Aug 15)*. Head to the Plaza de Armas to see colorfully dressed folk-dancing troupes on Arequipa's anniversary.

Yaku Raymi *(end Aug)*. Offerings are made to goddess Pachamama amid striking dances such as the Danzantes de Tijera (Scissors Dance) during this impressive Big Water Festival in Ayacucho.

NOVEMBER

△ **Día de Todos los Santos and Día de Los Difuntos** *(Nov 1–2)*. Picnics are held at cemeteries across Peru to commemorate All Saints' Day and All Souls Day.

Semana Jubilar de Puno *(first week Nov)*. Dancing, processions, and fireworks celebrate the founding of Puno.

DECEMBER

△ **Vispera de Navidad and Día de Navidad** *(Dec 24/25)*. Cusco's Plaza de Armas hosts the Santurantikuy market, with handcrafted Nativity scenes for sale.

A BRIEF
HISTORY

The origins of civilization in Peru can be traced back 20,000 years before the Incas, making the country one of the cradles of ancient cultures. Peru today is the result of a collision between the Andean and Western worlds, a process that began with the arrival of the Spanish in 1532.

First Human Traces

Peru's earliest settlers arrived via the Bering Strait during the last Ice Age (40,000 to 20,000 BC), leaving evidence of human civilization in Cueva de Pikimachay in around 20,000 BC. Later, the planting of crops established a system of agriculture and founded permanent settlements. Excavations of Caral, north of Lima, revealed a complex urban center in the Central Andes. Radiocarbon dating indicates that it was built around 2600 BC – 4,000 years before the appearance of the Incas. After 500 years of occupation, Caral was abandoned for reasons unknown.

1 A map of Peru from the 16th century.

2 Ruins found at the vast site of Caral, an impressive complex.

3 Golden mask from a Chimú jewelry collection.

4 The defeat of Huáscar by his brother Atahualpa during the civil war.

Timeline of events

11,000 BC
First nomadic communities roam the highlands hunting giant animals.

8000 BC
Potatoes are first cultivated by farmers near Lake Titicaca.

900–300 BC
Coastal societies disintegrate while the Chavín cult flourishes.

20,000 BC
Nomadic groups cross the Bering Strait from Asia to the Americas, gradually spreading south.

2627 BC
Caral, the oldest city in the Americas, is built in the Supe Valley.

Main Early Cultures

The Early Horizon (1000 BC–AD 200) saw the Chavín cult unite coastal and highland societies, but as their influence waned, various regional cultures arose, from the Nazca (100 BC–AD 700) in the south, to the Moche (AD 100–700) in the north. By the Middle Horizon period (AD 600–1000) two expansive states had emerged: the Wari, from Ayacucho and the Tiwanaku, based around Lake Titicaca. It was not until 1197, though, that a group in the Cusco Valley known as the Inca came to prominence.

The Inca

Little is known about the early Inca leaders, although legend tells that the first, Manco Cápac, founded the city of Cusco. The most important was the ninth, Pachacútec (1438–71), under whose leadership the Tahuantinsuyu (Land of the Four Quarters) expanded and covered nearly a third of South America, making it one of the largest empires in history. By the 16th century, civil war broke out when Huayna Cápac, the 11th Inca, died. The kingdom was divided between his son, Huáscar, and illegitimate son, Atahualpa, though the latter finally seized control.

THE CÁPAC ÑAN (ROYAL ROAD)

Roads were crucial to Pachacútec's program of unification. Under his reign alone, the Inca constructed some 25,00 miles (40,000 km) of stone roads, some scaling passes 16,500 ft (5,000 m) high. This Cápac Ñan network connected all four regions of the empire, running 3,500 miles (5,500 km) from Quito in Ecuador right down to Santiago in Chile.

650
The Wari-Tiahuanaco period begins.

1200
Cusco is founded by the first Inca, Manco Cápac.

AD 220–600
Moche culture thrives.

1400
Maximum expansion of the Chimú kingdom.

1438–71
The 9th Inca Pachacútec's 33-year reign begins.

1

The Spanish Conquest

In 1524, the conquistador Francisco Pizarro set out to conquer "Birú", a kingdom rich in gold and silver situated south of present-day Colombia. Returning to Spain with goods to prove the existence of "El Dorado", Pizarro was appointed Governor and Captain-General in 1529, and authorized to conquer Peru.

The Spanish invasion was one of the first and bloodiest clashes between European colonizers and people in the Americas. Pizarro and Almagro landed in Tumbes in 1532 during the civil war between Atahualpa and Huáscar over succession. Pizarro later executed Atahualpa and took over the leaderless empire.

Life Under the Spanish

The original leaders of the Spanish conquest perished in a bitter feud, with the execution of Almagro by Pizarro in 1538, which led to the assassination of Pizarro in 1541. Colonization and exploitation of the country's natural and human resources continued nonetheless. The conquistadors introduced new economic classes, as well as Catholicism and the Spanish language, which Peruvians still adhere to and speak today.

↑ Francisco Pizarro, Spanish conqueror of the Inca Empire

Timeline of events

1525
Huayna Cápac dies and his son, Huáscar succeeds; war with Atahualpa.

1532
Pizarro lands in Tumbes with 168 men and captures Atahualpa.

1533
Atahualpa is tried and executed; Cusco is sacked.

1535
Pizarro founds Lima on January 18.

2 3

The feudal encomienda system they introduced produced immense inequalities, and to reduce these, the Spanish king issued new laws. From 1542, civil war broke out between the conquistadors, who saw their livelihoods under threat, and the Viceroyalty, the Spanish administrative district that had been newly established by the Spanish Crown. After 10 years of conflict, the Viceroyalty triumphed. In 1574, Viceroy Francisco de Toledo reintroduced the Inca mit'a tax, forcing people to work unpaid, to their death, in mines.

Push for Independence

With the abdication of Spain's King Charles IV in the early 1800s, thoughts of independence spread throughout South America. In 1821, José de San Martín defeated the royalist forces in Peru and proclaimed its independence. After trying to introduce a new constitution, San Martín ceded control to Venezuelan general Simón Bolívar. The first elected president in Peru did not enter office until 1827. In the first 40 years after independence, the presidency changed hands 35 times, of which only four presidents were constitutionally chosen.

1 Spaniards burning Atahualpa in 1538.

2 Almagro loyalists murdering Francisco Pizarro in 1541.

3 General San Martín proclaiming Peru's independence.

15
—
The number of different constitutions written in the first 40 years after independence.

1600
Potosí mines reach population peak with 160,000 workers.

1767
Jesuits are expelled from the Spanish Empire.

1780–82
A descendant of Atahualpa, Túpac Amaru II, stages the final Inca rebellion and is executed.

1821
San Martín proclaims Peru's independence.

1

Post-Independence and the Modern Era

The War of the Pacific (1879–83) was sparked by a dispute over control of nitrate-rich beds in the northern Atacama Desert. Following a rising global demand for nitrates, a key ingredient in explosives and fertilizers, Bolivia attempted to tax Chilean companies operating in their territory. When Chile refused, Bolivia declared war, asking for aid from neighboring Peru. Much of the conflict played out at sea, through warships such as the iron-clad *Huáscar*. By 1883, Chile had won; Bolivia had lost its sea access, while Peru ceded substantial territory.

Early 20th Century

After the war, Peru oscillated between democracy and military dictatorship. In 1919, Augusto Leguía assumed the presidency in a coup, introducing a new constitution which gave the state wide-ranging power. In 1968, a military dictatorship was again enforced when General Juan Velasco Alvarado seized power. Democracy was restored in 1980 by Fernando Belaúnde. Intent on privatizing industry, his term was hampered by high inflation and the threat of guerrilla movements.

↑ Augusto Leguía, who served as president of Peru from 1919 to 1930

Timeline of events

1879–83
War of the Pacific.

1938
María Luisa Aguilar, Peru's first professional astronomer, is born.

1919–30
Leguía's 11-year civil dictatorship, marked by strong foreign investment and restrictions of civil rights.

1968–80
Twelve years of military dictatorship under General Juan Velasco Alvarado.

1980
Belaúnde is re-elected; Sendero Luminoso (Shining Path) initiates the guerrilla struggle.

Shining Path, Fujimori, and Civil Conflict

The growth of the extremist guerilla movement Sendero Luminoso (Shining Path), led by Abimael Guzmán, and of the Marxist Movimiento Revolucionario Túpac Amaru (MRTA), resulted in a guerrilla war. From 1980, vast stretches of the sierra and the Amazon were cut off from the rest of the country, and 70,000 Peruvians were killed during the conflict. In 1990, the new Cambio 90 party were elected. Their leader Alberto Fujimori, though initially popular, was sentenced to 25 years in prison in 2007 for corruption and human rights abuses.

Peru Today

Since 2001, Peru has been one of the fastest growing economies in Latin America, with poverty rates steadily reducing. However, many – especially Indigenous people in rural areas – are still not benefitting from the wealth. The first four presidents this century – Toledo, García, Humala, and Kuczynski – have all been implicated in major corruption scandals, and since 2017, Peru has had five presidents in five years. Despite this, Peruvians remain optimistic that public protest can usher in a new era.

1 The Battle of Angamos during the War of the Pacific. ↑

2 Juan Velasco Alvarado's presidency tour in 1971.

3 Workers cleaning up a bomb explosion in Miraflores in 1992, for which Guzmán was captured and tried for.

4 Alejandro Toledo, Peru's first Indigenous president, at a traditional blessing ceremony at Machu Picchu in 2001.

1999

Fujimori is elected president for an unprecedented third term.

2000

Fujimori flees the country and resigns via fax after a bribery scandal.

2017

Pedro Pablo Kuczynski (PPK) is elected president.

2017–2018

PPK narrowly survives an impeachment vote after he is implicated in Lava Jato. He resigns before a second vote in March 2018.

2018

The probe into the Odebrecht scandal continues, implicating the four last Peruvian presidents.

PERU'S INDIGENOUS POPULATION

Speaking 47 different languages, Peru's Indigenous population comprises around a fifth of the country's 31 million people. Most inhabit the Andes, dominated by Quechua groups, or the Amazon Basin, where the Asháninka make up the majority community. Common to all is the struggle to maintain their traditional customs and ways of life while trying to adapt to modern living on their own terms. Significant numbers have migrated to the big cities in recent decades, initially fleeing the violence of the 1980s, and latterly in search of employment. A visit to the highlands or the rainforest affords unique opportunities to learn from these ancient societies.

ANDEAN PEOPLES

Quechua and Aymara groups dominate Peru's Andean spine, and their beliefs permeate everything from labor practices to festivals, and food to fabric. *Pachamama* (Mother Earth) reigns as the supreme deity and guiding force, and ritual offerings made every August 1 kickstart a month of celebrations across the Altiplano. Since colonial times, the three-million plus Quechua and half a million Aymara have often worshipped Pachamama along with the Virgin Mary.

AMAZONIAN PEOPLES

Around 40 Indigenous groups inhabit the forested Amazon Basin, with some 55,000 Asháninka the most numerous. They, along with many others, are increasingly being forced off their lands by oil exploration and illegal logging and mining. Widespread among Indigenous Amazonian groups are animism and shamanism, the belief that all nature is imbued with spirits that can be contacted via spiritual leaders in altered states of consciousness.

↑ Feeding a llama in the Cusco area of Peru

> INSIDER TIP
> ### Homestays
> Avoiding the voyeuristic visits to Indigenous villages offered by tour operators, homestays *(p163)* offer a deeper intercultural exchange. Visit *www.peru.travel/en/experiences/experiential* to find out the best places for homestays.

↑ Islas Uros on Lake Titicaca, a great place to do a homestay

THE IMPORTANCE OF PLANTS

Plants have been crucial to traditional societies for centuries, whether making clothing, homes, and utensils, or used as medicines and during shamanic rituals.

Coca - Since pre-Columbian times sacred coca leaves have fulfilled social, ritual, and medicinal functions, combating diverse ailments such as hunger, fatigue, and altitude sickness.

Ayahuasca - This giant vine with hallucinogenic and purgative properties is used by shamans for medicinal and spiritual purposes.

Achiote - As well as possessing antibacterial properties, the crushed seeds from this tropical shrub's flowers produce a red dye, used for fabrics.

1 A colorful handmade bag used to hold coca leaves.

2 Ayahuasca leaves, found at a healing center in Peru.

3 The stunning flowers on an Achiote tree.

↑ Members of the Amazonian Yagua entering a traditional *maloca*

EXPERIENCE
LIMA

Enjoying the Circuito Mágico del Agua

3 Days in Lima 80

Lima Your Way 82

Central Lima 88

Miraflores and San Isidro 104

Barranco 116

Beyond the Center 126

Río Rímac

AVENIDA MORALES DUAREZ

AVENIDA ARGENTINA

AV. REPÚBLICA
DE VENEZUELA

Parque de las
Leyendas

AVENIDA LA MARINA

LA PERLA

AV. UNIVERSITARIA

SAN MIGUEL

AVENIDA LA PAZ
AVENIDA COSTANERA

MAGDALENA

EXPLORE
LIMA

This guide divides Lima into four
sightseeing areas: the three shown
on this map and Beyond the Center.

←

1 Lima's pretty main square.

2 Paragliding over Larcomar shopping mall.

3 Goldenberries on sale at Mercado Surquillo de Lima.

4 Enjoying the Circuito Mágico del Agua.

3 DAYS
in Lima

Day 1

Morning Begin your day absorbing Central Lima's colonial atmosphere in the Plaza Mayor (p102) and watch the changing of the guard at noon outside the Palacio del Gobierno (p97). Continue one block north to the Casa de Aliaga (p97), the oldest colonial mansion in the city and, allegedly, South America. Continue south to reach Chinatown (p100) for a traditional lunch at a *chifa*.

Afternoon Catch a cab across the city to the Museo Nacional de Arqueología, Antropología e Historia del Perú (p128), with its dazzling array of mummies from the Paracas culture. Once finished, head a few blocks away to the collection of pre-Columbian ceramics covering 3,000 years of history at the renowned Museo Arqueológico Rafael Larco Herrera (p131).

Evening For souvenir shopping, take a taxi south to Miraflores and browse the handicraft and antiques stalls clustered in the cat-filled Parque Kennedy (p110). Stroll south for dinner at one of the modern restaurants in the Larcomar shopping mall, which come complete with expansive ocean views.

Day 2

Morning One of the city's loveliest parts is the Miraflores' Malecón (p114), a cliff-side path punctuated by manicured parks and plenty of benches. Hire a bike for an early-morning spot of exercise. Continue on foot along the coast to reach Barranco (p116), strolling along Avenida Sáenz Peña to take in the neighborhood's exquisite 20th-century mansions.

Afternoon Head further north and grab lunch on the go as you explore the bustling Mercado de Surquillo, an unmissable Peruvian market experience. Pick your way between stalls laden with mouthwatering fruit, mountains of vegetables, and hook-slung meat. Afterward, take a *metropolitano* bus north for the Museo de Arte de Lima (p99), a museum with 34 galleries.

Evening For dinner, reserve a table at one of the branches of the perpetually-rammed Punto Azul (www.puntoazul restaurante.com), a chain of *cevicherías* offering some of the city's finest and most affordable dining.

Day 3

Morning From central Lima, hop on a bus heading south along the Pan-American Highway to reach Pachacámac (p133). A guided tour takes you around this temple complex, which dates back to AD 200.

Afternoon Back in Miraflores, grab a sandwich at La Lucha Sanguchería (p111) before taking in the Huaca Pucllana (p108), a pre-Inca adobe pyramid that offers excellent views across the city. Browse the neighborhood's boutique stores as you weave your way north into San Isidro for even more stylish shopping.

Evening Drop by the Parque de la Reserva for the Circuito Mágico del Agua (p95), an interactive water show where 15 lit fountains dance to music. Make a reservation for dinner at the renowned Astrid & Gastón (p111), one of the city's finest restaurants owned by celebrity chef Gastón Acurio and his wife Astrid.

OUTSIDE OF LIMA

In northern Peru's Museo de Arte Moderno *(p229)*, Gerardo Chávez's surrealist paintings don't make for comfortable viewing, but are still worth seeing. Down in the Amazon, Pablo Amaringo forged his own style known as Nuevo-Amazónico, which uses fluorescent colors to create vivid paintings based on ayahuasca visions.

→

El Beso sculpture epitomizing the love theme in the Parque del Amor

LIMA FOR
ART LOVERS

Lima's thriving contemporary art scene continues to gain momentum as small private galleries showcase exciting new talent in Miraflores and Barranco, while street art flourishes organically. With a wealth of sculpture, public art, and traditional paintings, Lima has pieces to suit every taste.

Painting:
Puka Wamani

Bold shapes and colors rooted in Indigenous Andean motifs are the hallmarks of Fernando de Szyslzo's paintings. Szyslzo is considered one of Latin America's greatest abstract artists, and his work is well worth a visit. *Puka Wamani* (1968) – one in a series of the same name – is one such oeuvre, which hangs in the Museo de Arte de Lima *(p99)*, alongside some of his other works.

←

Museo de Arte de Lima, where Szyslzo's paintings are on display

Sculpture: El Beso

One of Lima's most photographed sights, *El Beso* (The Kiss) is a gigantic stone sculpture in Miraflores by Limeño artist Victor Delfín, modelled on himself and his wife locked in a passionate embrace. Inaugurated on Valentine's Day in 1993, it remains the star attraction in the themed clifftop Parque del Amor (Park of Love) *(p111)*. More of his work is exhibited in his nearby studio-gallery *(www.victordelfin.com)*, where he gives tours.

TOP 3 MODERN ART GALLERIES

Museo de Arte Contemporáneo
This gallery is devoted to contemporary art and is expanding *(p122)*.

Revolver Galería
 San Isidro ⓦ revolvergaleria.com
Avant-garde space for local and international contemporary artists.

Wu Galería
Barranco ⓦ wugalleria.com
Encouraging emerging artists in all media.

Street Art: Hogar de un Suspiro

Sprawling across walls, bridges and shopfronts, up steps, or tucked away in courtyards, murals are a big deal in bohemian Barranco. Jade Rivera's *(www.museojaderivera.com)* striking *Hogar de un Suspiro* (Home of the Sigh), located near the Puente de los Suspiros *(p121)*, is one of the main sights in Barranco and celebrates the love in the neighborhood. If a camera snap is not enough, his art gallery on Malecón Castilla sells prints, and for serious enthusiasts, Tailored Tours *(www.tailoredtoursperu.com)* will guide you through the pick of Barranco's graffiti.

↑ The impressive *Hogar de un Suspiro* mural, painted in 2015

💬 INSIDER TIP
Circuito Mágico del Agua

For something different, catch the Magic Water Circuit (p95) in the Parque de la Reserva, a great technicolour sound and light fountain show.

LIMA
AFTER DARK

The capital's vibrant nightlife scene holds something for everyone, with little need to stray from the sophisticated clifftop barrios of Miraflores and Barranco. Whether you opt for a moonlit stroll along the malecón, indulge in a gourmet meal, or hit the bars, clubs, and peñas, Lima has it covered.

Experience Peñas

Originally community venues celebrating a shared heritage of great food and musical traditions, Lima's modern *peñas*, such as La Candelaria *(www.lacandelariaperu.com)*, are now more visitor-oriented, putting on well-choreographed shows of Afro-Peruvian or Andean folk music and dance. For a much more intimate experience, catch an unadulterated slice of criolla culture at Don Porfirio's on a Friday night *(Manuel Segura 115, Barranco)*.

←

Dancers performing at Barranco's popular *peña* Don Porfirio

An Evening at the Theatre

Lima's two standout venues offer plenty. The Teatro Municipal *(Jirón Ica 377)*, with its top-notch acoustics, is the perfect spot for fans of modern dance and classical music. The striking Gran Teatro Nacional de Peru *(www.granteatronacional.pe)* serves up a more varied programme, performing everything from rock to opera, and Broadway to ballet.

←

Dancers rehearsing for a performance at the Gran Teatro Nacional

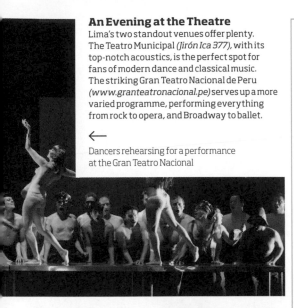

DRINK

Mango's
For a stellar sundowner, bag a clifftop table at this Miraflores bar with fantastic ocean views.

🅐D5 🄰Larcomar, Malecón de la Reserva 610 🅦mangosperu.com

Ayahuasca
Trendy Bohemian restobar set in a gloriously restored colonial mansion with creative cocktails and superb snacks.

🅐D5 🄰Av San Martin 130 🅦ayahuasca restobar.com

Bar-Hop in Barranco

When it comes to bar crawls, Barranco is the place to be, offering all manner of watering holes. Hip bars such as Café Victoria *(Pedro de Osma 135)* inhabit glorious colonial mansions, while family-run Juanito Barranco *(Av Almte Miguel Grau 270)* with its sedate decor attracts a more local crowd. All are conveniently packed round Parque Municipal *(p122)*.

→

The bohemian Bajada de Baños district in Barranco

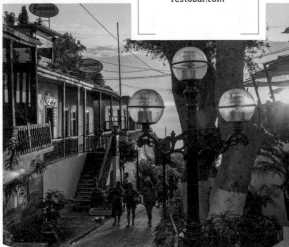

Dance Until You Drop

While dance venues abound in Lima, all require stamina, as the action only hots up around midnight and continues at full speed until almost dawn. Take your pick from intimate dance floors to vast laser-lit caverns, contemporary to retro, rock to reggaeton, and salsa to hip-hop. Miraflores in particular hosts a number of clubs, with the swankiest spots located in Larcomar.

←

Larcomar shopping center and surroundings lit up at night

LIMA'S COLONIAL ARCHITECTURE

A designated UNESCO World Heritage Site, the historical center of the "City of Kings" is known for its 16th to 19th-century architecture. Spanish and Indigenous design often merge in colonial architecture, resulting in a kind of Creole style seen all over Lima. The two grandiose main plazas and neighboring streets overflow with fine churches, palaces, and mansions. Though ravaged by earthquakes, many have been rebuilt in more earthquake-resistant adobe (bricks made from organic materials) and *quincha* (wood or cane covered in mud and plaster).

CASA DE ALIAGA

Dating from 1535, the opulence and Baroque artistry of Lima's oldest and best-preserved mansion *(p97)* are omnipresent, seen in the magnificently carved wooden coffered ceilings, pediments, and mouldings. *Azulejos* (painted tin-glazed ceramic tiles adapted from Islamic architecture) found here are a key decorative feature of both religious and secular colonial buildings.

PALACIO DE TORRE TAGLE

This 18th-century palace *(Jr Ucayali, 363)* was commissioned by the then treasurer of the Spanish fleet, Don José Bernardo de Tagle y Bracho. It features two of the city's most ornate balconies – a key feature of the time. *Mudéjar* (north African Islamic) architectural features inside include lobed arches and fine *azulejos*. The building has been home to the Ministry of Foreign Affairs since 1918.

CASA DE PILATOS

Built in 1590 for a Spanish merchant, the Casa de Pilatos *(Jr Ancash 390)* is based on the Sevillian house in Seville, Spain, of the same name. Currently housing offices of the Supreme Court, the mansion possesses a characteristic colonial courtyard, enclosed by a fine stone staircase. The original wooden balconies were replaced after an earthquake.

CASA DE OSAMBELA

Also known as Casa de Oquendo *(Jr Conde de Superunda, 298)*, Lima's tallest *casona* at the time uniquely has three storeys and is topped with a *mirador* (observation tower). The original owner, shipping merchant Martín de Osambela, would watch his galleons rolling into port from this *mirador*. Though first built in the early 19th century, the current facade displays later Neo-Classical characteristics with Rococo embellishments.

↑ Casa de Aliaga's impressive inner patio, complete with fig tree and fountain

Casa de Osambela's ↑ splendid facade lined with wooden balconies

LIMA'S CHURCHES

Iglesia San Pedro Relatively restrained on the outside, Iglesia San Pedro *(p98)* is jaw-droppingly ornate on the inside, and saturated in gold leaf. Built in its third, and current, incarnation in 1636, Churrigueresque *(p156)* ornamentation was added over time. Gold embellishes everything from the altarpieces and pulpit to the lateral naves and glorious coffered ceiling and cupola.

Iglesia de San Francisco Dating from 1664, the imposing facade of the Iglesia de San Francisco *(p92)* is a sight to behold. Flanked by twin towers, the facade presents a fine example of Spanish Baroque style, comprising a stone altarpiece-portal, decorated with niches, statues and pilasters.

1 Stunning gold embellishment inside San Pedro.

2 San Pedro's cupola, a common feature in religious buildings.

3 San Francisco's splendid facade.

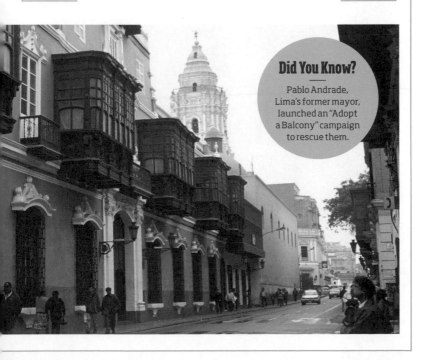

Did You Know?

Pablo Andrade, Lima's former mayor, launched an "Adopt a Balcony" campaign to rescue them.

CENTRAL LIMA

The area on which present-day Lima is located had been populated for thousands of years before the Spanish arrived. It was once home to a confederation of rural fiefdoms, which were later absorbed into the Inca Empire. The Incas also established three urban centers here: Carabyll to the north, Maranga in the center, and Surco, south of what is today Miraflores.

Lima, as we know it, was founded by Francisco Pizarro in 1535, and was the capital of the Spanish Empire in South America for almost two centuries. Dubbed the City of Kings, it was at the time the most important metropolis in the region, the center of power and wealth. Its coat of arms bears three crowns, representing the three kings of the nativity, and the motto proclaiming, "This is truly the sign of kings." Based on a Roman plan, the original 117 city blocks radiate out from Plaza Mayor, where the imposing presence of both church and state accent its pivotal role. Many of the buildings date from the 18th and 19th centuries, as an earthquake in 1746 razed most original structures. Private homes have since morphed into museums or government offices. Fervent devotion to the Catholic doctrine, introduced by the Spanish, means there is a Baroque-, Renaissance-, or Rococo-inspired church or convent on almost every street corner, from the beautiful Santo Domingo to the grand San Francisco.

CENTRAL LIMA

Must See

1 San Francisco

Experience More

2 Estadio Nacional
3 Circuito Mágico del Agua
4 La Catedral
5 Museo de Sitio Bodega y Quadra
6 Casa de Aliaga
7 Palacio de Gobierno
8 Museo Andrés del Castillo
9 San Pedro
10 Parque de la Muralla
11 Santo Domingo
12 Museo de Arte de Lima
13 Convento de los Descalzos
14 Chinatown
15 Plaza San Martín
16 Las Nazarenas
17 Museo de Arte Italiano
18 Museo Nacional de
la Cultura Peruana

Eat & Drink

1 L'Eau Vive
2 Restaurant Bar Cordano

❶ ⚜ Ⓜ 🛍

SAN FRANCISCO

📍 E2 🏛 Jirón Ancash, block 3 🕐 Church: 7–11am & 4–8pm daily; Museum & Convent: 9am–8:45pm daily 🌐 museocatacumbas.com

The striking yellow-and-white complex of San Francisco comprises a church, a convent, the chapels of La Soledad and El Milagro, and eerie catacombs. The facade alone is one of the best examples of 17th-century Baroque architecture in Peru. Inside, the complex also houses superb examples of Baroque sculpture as well as a valuable collection of treasures, from art with Andean touches to the first dictionary published by the Real Academia Española.

The original mud and wood church built in 1557 was destroyed in the 1656 earthquake, and the reconstructed church was completed in 1672 by Portuguese architect Constantino de Vasconcellos. With the exception of the stone altarpiece-portal and the lateral portal, the church is made of the earthquake-resistant *quincha* (rushes, mud, and plaster). The church itself is built on underground tunnels or catacombs, which were used as a cemetery until the early 19th century.

Being the preferred place of worship for the Spanish viceroy and his court, the church received generous donations, especially from the gold and silver mines of Peru. Some of these treasures vanished during the wars of independence in the 19th century, though many remarkable works of art, architecture, and literature remain. The Religious Museum is especially worth a visit, housing a series of the "Passion of Christ" paintings from the 17th-century Flemish painter Peter Paul Rubens. Portraits of the apostles from the studio of the Spanish painter Francisco Zurbarán hang in the Zurbarán Room.

↑ Dramatic circles of skulls and femur bones in the crypt

↑ The splendid convent library, home to centuries-old manuscripts and books

Highlights

The High Altar

△ Designed by the renowned Spanish architect Presbitero Matías Maestro, this impressive structure is carved in a Neo-Classical style.

Convent Library

△ This 17th-century library houses around 25,000 books from the 15th to 18th centuries, including many first editions and parchments.

Baroque Church Facade

△ Two towers flank a stone altarpiece-portal, a lavish mass of sculptures, niches, and more dating from 1664.

Convent Cloister and Garden

△ The tiled patio has a stunning ceiling made from mahogany, and the walls are painted with frescoes.

70,000

The estimated number of burials in San Francisco's bone-packed crypt.

↑ The stunningly ornate Baroque facade of the Complejo de San Francisco

Building San Francisco

In 1535, Emperor Charles I ordered Francisco Pizarro to put aside two sites in Lima so that the Franciscans could build a church and convent. Located on the banks of the Río Rimac, the sites were approximately one-eighth the area of the city, the largest church complexes in the Americas. The best artists of the day, from silversmiths to sculptors were brought in to add decoration. A factory was organized to produce *azulejos* (painted tiles). Impressive detailed decorative patterns can best be seen on the altarpieces, facade, domes, and towers in the church.

↑ Tiled walls, paintings, and ornate woodwork in the colorful mosaic hallway in the cloisters

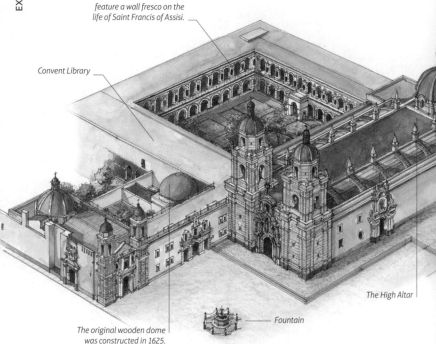

The convent cloisters feature a wall fresco on the life of Saint Francis of Assisi.

Convent Library

The original wooden dome was constructed in 1625.

Fountain

The High Altar

GUINEA PIG SUPPER

Guinea pigs are integral to Peruvian life and millions are eaten every year. The Incas reportedly sacrificed 1,000 guinea pigs and 100 llamas in Cusco's plaza each year for the safety of their fields. Small wonder that Diego de la Puente's *Last Supper*, displayed in San Francisco's Dining Hall, shows Jesus and his 12 disciples sitting down to *cuy chactado* (roast guinea pig). This painting is often mistaken for Marcos Zapata's of the same name *(p179)*.

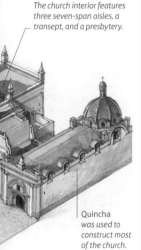

↑ The spectacular Mudéjar (Arabic-patterned) ceiling of the High Altar

The church interior features three seven-span aisles, a transept, and a presbytery.

Quincha *was used to construct most of the church.*

↑ The layout of the grand San Francisco complex, with its church, convent, and chapels

Did You Know?

Lima's largest collection of blue tiles, from Seville, Spain, dating back to 1620, lines the cloisters.

EXPERIENCE MORE

2

Estadio Nacional

📍 D5 📅 Calle José Díaz
📞 01 431 6190 🕐 For fixtures and events

The Estadio Nacional is a 40,000-capacity stadium and home ground of the Peruvian national soccer team. Built in 1952, it hosts international matches, including three of the six Copa America (South American Championship) tournaments held on Peruvian ground. It's also one of Lima's main music venues, hosting big international names.

On May 24, 1964, the stadium saw one of the most tragic soccer disasters in history. During an Olympic qualifying match against Argentina, tear gas was used to dispel pitch invaders and caused a stampede of spectators toward the exit, killing 300 people.

3

Circuito Mágico del Agua

📍 D5 📅 Between Av Arequipa and Av Paseo de la República 🕐 2–10pm daily (water shows at 7:10, 7:50, 8:30 & 9:10pm) 🌐 circuito magicodelagua.com.pe

The spacious Parque de la Reserva, designed by French architect Claude Sahut, is one of Lima's most enticing public areas. In 2007, after lengthy and controversially costly remodeling, 13 cybernetic fountains were installed to create the Circuito Mágico del Agua, an enchanting circuit of ornamental water features. At night, its splendid illuminated water show is Lima's most spectacular entertainment. The fountains are choreographed to light and music. Some spray water 260 ft (80 m) into the air, while others, such as the Túnel de las Sorpresas, form archways through which you can walk.

> 💬 INSIDER TIP
> ### Laberinto del Ensueño
>
> Be sure to protect your valuables when making your way through this fountain at the Circuito Mágico del Agua, as the shots of vertical water are likely to soak you.

↑ The Circuito Mágico del Agua's Túnel de las Sorpresas

Gilded vaulting above the naves of La Catedral ↑

La Catedral

⚲ E2 **⌂ Plaza Mayor**
☏ 01 427 9647 **◷ 9am-1pm & 2-5pm Tue-Sat**

With its imposing twin towers, the cathedral dominates the eastern side of Plaza Mayor. Founder of Lima Francisco Pizarro (1478–1541) carried the first log for the construction of the original adobe wall and the straw roof structure on this site in 1535.

Construction began on the current Baroque-Renaissance-style structure in 1564. Work stalled due to lack of funds and the devastating earthquakes of 1687 and 1746 but was finally completed in 1758. Further rebuilding followed the earthquake of 1940.

The cathedral has five naves and 10 side chapels, the smaller ones dedicated to religious figures. The chapel of John the Baptist has a carving of Jesus, said to be the most beautiful in the Americas. The remains of Francisco Pizarro lie in the mosaic-covered chapel to the right of the entrance. Highlights include

the ornate choir stalls, carved by Spanish sculptor Pedro Noguera, and the museum of religious art.

Museo de Sitio Bodega y Quadra

⚲ E2 **⌂ Jirón Ancash 213**
☏ 01 428 1644 **◷ 10am-3pm Tue, Thu & Sat**

Behind an unassuming exterior lies a journey into the past: a painstakingly excavated 17th-century colonial house.

Stripped walls and floors allow you to wander the layout and imagine how life was lived in that era. It was the home of Spanish merchant and Lima consul Thomas de la Bodega y Quadra and his Peruvian-born son Juan Francisco, the famous explorer and naval officer in the Spanish Armada. Juan Francisco explored California and discovered the Canadian Quadra Island (named after him) and Vancouver Island. The museum includes 10 interesting exhibition rooms, audiovisuals,

→

The grandiose facade of the president's residence, Palacio de Gobierno displays of china and pottery, and cutlery found in the excavations.

Casa de Aliaga

📍 D2 🏛 Jirón de la Unión, 224 🕐 10am–4pm daily, for pre-reserved tours only; call 01 427 7736 to reserve 🌐 casadealiaga.com

This *quincha* (earthquake-resistant material) mansion was built by Jerónimo de Aliaga, one of Pizarro's lieutenants. It is the oldest and best-preserved colonial-era home in the continent and is owned by the same family 17 generations later.

The ornate timber balcony offers the only external clue to the lavish 66-room house that lies within. Marble stairs lead to the second-floor patio and the main entrance. The part that is open to the public showcases a wide range of colonial art and decor from the 16th to 18th centuries, such as Louis XIV mirrors and furniture, family portraits, and Cusco School paintings *(p178)*. One of the two Andalusian patios has a bronze fountain.

INSIDER TIP
Take a Food Tour Downtown

Take a walking tour through the colorful Mercado Central. Devour delicious *papas rellenas* (spicy meat-filled potato croquettes) from a street stall, and sample citrusy ceviche. E-mail foodwalkingtour@gmail.com to reserve.

Palacio de Gobierno

📍 E2 🏛 Plaza Mayor 📞 01 311 3900 ℹ️ PR office, Jirón de la Unión 🕐 For pre-reserved tours only: 9 & 10am Sat & Sun; call 01 311 3900, ext 523, to reserve (Mon–Thu)

Known as the Casa de Pizarro, the Government Palace was built by Pizarro on the land once owned by Taulichusco, a pre-Hispanic chief of the Rimac Valley. It has been the seat of political power in Peru ever since, undergoing major reconstruction in the 1920s and 1930s following a fire.

Inaugurated in 1938, the palace is a grand example of colonial affluence. Rooms are adorned with mahogany and cedar carvings, French glass, Carrara marble, and Czech crystal. A marble staircase dominates the Grand Hall, flanked by busts of key figures in Peru's history. The gilded Salón Dorado (Golden Room) is modeled on the Palace of Versailles' Hall of Mirrors.

The interior is open for tours only, on weekend mornings, but the Changing of the Guard in front of the palace, which takes place daily at noon, is well worth seeing.

Museo Andrés del Castillo

📍 D3 🏛 Jirón de la Unión 1030 🕐 9am–5pm Mon–Sat 🌐 madc.com.pe

This beautifully restored 19th-century house is home to a private museum set up in memory of Andrés del Castillo, a young student of mining engineering who died tragically in 2006. The exhibits reflect Andrés' studies and interests, with a unique and vast collection of crystallized minerals from the Peruvian Andes; exceptional Chancay ceramics dating from AD 900 to 1500; and a fascinating collection of pre-Hispanic clothing and accessories, with robes, corsets, shoes, belts, hats, wigs, and jewelry.

⑨ San Pedro

📍 E3 📍 Jirón Azángaro 451
☎ 01 428 3010 🕐 7:30am–
12:30pm daily, 5-8pm Mon-
Fri (to 7pm Sat & Sun)

The only church in Lima with
three entrances (usually a
feature of cathedrals), the
Iglesia de San Pedro is a fine
example of early colonial
architecture in the city. Built
in 1636, it was consecrated
two years later. Inspired by
the Jesuits' Chiesa del Sacre
Nome di Gesù in Rome, it has
three naves.

The restrained exterior
is adorned with Churrigeur-
esque (Spanish Baroque) and
gilded altars, carvings of the
founders of various religious
orders, and Moorish balconies.
The side chapels, with their
glazed tiles, are awash with
paintings from the Lima,
Quito, and Cusco schools.

The impressive golden
main altar, designed by priest
Matiás Maestro (1760–1835),
features columns, balconies,
and sculpted figures.

A painting depicting the
coronation of the Virgin Mary
by Bernardo Bitti (1548–1610),
who worked with Michelangelo
in Italy and supervised the
construction of San Pedro,
hangs in the sacristy.

⑩ Parque de la Muralla

📍 E2 📍 Jirón Amazonas and
Jirón Lampa ☎ 01 433 1546
🕐 7am-6pm daily

Once a deprived area, this
park has become a popular
spot to exercise for locals and
visitors. Situated behind the
Iglesia San Francisco, next to
the Río Rimac, it exhibits the
remains of a 17th-century wall
that once protected the city
from pirates and enemies of
the Spanish crown. The park
has an outdoor gym, library,
a small exhibition of maps,
prints, and artifacts, and a
statue of Francisco Pizarro.

⑪ Santo Domingo

📍 D3 📍 Jirón Camaná 170
☎ 01 426 5521 🕐 9:30am-
1pm, 2-5:30pm Tue-Sat,
2-7pm Sun

Construction of the Basílica de
Santo Domingo began in 1540,
a few years after Francisco
Pizarro granted the land to
Dominican friar Vicente de

Valverde, who was with him
during his conquest of Peru.
Pizarro had sent Valverde to
meet the Inca ruler Atahualpa
(p190) in order to persuade
the Inca to convert to
Christianity or face a war
with the Spanish. However,
Valverde was unsuccessful.

Completed in the late 16th
century, the basilica features
an imposing dome and the
Retablo de las Reliquias, an
altar with relics of three
Dominican Peruvians who
attained sainthood – Santa
Rosa de Lima (1586–1617),
San Martín de Porras (1579–
1639), and San Juan Masías
(1585–1645).

To the right of the basilica
tower are the chapel and the
convent cloisters, said to be
the best preserved in Lima.

12 Museo de Arte de Lima

D4 Paseo Colón 125
10:30am–1pm & 2–6pm
Tue–Sun (to 5pm Sat)
mali.pe

Nestled in the Parque de la Exposición and surrounded by statues and gardens, the Neo-Renaissance Palacio de la Exposición (the Palace of the Exhibition) was built for the big industrial expo held in the city in 1872. The palace, once at the heart of Lima's most important 19th-century urban projects, is home to the city's Art Museum. Its collection of Peruvian art from the last 3,000 years ranges from ancient ceramics and textiles to contemporary jewelry, furniture, and paintings.

Highlights of the Colonial Art Gallery on the second floor include paintings by Juan de Santa Cruz Pumacallao, Diego Quispe Tito, and Juan Zapata Inca. These paintings of the Cusco School (p179) combine Andean mythology with Catholic symbols and contrast marvelously with the conventional religious parables depicted by Bernardo Bitti (1548–1610).

The collection includes Nazca ceramics, Inca cups, and colonial dresses. Also on view are portraits of wealthy 19th-century families by José Gil Castro (1785–1841) and Carlos Baca Flor (1867–1941), renowned for his paintings of eminent people such as Pope Pius XII, US banker J.P. Morgan, and fashion designer Charles Frederick Worth. Challenging works by 1960s vanguardists, such as Jesús Ruiz Durand, are also on display.

Parque de la Exposición, also known as the Parque de la Cultura, provides a welcome respite from Lima's traffic. The park houses an amphitheater, a children's puppet theater, and other performance areas. There is a peaceful Japanese garden and an artificial lake with paddleboats. Monuments here – such as the Chinese fountain, the Byzantine Pavilion and the attractive Moorish Pavilion – all celebrate Peru's centenary of independence.

Exercise caution here as thieves have been known to frequent the park. Avoid visiting after dark.

←
A riot of gilded Baroque decoration in the vestry of the Iglesia de San Pedro

SANTA ROSA DE LIMA

The Americas' first saint, Lima-born Isabel Flores de Oliva, was nicknamed "Rose" due to her beauty. She rubbed hot peppers on her cheeks to make herself less attractive, and used the pain to focus solely on God. Isabel joined the Third Order of St Dominic and her penances became more rigorous. She worked tirelessly for Lima's poor and advocated rights for Indigenous people. On her feast day, thousands flock to the Sanctuario de Santa Rosa de Lima, built near the house she was born in. Letters asking for her help are thrown into the same well that she threw the key of the iron chain she wore around her waist.

13 Convento de los Descalzos

E1 Calle Manco Cápac 202-A, Alameda de los Descalzos 01 481 0441
10am–1pm & 2–5pm daily

Founded in 1592 by Andrés Corso, a Corsican priest, the Convent of the Shoeless Ones was named after the barefooted Franciscan monks who lived a silent, spartan life in this spiritual retreat, relying on donations to meet their needs. Missionaries who took over the convent in 1852 said it breathed "poverty, orderliness and thrift, in contrast to the ostentation of other religious establishments."

Today, it is home to a priceless collection of religious and colonial paintings from the 17th and 18th centuries, which includes a work by Murillo (1617–82), of Saint Joseph with Jesus. The convent regularly holds music and art events.

The chapel has a gold-leaf altar, a kitchen, a refectory, an infirmary, and monks' cells. Seville tiles adorn the patio walls and Cusco School (p179) paintings hang in the chapel dedicated to Nuestra Señora de la Rosa Mística.

Take a taxi and ask it to wait as assaults have been known to happen in this area.

↑ Colorful curios displayed in a shop in Lima's Chinatown district

EAT

L'Eau Vive

A French order of nuns serves delicious cooking in a beautifully restored 18th-century home. The fixed-price lunch is a bargain. Proceeds go to charity.

📍E3 🏠Jirón Ucayali 370 📞01 427 5612 🕐3-7:30pm & Sun

Restaurant Bar Cordano

This is one of the oldest bars in the country. While dining options here are limited to traditional ham sandwiches loaded with criolla sauce, this restaurant delivers a perfect slice of Limeño history.

📍E2 🏠Jirón Ancash 202 📞01 427 0181 🕐9am-8:30pm daily

14 🍴🏠
Chinatown

📍E3 🏠Calle Calpón, between Jirón Andahuaylas and Jirón Paruro

Covering a few blocks of downtown Lima, Chinatown is one of the city's most intriguing neighborhoods. Chinese immigrants arrived in waves during the late 1800s, enticed by the offer of jobs building Peru's new railway. Today, the Chinese community is thought to make up just over 1 per cent of Peru's population.

The entrance to Chinatown is marked by an ornate, 26-ft- (8-m-) high Chinese archway where Jirón Ucayali and Jirón Andahuaylas converge. While few tourists venture to the area, it's home to some of Lima's best *chifas* (Chinese restaurants), and is unmissable at Chinese New Year.

15
Plaza San Martín

📍D3

Built in 1921 to commemorate 100 years of independence, Plaza San Martín has a distinct French architectural influence which can be seen in the exclusive men-only Club Nacional and the Gran Hotel

Bolívar, of 1924. At its center is a statue of the Argentinian liberator of Peru, General José de San Martín, crossing the Andes on horseback. A statue of Madre Patria, the symbolic mother of Peru, stands beneath the nation's protector. She should have been adorned with a *llama*, or crown of flames. Instead she has a little Peruvian llama – the animal – sitting on her head. The double meaning of the word was obviously lost on the artist who crafted the image in Spain.

16
Las Nazarenas

📍D2 🏠Jirón Huancavelica 515 📞01 423 5718 🕐7:30am-6pm daily

The Church of the Nazarene was built in the 18th century outside the city's walls in Pachacamilla, a neighborhood then inhabited by people from Angola who had been freed from enslavement and Pachacámac people. It was constructed around a local freed person's painting of Christ on an adobe wall, *El Señor de los Milagros* (Lord of Miracles), which inexplicably survived three major earthquakes, in 1655, 1687, and 1746. Sensing a miracle, people began to flock to see the painting, and the church sprang up at the site. Today, behind the altar, is a replica in oils of *The Cristo Púrpura (Purple Christ)*, as it is also known.

A copy of the image is paraded through Lima's streets

EARTHQUAKES IN LIMA

Peru is prone to earthquakes due to its location on a geological fault and Lima has endured its fair share over the centuries. On October 28, 1746, a colossal tremor rattled the country for four minutes. More than 15,000 people died in the capital, many vanishing in the tsunami that swallowed Callao, sinking all the boats in the harbor and reportedly carrying one vessel a mile (2 km) inland. Lima was in ruins, its 74 churches, 12 monasteries, and all but 20 of its 3,000 private houses severely damaged. In the aftermath of the quake, one account said of Lima's 40,000 survivors that "it was not life they were living but death they were enduring." Most of the buildings seen today date from after 1746. Lima's last major earthquake, of May 1940, demolished 23 per cent of its buildings.

on a one-ton silver litter during the El Señor de los Milagros procession in October *(p66)*. The procession, which takes different routes on three different days, draws thousands of devout believers dressed in purple robes.

Museo de Arte Italiano

📍 D4 🏛 Paseo de la República 250 🕐 10am–2pm Tue, Wed & Sat
🌐 museos.cultura.pe

The Italian Art Museum was gifted to Peru in 1921 by the Italian community living in Lima to mark the centenary of the country's independence. Designed by the Milanese architect Gaetano Moretti (1860–1938), it has a grand, white Renaissance-style facade that features the coats of arms of major Italian cities and reliefs made of marble. Two detailed mosaic panels depict illustrious figures from Italian history.

Inside, there are decorative details inspired by Italian masters such as Donatello, Michelangelo, and Botticelli. More than 300 works by about 100 Italian artists of the 20th century include paintings, engravings, sculptures, and drawings, as well as ceramics.

Museo Nacional de la Cultura Peruana

📍 C2 🏛 Av Alfonso Ugarte 650 🕐 10am–2pm Tue, Wed, Sat & first Sun of month
🌐 museos.cultura.pe

The National Museum of Peruvian Culture was set up in 1946 to conserve Peru's ethnographic heritage. The building's design was inspired by the iconography of the Tiahuanaco culture, which flourished around Lake Titicaca in 300 BC.

Folkloric and ethnographic exhibits gathered from all over the country include objects from the 40 different groups that inhabit the Amazonian jungles, and from the Andes are works from Ayacucho, Cusco, Cajamarca, and Puno. Other sections are devoted to functional and traditional objects, including musical instruments. Folk art lovers should not miss the miniature *retablo* depicting the *marinera*, Peru's national dance, by Joaquín López Antay (1897–1981). The engraved gourds, particularly the donkey pen by Alicia Bustamante, and the ceramics of the Shipibo people, are also spectacular.

→ Italianate garden in front of the decorated facade of the Museo de Arte Italiano

A SHORT WALK
PLAZA MAYOR

Distance 2 miles (3 km) **Time** 30 minutes
Nearest station Desamparados

Formerly called the Plaza de Armas, it was here that Francisco Pizarro founded Lima. A stroll of this part of the city takes you to various major institutions established here, and which today form part of Lima's historic center, such as La Catedral, the Palacio Arzobispal (Archbishop's Palace), the Municipalidad (City Hall), and the Palacio de Gobierno (Government Palace). The plaza has witnessed many significant historical events including the declaration of Peru's independence (p71) in 1821. The large bronze fountain in the center, erected in 1651, is the square's oldest feature.

Palacio de Gobierno was the president's residence and was remodeled and inaugurated in 1938.

JIRÓN ANCASH

START

JUNÍN

Casa de Aliaga is the oldest piece of family-owned real estate on the continent, and was built on top of an Inca shrine in 1535 (p97).

JIRÓN CONDE DE SUPERUNDA

FINISH

JIRÓN

Municipalidad

This **bronze fountain** was commissioned by the Count of Salvatierra who was also the Viceroy of Peru, in 1650.

JIRÓN CALLAO

JIRÓN CAMANÁ

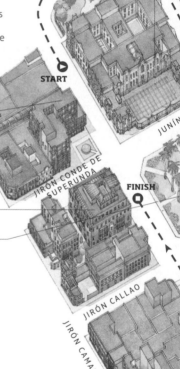

Jirón de la Unión links Plaza Mayor with Plaza San Martín via a busy thoroughfare (p100).

JIRÓN ICA

↑ Visitors relax outside the grand Palacio de Gobierno

Named after the original owner, writer Don José de la Riva Agüero, the 19th-century **Casa Riva-Agüero** houses a fine library and the Museo de Arte Popular (Folk Art Museum). It is now run by Lima's Catholic University.

Home to the Archbishop of Lima, **Palacio Arzobispal** was reconstructed in 1924. It is famed for the Moorish-style carved balconies that decorate its imposing facade.

Museo de Arte Religioso de la Catedral is housed inside a cathedral.

Did You Know?

The Spanish Inquisition used this square to execute their condemned.

Plaza Mayor

CENTRAL LIMA

Locator Map
For more detail see p90

Ambitious building plans combined with earthquakes saw the rebuilding of **La Catedral** several times, until it was finally reconstructed in 1758. The choir chairs are one of the greatest works of Peruvian art (p96).

The **Palacio Torre Tagle**, considered the best representation of 18th-century Lima architecture, was built in 1735. It is famed for its carved wooden balcony and stone entrance.

JIRÓN CARABALLA

HUALLAGA

JIRÓN LAMPA

Museo del Banco Central de la Reserva specializes in pre-Columbian archeology and displays 19th- and 20th-century Peruvian art. There is also an exhibition of Peru's currency.

JIRÓN CARABALLA

| 0 metres | 100 |
| 0 yards | 100 |

N

Iglesia de la Merced is where Lima's first Latin mass was held.

JIRON HUANCAVELICA

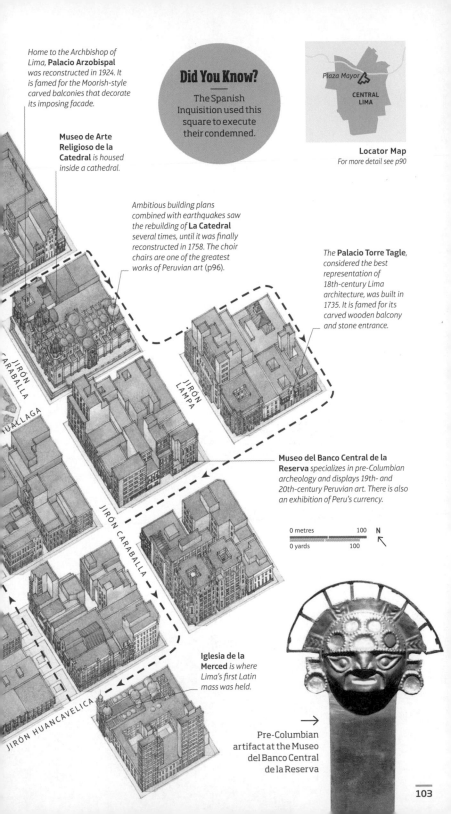

→
Pre-Columbian artifact at the Museo del Banco Central de la Reserva

MIRAFLORES AND SAN ISIDRO

Officially established in 1857, Miraflores quickly developed into Lima's prosperous commercial hub. With a history dating back thousands of years, vestiges of the area's ancient past remain in the form of the Huaca Huallamarca and the Huaca Pucllana – ancient adobe pyramids dating back to AD 200 and 400 respectively. After Francisco Pizarro founded Lima in 1535, the area became known for leisure, with its flower-filled parks and the beaches that line Miraflores' Costa Verde or Green Coast.

Close to Miraflores, San Isidro is the city's garden district. An olive grove was planted here in 1560, and still thrives today. In the 1920s, the establishment of a country club, golf club, and polo field helped make the area the preferred address of Lima's upper echelons of society, and it still is today.

MIRAFLORES AND SAN ISIDRO

Must See
1. Huaca Pucllana

Experience More
2. Parque Kennedy
3. Larcomar
4. Miraflores Clifftops
5. Casa Ricardo Palma
6. Museo Amano
7. Huaca Huallamarca
8. Lugar de la Memoria (LUM)
9. Bosque El Olivar

Eat
1. Astrid & Gastón
2. La Rosa Náutica
3. Malabar
4. La Mar
5. La Lucha Sanguchería

Stay
6. Westin Lima
7. Hostal El Patio
8. Lighthouse B&B

❶ HUACA PUCLLANA

📍 J8 🏠 Calle General Borgoño, block 8 🕐 9am–4:15pm Wed–Sun
🌐 huacapucllanamiraflores.pe

Right in the heart of the Miraflores district lie the ruins of the Huaca Pucllana, an adobe-brick pyramid thought to have served as both an administrative and ceremonial center for the Lima culture civilization. Several of the oldest mummies in Lima have been unearthed here, making it the most popular archeological site in the city.

Huaca Pucllana was an important temple constructed in the shape of a truncated pyramid in around AD 400. While it was reserved for priests, the lower buildings and plazas at its base were open to all citizens.

It has been used by different civilizations over the centuries. After it was abandoned in AD 800, likely due to the rise of new ideas and religions, the Wari occupation began. They destroyed much of the original architecture,

turning it into a cemetery. After this culture collapsed around AD 1100, the Ychsma arrived. They restored elements of the temple and used it as a cemetery and a spiritual place.

The museum contains artifacts uncovered since excavations began in 1967. Wari ceramics, many of which depict sea themes, and Ychsma pottery depicting women – potentially used as offerings in lieu of human sacrifices – are on display.

Did You Know?

Small handmade adobe bricks were arranged like books in shelves to build platforms for the main pyramid.

Highlights

Wari Textiles

△ The Wari fabrics were characterized by geometric and animal shapes. Wari textiles are among the most vibrant and finely woven in the world.

Ceramics

△ The ceramics in the museum are mainly sea-themed. This two-headed shark is considered the bringer of life and death.

Wari Mummy

△ The dead were buried in a sitting position, wrapped in elaborate bales of fabric and tied with rope. The oldest mummy found here is 1,300 years old.

Pyramid

△ Religious rites and ceremonies were performed at the pyramid and plazas by the priests, who served as governors.

↑ The impressively arranged adobe bricks at Huaca Pucllana

LIMA CULTURE RITUALS

Mannequins around the site *(pictured)* recreate ritual ceremonies that formed part of paying tribute to the gods. Religious rites were performed by the priests, and it was believed that breaking jars and sacrificing children and women helped maintain community cohesion. Many of the jars and ceremonial plazas were decorated with marine symbols such as waves to symbolize movement, sea lions, and even two-headed sharks.

EXPERIENCE MORE

2

Parque Kennedy

K9 Cnr of Av Benavides & Calle Schell, Miraflores

The shady, tree-lined Parque Kennedy and the adjoining Parque 7 de Junio offer a welcome escape from Lima's jostling crowds and lurching traffic. Its modern playground is a bonus for families. Local artists line the pedestrianized street in front of the Iglesia Virgen Milagrosa, proffering colorful canvases of Peru's landscapes and street scenes. Food vendors and shoeshiners ply their trade across the park.

The weekends are even more lively, with all kinds of entertainment. A small but colorful market springs up in the center of the park in the Rotonda de los Artesanos, selling a wide variety of Peruvian crafts, and the small amphitheater in the park is transformed into a dance arena. Couples take to the floor sashaying to everything from salsa beats and Andean pipes to Latin American pop.

PICTURE PERFECT
Sunset from the Miraflores Clifftops

Catch the sun setting from Parque Raimondi on the western edge of the Miraflores cliffs, where the sun slips beneath the sea horizon with the silhouettes of floating paragliders in the foreground.

3

Larcomar

K10 Av Malecón de la Reserva 610, Miraflores
7am-11pm daily
larcomar.com

Built in 2002, Larcomar is a shopping mall, comprising three terraces carved into the Miraflores cliffs. It has boutiques specializing in Peruvian handicrafts, a 12-screen cinema complex, cafés, bars, clubs, restaurants, a bowling alley, and gaming arcade. Limeños are in two minds about the mall. Some lament that it replaced a once-tranquil park, while others consider it a great addition to the neighborhood. Whatever they think of it, most locals find themselves here during the week.

4

Miraflores Clifftops

J9 Malecón Cisneros & Malecón de la Reserva

The clifftops overlooking the Pacific Ocean form one of Lima's most popular outdoor destinations. The weekends are particularly crowded with picnickers, skaters, paragliders, ice-cream vendors, and rehearsing musicians and dancers. At the northern end, colorful flower beds in the shape of the Nazca Lines,

← Serpentine mosaic bench at the Parque del Amor on the Miraflores clifftops

the mysterious "drawings" in the desert *(p140)*, dominate the view at the Parque Grau. On summer Sundays, tango dancers gather on a paved area overlooking the sea to show off their skills.

Southward is the black-and-white striped La Marina lighthouse. The nearby skate park swarms with padded-up BMX bikers, boarders, and bladers on the weekends.

The pretty Parque del Amor, or Love Park, inaugurated on February 14, 1993, is devoted to the old Peruvian custom of courting in public gardens. In the center is a colossal sculpture of a kissing couple.

Across the Puente Villena Rey bridge is the imposing *Intihuatana* sculpture by abstract artist Fernando de Szyszlo, celebrating the Incas' sacred stone *(p187)*. *Intihuatana* in Quechua translates as "hitching post of the sun."

Casa Ricardo Palma

📍K8 🏠General Suárez 189, Miraflores ⏰9am–12:45pm & 2:30–5pm Mon–Fri 🚫Public hols 🌐ricardopalma.miraflores.gob.pe

Peruvian writer Ricardo Palma's witty historical anecdotes or *tradiciones* have won him a prominent place in Latin American literature. His love for writing and books was reflected in his efforts to rebuild Lima's National Library. He was director of the library from 1884 until his retirement in 1912. He is said to have recovered several books that had been removed by Chilean soldiers, which he found by chance in the possession of some street vendors.

Built at the beginning of the 20th century, the house where Palma spent his last years celebrates his life and works. Palma became such an institution in Lima that a pilgrimage to his home was deemed essential for connoisseurs of Latin American literature. His bookshelves were filled with Voltaire's works in particular. The writer's desk, favorite chair, manuscripts, letters, photographs, and even an X-ray of his hand, dating from 1899, have been preserved for posterity.

Visitors can explore the music room, study, and bedroom to get a glimpse of Palma's life. His binoculars and books are placed exactly where he left them.

↑ The house of Peruvian author and scholar Ricardo Palma

EAT

Astrid & Gastón
Celebrity chef Gastón Acurio and wife Astrid blend contemporary cooking with traditional Andean ingredients.

📍J6 🏠Av Paz Soldán 290 ⏰1–3:30pm & 7–11pm Mon–Sat, 11am–4pm Sun 🌐astridygaston.com

💲💲💲

La Rosa Náutica
Great seafood on a charming pier. Stop by for a sundowner and stay for dinner.

📍J10 🏠Espigón 4 🌐larosanautica.com

💲💲💲

Malabar
This restaurant plates up rare Amazon jungle ingredients with traditional Peruvian fare.

📍J6 🏠Av Camino Real 101 ⏰12:30–3:30pm & 7–11pm Mon–Sat, 9am–5pm Sun 🌐malabar.com.pe

💲💲💲

La Mar
No reservations at this trendy seafood restaurant, so arrive by noon or prepare to wait in line.

📍H8 🏠Av La Mar 770 🌐lamarcebicheria.com

💲💲💲

La Lucha Sanguchería
Fantastic, inventive sandwiches and crusty rolls. Wait in line for a table or opt for takeout.

📍K9 🏠Diagonal 308 ⏰7:30am–9:30pm 🌐lalucha.com.pe

💲💲💲

↑ The ancient slopes of San Isidro's Huaca Huallamarca

Museo Amano

📍 J8 🏠 Retiro 160, Miraflores 🕙 10am-5pm Tue-Sun; Mon: by appt only 🌐 museoamano.org

The house of Yoshirato Amano (1898–1982), and his collection of exhibits, was opened to the public in 1964 as the Museo Amano. A Japanese businessman turned archeologist who settled in Peru, Amaro

↑ Ceramic bottle with geometric patterns in the Museo Amano

traveled the country in search of cultural artifacts, amassing what is one of the most comprehensive private collections of pre-Hispanic textiles and handicrafts in Lima.

The ceramics section has objects from the Kotosh, Moche, Chimú, Cupisnique, and Nazca cultures and charts the development of pottery in Peru through the ages. The exhibits are organized chronologically, illustrating the differences, and the advances made, between one culture and the next. They reveal how people in the north, such as the Moche, focused more on sculptural images, while those in the southern areas, the Nazca for example, used vibrant and vivid colors.

However, the section dedicated to pre-Hispanic textiles is what draws the crowds. Among the myriad items on display are beautiful woven pieces by the Chancay people, some of which resemble fine lacework, and an ancient Incan *quipu*, their unique system of recording events and keeping track of livestock with multicolored threads and knots.

Huaca Huallamarca

📍 J6 🏠 Nicolás de Ribera 201, San Isidro ☎ 01 222 4124 🕙 10am-3pm Tue, Thu & Sat

Also known as the Sugar Loaf or Pan de Azúcar, the Huaca Huallamarca is a fully restored ancient adobe pyramid dating from AD 200 to 500. In the Quechua language, *marca* denotes "region or town" and consequently *huallamarca* means the "place or residence of the Hualla people."

Experts believe it to be a ceremonial center. The floors show little sign of wear, indicating that it was used only by the religious elite.

The tombs uncovered in the *huaca* (shrine) show the changes in funerary practices from AD 300 up to the 15th century, when the center was finally abandoned. During the Early Intermediate Period (AD 200–600), bodies were laid on their backs on reed mattresses. Later, the dead were put in a fetal position and wrapped in fine fabrics. During the Middle Horizon (AD 600–900), burials became more elaborate and wrapped bodies had a mask of wood or painted fabric placed over the head.

Archeologists have recovered farming tools, children's games, crockery, woven cotton, and sewing baskets from the tombs. The presence of the latter emphasizes the importance of women within these ancient communities.

Some of the mummies, as well as the artifacts found with them, are on display at the on-site museum. The ceremonial platform located on top of the *huaca* provides a vantage point for an excellent view of San Isidro.

8

Lugar de la Memoria (LUM)

📍G7 🏠Bajada San Martin 151, Miraflores ⏰10am–5pm Tue–Sun 🌐lum.cultura.pe

This museum looks at the 20 years of internal conflict instigated by the Sendero Luminoso (Shining Path) rebel group in the 1980s and 1990s that resulted in the death of 70,000 Peruvians. The museum includes the Yuyanapaq exhibit, a powerful collection of photographs that record this violent period of history. It also has multimedia exhibits which are part of the findings of the Truth and Reconciliation Commission.

9

Bosque El Olivar

📍J7 🏠Av La República, San Isidro

Spread over a large area in central San Isidro, the beautiful Bosque El Olivar (Olive Grove) was declared a national monument in 1959. Antonio de Rivera, a former mayor of Lima, introduced the olive tree to Peru in 1560. Of the numerous saplings he brought from Seville, only three survived the journey, and he planted them here.

By 1730, when Nicolás de Ribera, a descendant, decided to build his hacienda – Los Condes de San Isidro – among the olive trees, along with a grinding mill and an olive press, the number of trees had swelled to over 2,000.

Today, the garden contains over 1,600 olive trees, many of them centuries old, and over 200 other species. The grove is also home to around 25 species of birds.

Spending time lazing under the sprawling branches is a favorite with picnickers during the day. When the sun goes down, the central pathway, spanning several blocks, is perfect for a leisurely evening stroll.

Olive trees, some four centuries old, in the Bosque El Olivar ↑

A SHORT WALK
MALECÓN DE MIRAFLORES

Distance 2 miles (3 km)
Time 45 minutes **Terrain** Easy,
mostly flat **Nearest bus and coach
station** Hostal Torreblanco

Clinging to the coastal edge of the
city, the Malecón de Miraflores is a
manicured, park-lined promenade,
showcasing Lima's greener side.
Following the curve of the coastline,
this clifftop walk connects palm- and
sculpture-studded parks and fine,
sweeping views of the Pacific Ocean
below. Popular among joggers,
families, and those on a romantic
stroll, this route is even more
spectacular at sunset.

MILAFLORES
AND SAN ISIDRO

*Malecón de
Miraflores*

*Parque Grau
Miraflores*

Locator Map
For more detail see p106

▶ **START**

MALECÓN CISNEROS

BERLÍN

CIRCUITO

TUPAC AMARU

AVENUE

*Parque
Tres Picos*

*Parque
El Libro*

DE

PLAYAS

La Marina
Lighthouse

Parque Grau Miraflores, *a
leafy park named after
Peru's most esteemed naval
figure, tends to display
brilliant art exhibitions.*

The striking Entre El
Tiempo *sculpture by
Limeño artist José Tola in*
Parque El Libro *has two
faces: one watches the sun-
rise, the other the sunset.*

*This iconic, black-and-
white striped* **La Marina
Lighthouse** *started life at
Punta Coles near Tacna,
but was moved to its
present location in 1973.*

0 meters   250

0 yards   250

N
↑

Did You Know?
—
The Paddington Bear
statue was designed by
British comedian Stephen
Fry and wears a Union
Jack coat.

↑ The black-and-white striped La Marina
lighthouse at sunset

Victor Delfín's sculpture *El Beso* in the themed Parque del Amor, or Love Park

Described as the "green lung" of the city, **Parque Antonio Raimondi** has fine sea views and is the spot for watching paragliders leaping into the air.

JOSE GALVEZ

AV COMANDANTE ESPINAR

BOLOGNESI

FRANCIA

MADRID

GRAU

ITALIA

TRÍPOLI

Parque Antonio Raimondi

VENECIA

MALECÓN BALTA

MALECÓN CISNEROS

NIACIÓN

Playa Waikiki

Parque del Amor

Intihuatana

Beso Francés Creperia

Playa Makah

El Amarre

PORTA

FANNING

OCHARAN

FERRÉ

GONZÁLES

CRISTOBAL COLÓN

AV JOSE LARCO

Parque San Marcelino Champagnat

MALECÓN DE LA RESERVA

CIRCUITO DE PLAYAS

MALECÓN DE LA RESERVA

Paddington Bear Statue

FINISH
Larcomar

Victor Delfín's El Beso, *a sculpture of two lovers kissing, and Gaudí-inspired mosaics are among Lima's most emblematic art, found in* **Parque del Amor** (p111).

Peruvian artist Fernando de Szyszlo's dramatic concrete sculpture, **Intihuatana**, *represents an Inca stone thought to have been used for rituals or as a solar clock (p111).*

The award-winning sculpture **El Amarre** *in travertine marble by Limeña artist Sonia Prager was accused of being "unintelligible" when installed in 1986.*

Stop for a sweet or savory crepe at the **Beso Francés Crepería**, *a coffee shack with sublime ocean views.*

Honoring French priest Saint Marcellin Champagnat, the eponymous, **Parque San Marcelino Champagnat** *overlooks a historic pier home to Lima's famed restaurant, La Rosa Nautica.*

The **Paddington Bear Statue** *was a gift from the British embassy in July 2015.*

Finish the walk by browsing the boutique stores of Lima's flashiest shopping centre, **Larcomar** (p110).

BARRANCO

Just a stone's throw from Miraflores, Barranco is located on the cliffs at the southern tip of Lima Bay. When the Spanish first arrived here in 1533, they encountered a community of Indigenous farmers and fisherfolk. The area was handed over to one of the companions of conquistador Francisco Pizarro, the leader of the Spanish invasion, and the local people were soon drawn into the colonizers' *encomienda* labor system. It was a quiet windmill-dappled hamlet until the 19th century, when Lima's elite moved in and began to build grand summer mansions, spurred on by the new fashion of bathing in the sea. Small communities of Europeans, mainly English, French, and Italians, settled here, adding their own stylistic traits to local architecture.

The area's most famous sights, the Bajada de los Baños footpath – a scenic walkway down to the beach – and the Puente de los Suspiros, or Bridge of Sighs, were constructed in the 1870s. During the 20th century, the district became a bohemian area, popular with Peruvian writers and artists. The Parque Municipal, and many of Barranco's cafés, restaurants, and bars retain a hint of the refined airs of days gone by.

J

K

Parque
Salazar

AV. ARMENDÁRIZ

CIRCUITO DE PLAYA

Playa
Redonda

Nstra. Sra.
de Fátima

Playa
La Estrella

Playa
Las Piedritas

BARRANCO

*Pacific
Ocean*

11

BARRANCO

Experience

❶ Museo de la Electricidad
❷ La Ermita
❸ Puente de los Suspiros
❹ MATE - Museo Mario Testino
❺ Museo de Arte Contemporáneo
❻ Parque Municipal
❼ Museo Pedro de Osma

Eat

① Central
② Isolina
③ El Muelle de Barranco

Drink

④ Barranco Beer Co.
⑤ Bodega Piselli
⑥ Del Carajo

12

13

K

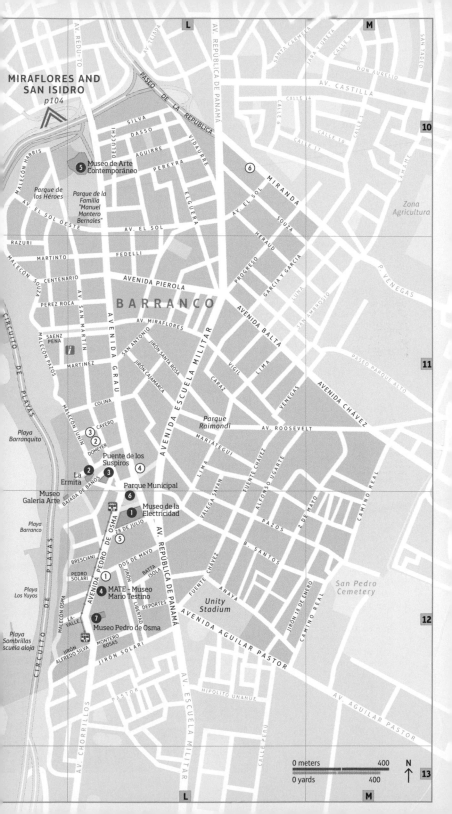

MIRAFLORES AND SAN ISIDRO
p104

BARRANCO

5 Museo de Arte Contemporáneo

Parque de los Héroes

Parque de la Familia "Manuel Montero Bernales"

6

Zona Agricultura

Playa Barranquito

3
2

2
3
4 Puente de los Suspiros

La Ermita

Museo Galería Arte

6 Parque Municipal

1 Museo de la Electricidad

5

Playa Barranco

1

4 MATE – Museo Mario Testino

7

Museo Pedro de Osma

Playa Los Yuyos

Playa Sombrillas scuéla aloja

Unity Stadium

Parque Raimondi

San Pedro Cemetery

L
M

10

11

12

13

0 meters   400
0 yards   400

N

EXPERIENCE

1

Museo de la Electricidad

📍L12 🏛 Av Pedro de Osma 105 📞01 477 6577 🕐9am–5pm daily

The charming, restored tram outside the Museo de la Electricidad (Museum of Electricity) entices visitors into this small but interesting museum. The tram was rebuilt from an abandoned car that was found in a city scrapyard. It bears the number 97 in honor of the year it was restored, in 1997, some 30 years after the last tram stopped running in Lima.

Photos and further details of Lima's trolley and tram system are given inside the museum. The city's tram cars were built in the 1920s in Italy and operated in the center of the city, while larger carriages served Barranco.

Beyond electrically powered transport, exhibitions at the museum also cover the history of electricity both globally and locally. There are displays of a wide array of electrical appliances and machines that have been used by people of the area over the years, including an old Wurlitzer jukebox and ancient television, radio, and telephone models. The museum's interactive room is particularly popular with school groups.

BARRANCO, THE SEASIDE RESORT

The early 20th century saw Barranco transform from a simple seaside hideaway into the most popular summer address for aristocratic Peruvians and expatriates escaping Lima's heat. Its pier, built in 1906, has a huge restaurant with a dance floor that played host to the best orchestras of the day. Postcards from 1915 show women in extravagant hats and white dresses promenading on the pier, escorted by men in straw boaters and crisp, pressed suits. A funicular took patrician families from the clifftops to the beach. Windmills, used to draw water for the houses, dot the area.

2

La Ermita

📍L11 🏛 Jirón Ermita 🚫To the public

The Church of the Hermitage is a famous Barranco landmark, although one in desperate need of restoration. According to legend, a group of fishers, lost in a winter mist blanketing Lima's coast, prayed to be rescued. They rowed toward a glow that suddenly appeared in the distance and, once on land, they found only a wooden cross in the place from where the light had emanated. Believing that divine intervention had spared them, the fishers erected La Ermita on that spot.

In front of La Ermita is a statue commemorating Peruvian singer Chabuca Granda, most famous for her tribute to the Puente de los Suspiros. A pathway bordering the side of the

💬 INSIDER TIP
Barranco's Graffiti

Take a stroll along Calle 28 de Julio to appreciate Barranco's murals, which have transformed its streets into an open-air gallery. Many offer political commentary, with several works by acclaimed Limeño artist Jade Rivera (p83).

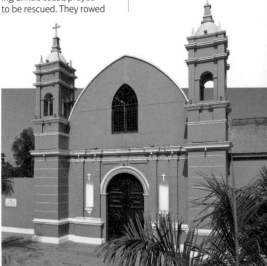

↑ Colorful and bustling Puente de los Suspiros

church, built in 1988, leads past colorful houses and cafés to El Mirador Catalina Recavarren, a lookout point offering panoramic ocean views.

---

③
Puente de los Suspiros

 L11 ⊕ Between calles Ayacucho and La Ermita

The 19th-century "Bridge of Sighs," which survived the earthquake of 1940, is steeped in legend. It derived its name from the thwarted love of a beautiful girl who lived on the Bajada de los Baños. She fell in love with a lowly street sweeper, but her father forbade her to see the boy and she spent the rest of her days gazing out of the window hoping for a glimpse of him. People crossing the bridge used to hear her sighing for her lost love.

The Bajada de los Baños, a pretty 19th-century walkway, slopes gently to the

sea connecting the streets of Ayacucho and La Ermita. Built to give Barranqueños access to the beach, the walkway starts below the Puente de los Suspiros and leads down to the sea in a combination of steps and sloping pathway. Bustling with locals at weekends, the path is bordered by small cafés and ice-cream shops, interspersed with crumbling buildings, colorful vegetation, and jewel-bright murals and graffiti. Closer to the sea, a viewing platform provides the perfect spot to watch the surfers bobbing like seals in the bay below.

During the late 19th and early 20th centuries, many upper-class Peruvian families built fancy country homes in Barranco. Wooden baths were built in 1876, and then rebuilt in 1906 following their destruction during the War of the Pacific (p72). Unfortunately, the baths were razed in the 1960s to make way for a coastal road.

Today, most of these homes have been transformed into restaurants, cafés, and bars but their balconies and carved ceilings are a reminder of their colonial grandeur.

← The bright paintwork of La Ermita, typical of the Barranco district

---

DRINK

Barranco Beer Co.
This family-run and award-winning brewery serves ten flagship beers on tap.

 L12 ⊕ Av Grau 308 ⊕ barrancobeer company.pe

Ⓢ Ⓢ Ⓢ

Bodega Piselli
Largely unchanged since 1915; a great spot for a quiet pisco sour among the locals.

L11 ⊕ 28 de Julio 297 ℂ 01 252 6750

Ⓢ Ⓢ Ⓢ

Del Carajo
A classic peña, with criolla dancing, performances from top Peruvian musicians, and inexpensive beer.

 K12 ⊕ Jirón Catalino Miranda 158 ⊕ delcarajo.com.pe

Ⓢ Ⓢ Ⓢ

EAT

Central

World-class tasting menus take inspiration from across Peru; reserve ahead.

 L11 ☑ Av Pedro de Osma 301 🕐 12:45–1:45pm & 7-8:30pm Mon-Sat Ⓦ central restaurante.com.pe

Ⓢ/Ⓢ/Ⓢ/

Isolina

Dishes draw on creole cooking at this shabby-chic tavern.

 L11 ☑ Av Prolongación San Martín 101 Ⓦ isolina.pe

Ⓢ/Ⓢ/Ⓢ/

El Muelle de Barranco

Perfect for inexpensive seafood dining.

L12 ☑ Av Alfonso Ugarte 225 ☎ 01 252 8643

Ⓢ/Ⓢ/Ⓢ/

Latin American art at the Museo de Arte Contemporáneo ↑

---

④ MATE - Museo Mario Testino

L12 ☑ Av Pedro de Osma 409 🕐 10am-7pm Tue-Sat ☒ Public hols Ⓦ mate.pe/en

Lima-born Mario Testino, one of the most influential photographers in the world, founded this museum in 2012. Set in a 19th-century townhouse, MATE reflects the history of Barranco as the cultural hub of Lima. Its mission is to promote Peru's artists, their culture, and their heritage. MATE also showcases iconic works by Testino, including his popular *Alta Moda* series and portraits of Diana, Princess of Wales and other international celebrities.

⑤ Museo de Arte Contemporáneo

L10 ☑ Av Grau 1511 🕐 3-7pm Tue-Sun Ⓦ maclima.pe

This modern, glass-walled museum set within a public park houses a permanent collection of more than 120 contemporary paintings, sculptures, and installations by some of today's leading Peruvian and Latin American artists, including Fernando de Szyszlo, Ramiro Llona, Oswaldo Guayasamín, Sonia Praga, Lika Mutal, and José Tola. The museum also hosts temporary exhibitions and events, and has a research library. Visitors to the museum also have access to the gardens, where sculptures are displayed. The "Sundays in the MAC" program offers weekend art workshops and guided tours for children.

⑥ Parque Municipal

L12 ☑ Av Grau

Inaugurated in February 1898, Barranco's Parque Municipal, with its wooden benches, towering palms, and colorful flower beds, is a favorite stop for locals, especially after Mass in the nearby Iglesia de la Santísima Cruz.

During the late afternoon, resident artists often display their canvases under the watchful gaze of the Carrara marble statue of *La Donaide*, or *Daughter of Venus*. She floats over the waters of the central pool alongside two small angels, or putti. An exquisite Etruscan vase – Barberini's *Candelabro* – also in marble, sits nearby.

The striking crimson-colored Biblioteca Municipal, constructed between 1895 and 1899 and opened in 1922, dominates this popular park.

> During the late afternoon at Parque Municipal, resident artists often display their canvases under the watchful gaze of the Carrara marble statue of *La Donaide*.

Lima School, also line its walls. Of particular interest are the bleeding head of John the Baptist and Adam and Eve reaching for the apple. The second building, set among palm trees, geranium beds, and marble sculptures in the back garden, was originally the dining room. It now houses photographs and dinnerware belonging to the Osma family. A third building is home to an impressive collection of silverware.

The tower, which was added in 1911, displays the Barranco crest and a clock. Designated a "historic monument of exceptional worth" by Peru's Ministry of Culture, the Biblioteca organizes regular lectures in Spanish, on diverse topics ranging from Peruvian identity and gastronomy to art and theater.

On weekends, a food market takes over the plaza opposite the park, where a number of Peruvian cooks show off their baking, roasting, frying, and selling skills.

Paintings from the Cusco School, melding Spanish Baroque with Andean imagery, offer fascinating examples of subversion, such as the Virgin Mary portrayed with dark Andean hair. Outstanding religious sculptures, many from the

Museo Pedro de Osma

⦿L12 ⌂ Av Pedro de Osma 423 ⊙10am-6pm Tue-Sun ⊕museopedrodeosma.org

This sugar-white structure is one of Barranco's oldest summer homes, built in the early 20th century for the Osma family. The main building houses a fine collection of colonial art and furniture and pre-Hispanic and colonial works and objects from the southern Andes.

BOHEMIAN BARRANCO

Barranco has long been a popular spot with artists and intellectuals. From 1913 through the 1950s, it saw memorable partying, especially during Carnaval. One of Peru's most beloved singers Chabuca Granda *(right)* lived here, praising it thus: "The founder of Barranco was none other than God." Today, it is Lima's evening haunt, with music spilling out of hole-in-the-wall bars, posh nightclubs, and busy *peñas*. Gian Marco, local pop icon and popular Latin music composer, honed his skills here with bar gigs, and after a stint abroad returned to live in his favorite *barrio* (district). While writer Mario Vargas Llosa's seafront house has been replaced by an apartment block, other homes remain, such as that of sculptor and artist Víctor Delfín.

A SHORT WALK
BARRANCO

Distance 1.2 miles (2 km) **Time** 25 minutes
Nearest bus station Estadio Unión

While wandering along the stately Avenida Sáenz Peña, dotted with mansions and leafy side streets, it is easy to visualize Barranco's previous life as an aristocrats' playground. Some of these buildings, however, are crumbling and Barranco has launched an "Adopt a Facade" program to promote private investment as a means of restoring the neighborhood's beauty. Colorfully painted facades along Calle Junín, Avenida Grau, and Bajada de los Baños merge the past with the present.

Avenida Sáenz Peña is lined with graceful old mansions of sepia, rose, ochre, or lapis lazuli painted facades that recall the bygone era.

FINISH

AV. SÁENZ PEÑA

JIRÓN MARTÍNEZ DE PINILLOS

CALLE JUNÍN

COLINA

ALFONSO UGARTE

The exhibits at **80m2 Livia Benavides** specialize in Peruvian art.

The present-day bajada (slope) corresponds with the path of a stream once followed by fishers down to the ocean. Over time it has morphed into **Bajada de los Baños**, a lane of summer homes and restaurants (p121).

↑ Barranco's famous bridge, Puente de los Suspiros, lit up in the evening

The devastating 1940 earthquake considerably damaged **La Ermita** church (p120); the disintegrating roof is a reminder of the tremor's ferocity.

START

Locator Map
For more detail see p118

↑ The bright colonial facade of La Ermita church, surrounded by abundant flora

The vintage store and furniture refurbisher **Cuatro en un Baúl** *sells unique treasures, from art to children's books. It's the perfect spot to go on the hunt for antique pieces to bring home and great for fans of creative upcycling.*

Did You Know?

The Puente de los Suspiros inspired the song "El puente de los Suspiros" by Chabuca Granda.

PUNA Tienda Galería, *a small arts and crafts store and gift emporium, sells local art and plenty of treasures.*

Following the destruction of La Hermita in 1940, prominent local parishioners asked the Archbishop of Lima to authorize the building of a new parish church in the municipal plaza. The first stone of the **Iglesia Santisima Cruz** *was laid in 1944 and the church was finally consecrated in 1963.*

The **Puente de los Suspiros** *(p121), a symbol of romantic Barranco, was remodeled in 1921. Legend has it that anyone who crosses this bridge for the first time while holding their breath will be granted their wish.*

The **Biblioteca Municipal** *(Municipal Library) opened in 1922 and functioned as the Barranco Town Hall for many years. The columns at the entrance and along the facade are repeated on each side of the elongated windows.*

0 metres 50
0 yards 50

N ↑

Must See

❶ Museo Nacional de Arqueología, Antropología e Historia del Perú

Experience More

❷ Fortaleza del Real Felipe
❸ Museo Naval del Perú
❹ Museo de Sitio Submarino Abtao
❺ Museo Arqueológico Rafael Larco Herrera
❻ Museo de Oro del Perú
❼ Museo del Automóvil Colección Nicolini
❽ Pachacámac
❾ Pantanos de Villa

BEYOND THE CENTER

Beyond the key areas of Central Lima, Miraflores, and Barranco, the sights of interest are somewhat dispersed. The village-like suburb of Pueblo Libre, to the south of Central Lima, is home to a number of museums that chronicle Peru's intriguing past. Far away from the confines of the city is the archeological site of Pachacámac, once inhabited by both Wari and Inca cultures. Stately houses in the nearby district of La Punta are a reminder of the area's popularity with Lima's aristocracy from the 19th century to the 1940s.

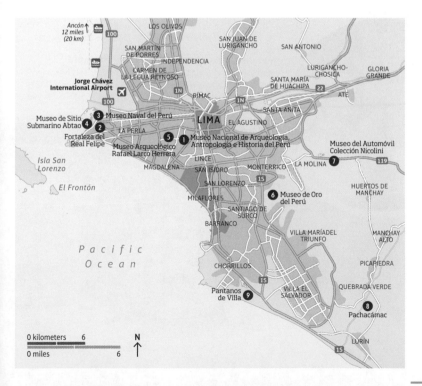

❶ 🏛️ 🖼️ 🛍️

MUSEO NACIONAL DE ARQUEOLOGÍA, ANTROPOLOGÍA E HISTORIA DEL PERÚ

📍 Plaza Bolivar, cnr of San Martín & Vivanco, Pueblo Libre 🕐 8:45am-4pm Mon-Sun (to 3pm Sun & public hols) 🌐 mnaahp.cultura.pe

Containing within its grounds the mansion Quinta del Virrey Pezuela, used by Peru's liberators, this comprehensive collection of Peruvian historical artifacts charts the country's history from the pre-Hispanic Paracas, Nazca, Wari, and Inca periods to colonial and republican times. It has around 70,000 ceramics and Peru's most important collection of ancient human remains, plus a series of viceroy portraits from the 18th and 19th centuries.

The Collection

The rooms in the museum are arranged chronologically by Peruvian culture. Displaying some of the oldest objects, the Chavín Room (1200 BC–AD 200) houses carved stone obelisks used for ceremonial and agricultural purposes.

The exceptional pottery of the Nazca culture (100 BC–AD 800) evidences meticulous designs, stylized naturalistic themes, and an extensive variety of colors. The Moche (AD 100–700) also excelled in ceramics, depicting people, animals, and deities hunting and fighting. Several of the mysterious *quipu* (knotted strings) used by the Inca (1438–1532) are also on display.

Quinta del Virrey Pezuela

Built in the late 18th century, this building is where liberators José de San Martín (1821–1822) and Símon Bolívar (1823–1826) stayed

← Variety of expressive Inca statues on display

↑ Artifacts found in one of the many rooms inside the museum

during the Peruvian War of Independence (*p71*). It is now part of the museum, and houses a collection of personal objects belonging to the two men. It can be accessed via the final gallery to the right of the entrance.

It has around 70,000 ceramics and Peru's most important collection of ancient human remains.

← Large neck-face jars, made and used by the Wari culture

Museum Highlights

Estela Raimondi

▷ This enormous stone obelisk was recovered from Chavín de Huántar. Carved with intricate images of snakes, condors, jaguars, and the Staff God, it is one of the most important pieces in the museum.

Obelisko Tello

Also from the Chavín cult, this obelisk was named after the archeologist who discovered it. It was used to mark the beginning and end of the agricultural year.

Lithics

The Lithics Gallery contains around 22,100 stone artifacts (lithics) from all over Peru. Some of these date from 12,000 BC and the collection comprises knives, hammers, grinding stones, sculptures, beads, and bowls.

Mummies

The Paracas culture (800 BC–AD 200) buried their dead in a sitting position, wrapped in layers of fabric, otherwise known as burial blankets. These *fardos funerarios* (wrapped bodies) are said to be among the best preserved in the world due to the freeze-drying effect of the coast's arid climate.

Manos Cruzados

◁ The Crossed Hands stone from Kotosh is over 5,000 years old and shows two hands crossed over one another, thought to symbolize duality - an important concept in Andean ideology.

Chavín Ceramics

▷ Chavín pottery is known for its unique globular shapes, intricately marked sculptural elements, and black, red, or brown colors. This black stirrup handled terra-cotta vase, dating from 200 AD, is a fine example.

EXPERIENCE

2

Fortaleza del Real Felipe

📍 Plazuela de la Independencia, Callao
☎ 01 429 0532 ⏰ 9am–4pm daily (nighttime visits on Fri & Sat; reservations required) 🚫 Public hols

The stone-walled Royal Felipe Fort is one of the largest forts built by the Spanish in the 18th century. Of interest to both the visitor and the historian, it was designed by Frenchman Luis Gaudin. The fort was named in honor of Felipe V, the first Bourbon king of Spain, who died in 1746.

The austere, pentagon-shaped fort was intended to defend against pirate attacks. During the 19th century, Callao, where the fort stands, was considered to be the most protected port on the west coast of South America. Real Felipe had been "war-ready" since colonial times, and had repelled many

↑ Remnants of the military past at the Fortaleza del Real Felipe, Callao

attacks. The fort had been besieged five times but never conquered. It also played a pivotal role in Peru's War of Independence (p71), acting as the first line of defense.

Covering more than 84,000 sq yards (70,000 sq m), the fort contains brass and iron cannons, military tanks, the Governor's House, Towers of the King and Queen, as well as the Museo del Ejército (Military Museum), with its impressive collection of weapons, documents, military uniforms, and relics.

3

Museo Naval del Perú

📍 Av Jorge Chávez 123, Callao ☎ 01 429 4793
⏰ 9am–4pm Tue–Sun

The Naval Museum, near the Fortaleza del Real Felipe, is a key site for seafaring history buffs. Instigated by Capitán de Navío Julio J. Elías Murguía, a Peruvian naval figure, the museum has an important collection of historical naval documents, oil paintings, uniforms, and relics from the 1879–83 War of the Pacific (p72). Also included are many personal objects of those involved in the conflict, photographs, weapons, and navigational instruments.

Prized items are belongings of one of Peru's most famous military figures, Admiral Miguel Grau, who died in the Battle of Angamos. Also known as the Caballero de los Mares (Gentleman of the Seas), his letters, navigational charts, and medals, as well as a sarcophagus containing a fragment of his shinbone, his only remains found after the battle, are displayed here. One room is devoted entirely to model ships, showcasing vessels from different eras and several other countries.

EAT

EAT

Café del Museo Larco

This delightful restaurant in the grounds of the Museo Arqueológico Rafael Larco Herrera has seating on a glorious floral terrace. Snack on tamales or enjoy a meal of beautifully presented sea bass and deep-fried squid.

📍 Av Bolívar 1515, Pueblo Libre
🌐 museolarco.org

4

Museo de Sitio Submarino Abtao

📍 Jorge Chávez 120-A, Callao ⏰ 9:30am–4:30pm Tue–Sun 🌐 museosub marinoabtao.com

A short walk away from Museo Naval del Perú and moored against the quayside lies a unique museum housed in a Sierra Class submarine which was built at the Electric Boat Company shipyard in the United States. It was

🔍 HIDDEN GEM
El Frontón

Visible from the Fortaleza del Real Felipe, the prison island of El Frontón offers a large rock formation with an abundance of marine salt easily seen from a boat. Tours depart from the Muelle de Guerra in Plaza Grau.

→ Artifacts on show at the Museo Arqueológico Rafael Larco Herrera

launched in New London, Connecticut, in 1953 as the BAP *Tiburón*.

The submarine was one of four commissioned by the Peruvian Navy, and was rechristened later as the BAP *Abtao* in commemoration of the Battle of Abtao, off the coast of Chile in 1866. The submarine carried a crew of 40 and was in service for 48 years, until 2001.

An interactive tour on board explores the sections of the vessel – the torpedo compartments with bunk beds and lockers, the engine room, the command center, ammu-nition storage, and radio room. Visitors can oper-ate the periscope and drive the 5-inch gun on the deck.

A light and sound show enabling visitors to experience underwater submarine combat marks the end of the tour.

Museo Arqueológico Rafael Larco Herrera

🏛 Av Bolivar 1515, Pueblo Libre 🕐 9am–10pm daily 🌐 museolarco.org

A grand 18th-century mansion built on a pyramid dating back to the 7th century AD provides more than a fitting home for 5,000 years of ancient history. El Museo Larco Herrera, founded in 1926, houses the biggest private collection of Peruvian pre-Columbian art – 45,000 pieces – amassed by sugar baron Rafael Larco Hoyle.

The Culture Hall is a good starting point as it gives a comprehensive overview of the cultures that existed from 7000 BC to the 16th century.

In the Andean world, the beauty and durability of metals gave objects an almost divine value. They were desig-ned to be offered to the gods. The Incas, as representatives of the gods, wore them or took them to their graves on their way to the other world.

The gold and silver collec-tion, which is nothing short of heavenly, comprises head-dresses, beads the size of golf balls, and chest plates inlaid with precious stones. Huge ear plugs, nose ornaments, crowns with quartz and turquoise, funerary masks, and a shirt made of gold discs are also displayed.

There are ancient textiles, including a fragment from a Paracas weaving showing 389 threads to 1 inch (2 cm) – a world record. Other exhibits range from a Wari loom-woven wall-hanging made from parrot feathers, to an Inca *quipu*, the ancient way of recording facts and events with colored threads and knots. The museum also showcases tools, kaolin, clay, molds, and paints.

Separate from the main house is a gallery of erotic art, with clay vessels made by the ancient Moche over 1,500 years ago, depicting different facets of their sex lives.

RAFAEL LARCO HOYLE

Born in 1901 on a sugar plantation in Trujillo, Rafael Larco Hoyle rose to be one of Peru's most noted businessmen; his family hacienda broke production records when he mechanized it after studying in the USA. He had a passion for collecting Peru's ancient artifacts – ceramics, metalwork, and textiles – exploring and excavating sites in northern Peru in search of the rarest and finest pieces. He once commandeered the largest swimming pool on the hacienda to wash salt from a newly acquired 8,000-piece collection.

BEACHES IN AND AROUND LIMA

With more than 1,156 miles (1,860 km) of shoreline, Peruvians have long worshipped the Pacific Ocean, as testified by friezes found at 2,000-year-old archeological complexes along the coast. Come December, when Lima's grey haze finally lifts, Limeños head south on weekends. By January, most city-dwellers move for the summer to one of the string of beaches stretching down the coast. Here, golden sands, headlands, and coves are plentiful, providing ample opportunity for surfing and swimming.

The beaches near the bustling resort town of Punta Hermosa offer consistent waves, making this Lima's top surfing destination. Punta Rocas, with its world-class exposed reef break, is also a draw; this bay hosts international surfing competitions. San Bartolo is a popular beach, with clear water and some excellent seafood restaurants, but for sun-seeking Limeños, the pick of the seaside towns is the traditional fishing village of Pucusana. Rent a boat here for a chance to see a colony of basking sea lions.

Museo de Oro del Perú

🏠 Alonso de Molina 1100, Monterrico-Surco ⏰ 10:30am–6pm daily 📅 Jan 1, May 1, Jul 28 & Dec 25 🌐 museoroperu.com.pe

Miguel Mujica Gallo's massive private Gold Museum displays numerous ceremonial knives and vases studded with turquoise. Ornate funerary masks, crowns, helmets, figurines, earrings, necklaces,

← A gold funerary mask adorned with pendants at the Museo de Oro del Peru

an impressive gold ceremonial bag, and a tunic appliquéd with gold are also on view.

Labeling on the exhibits, unfortunately, is poor, with inadequate explanation in Spanish, and almost none in English, making an audio guide essential.

The building's upper floor is set aside for Armas del Mundo (Arms of the World), a vast collection of ancient firearms and military paraphernalia. On view is an 1812 sword of Russian Tsar Alexander I, and the pistol that belonged to Chilean President Salvador Allende.

In 2001, the museum was rocked by scandal, with the National Institute of Culture and the Tourism Protection Bureau declaring that almost all its estimated 7,000 pieces were replicas. However, the owners claim to have only genuine gold pieces on display now.

7️⃣

Museo del Automóvil Colección Nicolini

🏠 Av La Molina ⏰ 10am–7pm daily 🌐 museode autosnicolini.com

Packed into a warehouse on the eastern outskirts of the city, this museum takes visitors on a virtual road trip through the 20th century with its collection of 120 beautifully polished vintage cars. Lovingly restored by the owner, Jorge Nicolini, the cars now comprise the largest collection of antique vehicles in Peru.

A Lincoln 1925, which was discovered being used as a taxi, was the first vehicle acquired by Nicolini in 1962. The oldest in the collection is a 1901 French-made Boyer, while other notable cars include a 1966 Corvette Stingray, number 214 of only 525 ever manufactured, and a 1903 Clement.

8

Pachacámac

⌂ Pan-American Hwy South, KM31.5, Lurín ◷ 9am–5pm Tue–Sat, 9am–4pm Sun Ⓦ pachacamac.cultura.pe

Dating from AD 200, this complex of adobe pyramids rising out of the Lurín Valley was a key pilgrimage center on Peru's central coast, and home to a much-venerated oracle. It flourished through the centuries and pilgrims traveled great distances to pay homage to the god Pachacámac (He who Enlivens the Universe and Everything).

Pachacámac was expanded by the Wari and their designs can be seen on the ceramics and textiles found here.

However, most of the compounds and pyramids date from after their downfall.

When the last Inca king, Atahualpa, was imprisoned by Pizarro, he complained that the oracle had falsely predicted his victory. His account of gold at the site led soldiers there but they were disappointed by the "ugly" idol they found instead.

The Incas built five separate complexes, including the Templo del Sol (Temple of the Sun) and the Palacio de Las Mamaconas (House of the Chosen Women), which has stonework on its entrance gate, a rarity on the coast.

The on-site museum houses a collection of pre-Hispanic relics, including Paracas textiles, ceramics, and a two-faced image of Pachacámac. The much-vaunted Museo Nacional del Perú, which reportedly has space for 500,000 artifacts, is found over the road from Pachacámac. Despite being officially inaugurated in 2021, it is unlikely to be open to the public until 2023.

Did You Know?

Some say the women of Pachacámac hid some of the Inca gold so cleverly that it is still to be discovered.

9

Pantanos de Villa

⌂ Av Hernando LaValle s/n, Chorillos ⊞ From Lima ◷ 8:30am–5pm daily Ⓦ gob.pe/prohvilla

This wetland area, located 11 miles (18 km) south of Lima, is one of the main coastal refuges for more than 210 bird species, including the majestic great egret. With its *totora* reed-lined pools and seven beautiful lagoons, Pantanos de Villa is Lima's last remaining natural reserve. There are signposted trails and lookout towers for bird-lovers here.

← Visitors approaching the on site museum at Pachacámac

EXPERIENCE PERU

The Southern Coast 136

Arequipa and Lake Titicaca 150

Cusco and the Sacred Valley 170

Central Sierra 196

Cordillera Blanca 206

The Northern Desert 222

The Northern Highlands 236

The Amazon Basin 248

THE SOUTHERN COAST

Remains uncovered in this dry tract reveal a fascinating blend of cultures, dating back at least 5,000 years. The Paracas civilization fashioned textiles in 300 BC with an artistry that still resonates today. The Nazca people created their mysterious giant drawings in the desert some 2,000 years ago, and the purpose of these enormous geoglyphs puzzles experts to this day. The aqueducts they built remain in use, and the ceramics they produced are among the finest of the pre-Columbian era. Despite the aridity of the land, agriculture thrives here thanks to the centuries-old systems of irrigation that use underground water supplies. The Spanish first introduced grape stocks in the 1550s and such was the success that the district around Ica is now Peru's wine basin and home to the national drink, pisco. The region also played an instrumental trading role in the 19th century due to its island deposits of *guano* (bird droppings), then a sought-after fertilizer.

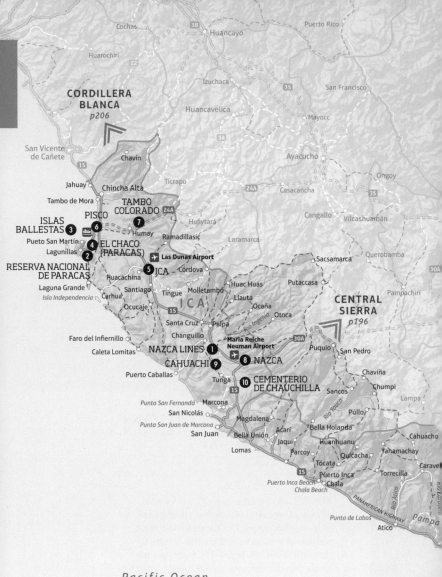

Cochas

Puerto Rico

HUANCAYO

Huarochiri

22

Izcuchaca

Huancavelica

San Francisco

35

CORDILLERA
BLANCA
p206

Ayacucho

Ongoy

San Vicente
de Cañete

Chavin

Ticrapo

Casacancha

Mayocc

Querobamba

30A

15

Jahuay

Chincha Alta

24A

Cangallo

Vilcashuamán

Tambo de Mora

Huaytará

Laramarca

Sacsamarca

PISCO

TAMBO
COLORADO ⑦

24A

Ramadillasic

Cangallo

Vilcashuamán

Humay

ISLAS
BALLESTAS ③

⑥

EL CHACO
(PARACAS)

Las Dunas Airport

Córdova

Putaccasa

Pampachiri

Pueto San Martín ④

Lagunillas

②

ICA ⑤

ICA

Huac Huas

CENTRAL
SIERRA
p196

RESERVA NACIONAL
DE PARACAS

Huacachina

Santiago

Llauta

Ocaña

Otoca

Laguna Grande

Carhua

Tingue

Molletambo

Isla Independencia

Ocucaje

15

Santa Cruz

Palpa

Rio Ingenio

Puquio

San Pedro

Faro del Infiernillo

Changuillo

30A

Chaviña

Caleta Lomitas

NAZCA LINES ①

María Reiche
Neuman Airport

Chumpi

CAHUACHI ⑨

⑧ NAZCA

Sancos

Lampa

Puerto Caballas

Tunga ⑩

CEMENTERIO
DE CHAUCHILLA

Púllo

Cahuacho

Punta San Fernando

Marcona

15

Magdalena

Rio Yauca

San Nicolás

Acarí

Bella Holanda

Punta San Juan de Marcona

San Juan

Bella Unión

Jaqui

Huanhuanu

Quicacha

Yahamachay

Lomas

Parcoy

Tócata

Torrecilla

Caravelí

15

Puerto Inca

Puerto Inca Beach

Chala

Rio Atico

Pampa

Chala Beach

PANAMERICAN HIGHWAY

Punta de Lobos

Atico

Pacific Ocean

THE SOUTHERN
COAST

0 kilometers   60

0 miles   60

N
↑

THE SOUTHERN COAST

Must Sees
1 Nazca Lines
2 Reserva Nacional de Paracas

Experience More
3 Islas Ballestas
4 El Chaco (Paracas)
5 Ica
6 Pisco
7 Tambo Colorado
8 Nazca
9 Cahuachi
10 Cementerio de Chauchilla
11 Tacna
12 Petroglifos de Miculla
13 Tarata
14 Baños Termales de Putina

EXPERIENCE The Southern Coast

①

NAZCA LINES

🅰 E6 🏠 12 miles (20 km) N of Nazca, Pan-American Hwy South, KM420 🚌 In Nazca 🛈 Nazca Municipalidad (Town Hall); 056 522 418

Dispersed over the high desert plateau between the towns of Nazca and Palpa, this collection of geoglyphs comprises more than 70 human figures and stylized animals, and 10,000 lines. First noticed from the air in 1927, these ancient enigmatic lines remain one of the world's greatest archeological mysteries.

It almost never rains on the Peruvian coast which is why the remarkable Nazca Lines have survived so many centuries, preserving the secrets of an ancient culture. Etched into the plains between 500 BC and AD 500, they were declared a UNESCO World Heritage Site in 1994. German mathematician and astronomer Maria Reiche began studying the Nazca Lines in the 1940s and devoted her life to uncovering their mysteries. She believed the lines were created by tying a chord to an axis, just as a compass is used to draw a circle. Debate continues about their original purpose, with theories including a giant astronomical calendar, ceremonial center, or alien landing strip.

> 🔍 HIDDEN GEM
> **Palpa Lines**
>
> Etched on the desert by the Paracas culture 1,000 years before the Nazca Lines, these lines are just as puzzling. Found around a 30-minute drive from Nazca, they can be viewed from the platforms at Palpa.

Highlights

Whale

△ The first geoglyph to be discovered, it probably depicts a killer whale (or orca). The Nazca were a coastal culture, and here they favor the largest creature of the ocean.

Spider

△ The spider is identified as being both a symbol of rain and fertility, and a representation of the soothsayers, who used these creatures to predict the future.

Monkey

△ Regarded as a divine being, the monkey also appears on Nazca ceramics. The geoglyph has only nine fingers and Reiche suggested it may have been made to mark the equinoxes.

Hummingbird

△ Measuring 315 ft by 217 ft (96 m by 66 m), this is one of the best-known geoglyphs. The Nazca believed hummingbirds were messengers between men and condors, which they considered to be gods.

↑ The geometric patterns of the enigmatic Nazca Lines, as seen from above

VIEWING THE LINES

You can admire the lines from the viewing platform at KM420 *(pictured)*, or visit one of the cheaper viewing platforms, where on-site guides provide brief details in Spanish. Another way to see the lines is from one of the three- to nine-seater planes flying out of Nazca airport. Prices start from around US$90 for a 35-minute flight, but it will be US$240 if you want to include the Palpa Lines. Aero Nasca *(www. aeronasca.com)* is a reputable air carrier.

2 🚴 Ⓜ 🍴

RESERVA NACIONAL DE PARACAS

🅰 D6　🄰 177 miles (285 km) S of Lima　🚌 From Pisco　📞 956 750 765　🕘 9am–4pm daily

The desert meets the sea at Peru's largest piece of protected coastline, where towering cliffs border beaches swarming with wildlife. A cycle circuit is the best way to take in the reserve's key sites, including the impressive El Candelabro geoglyph and the Paracas Necropolis burial ground.

The country's first designated national reserve provides a habitat for more than 1,800 species of plants and animals. Birdlife is particularly rich, and here visitors can find flamingos, Humboldt penguins, pelicans, and terns. Occasionally, condors can be seen overhead, along with red-headed turkey vultures.

The Islas San Gallán and La Vieja, lying just off the coast, are the only places for the endangered *potoyunco* (Peruvian diving petrel) to reproduce in Peru.

Touring the Reserve

A morning boat trip to the nearby Islas Ballestas (*p144*), a separate part of the reserve, is normally combined with an afternoon in the reserve, although renting a bike or quad grants greater freedom for exploring the latter. At the reserve, an 18-mile (30-km) biking circuit starts at a viewpoint for the rock formation La Catedral and continues south to Playa Roja, a curiously red-sand beach formed from particles of granodiorite rock. Nearby, the restaurants of Lagunillas serve up fresh seafood. Heading north, the Museo de Sitio Julio C. Tello displays textiles, ceramics, and skulls from the Paracas culture (700 BC). Not far from here is El Candelabro, a 595-ft (180-m) geoglyph stamped into the hillside. In the surrounding waters, also a part of the reserve, marine mammals abound, including sea lions, dolphins, and the endangered marine otter.

Did You Know?

Flamingos found here inspired the colors of the Peruvian flag after Liberator San Martín visited the bay.

Must See

TOP 3 PLACES TO SPOT WILDLIFE

Punta Arquillo
⬛ 9 miles (15 km) SW of park entrance
This cliff lookout is perfect for spotting fur seals and the rarer marine otter.

Bahía de Paracas
⬛ Behind the Museo de Sitio Julio C. Tello
The shoreline behind the museum is great for spying birds like flamingos, gulls, and heron from June to November.

Lagunillas
⬛ 5.5 miles (9 km) SW of park entrance
Keep an eye out for South American sea lions and fur seals in the waves in the bay.

←
Hikers exploring the vast golden stretch of the Reserva Nacional de Paracas

① Facade of the Museo de Sitio Julio C. Tello which displays paraphernalia from the Paracas culture.

② The three-pronged El Candelabro is thought to have been a navigational aid or a Nazca ritual symbol. It is best appreciated from the water.

③ Beautiful brown pelicans and guanay cormorants regularly inhabit the rocks at the reserve.

EXPERIENCE MORE

3

Islas Ballestas

D6 162 miles (261 km) S of Lima From El Chaco

The Ballestas Islands are among the most popular draws on the southern coast. They're dubbed the "Poor Man's Galapagos," because the arches and caves of these islets shelter more than 160 species of marine birds, including Humboldt penguins, boobies, and pelicans, as well as immense numbers of sea lions. Dolphins, whales, and sea turtles sometimes appear in the surrounding waters, too. Old, rusted factory remains on the islands are a throwback to the 19th century when guano (mineral-rich bird droppings) was an important fertilizer and provided a vital source of revenue for the country.

It is possible to take a boat tour around the islands, but visitors are not allowed to disembark. On the way, look out for El Candelabro de Paracas (p142), a 595-ft (180-m) geoglyph within the Reserva Nacional de Paracas (p142), that is only fully visible on the way to and from the islands. Some claim it is a pirate's sign.

💬 **INSIDER TIP**
Watch the Birdie

Boats to the Islas Ballestas are uncovered, so take a hat with a visor or wide brim. Guano harvesting may have ceased here, but no one has told the avian inhabitants, and "bird-bombings" have disrupted many a perfectly aligned photo.

4

El Chaco (Paracas)

D6 158 miles (254 km) S of Lima From Lima iPerú Av los Libertadores; 980 894 433; 7am–12:30pm & 1:30–4pm Wed–Sun

A former seaside getaway for Lima's well-heeled, El Chaco, also known as Paracas, is still a favorite among holidaying Peruvians. Exclusive harbor-side hotels with tempting swimming pools line the shores of the pelican-studded harbor, and a stroll along the promenade at sunset is an excellent way of soaking up the town's mellow atmosphere. It's a nicer place to stay than

neighboring Pisco, although pollution from nearby fishmeal factories means swimming in the bay is not recommended. However, kayaking and wind-surfing are popular water activities, as are the boat trips to the Islas Ballestas, which generally leave at 9–10am.

5

Ica

D6 192 miles (310 km) S of Lima Charter services from Lima From Lima Dircetur Av Grau; 056 238 710 (ext 29); 8am–12:30pm & 2–4:30pm Mon–Fri

Founded by the Spanish in 1563 as Villa de Valverde, this village was renamed in 1640, and is now Peru's premier wine center, with

Did You Know?

El Chaco is where General San Martín's army made landfall in 1820 to liberate Peru from the Spanish.

↑ Boats in the beautiful El Chaco harbor, where trips depart for Islas Ballestas

→ The adobe walls of Tambo Colorado, once colored with bright pigments

vineyards dating back to the 16th century. Its Vendimia (grape harvest festival) takes place in the first two weeks of March, and pisco-soaked raisins sometimes feature in *tejas*, Ica's delicious traditional confectionery.

Known as the "city of eternal sun" due to its dry weather, Ica was badly affected by the 2007 earthquake, Peru's worst since 1974. A chapel in the Neo-Classical Sanctuario del Señor del Luren collapsed during evening Mass, killing several people and injuring dozens. While over 2,800 pre-Hispanic artifacts in museums across the Ica region also suffered extensive damage, Ica's Museo Regional Adolfo Bermúdez Jenkins escaped virtually unscathed. It houses an interesting collection of Paracas, Nazca, Ica, Wari, and Inca artifacts, including mummies and skulls that show evidence of ancient surgical techniques.

The oasis of Huacachina, a green lagoon attractively situated amid towering dunes, is just 3 miles (5 km) from Ica. The water is not clean enough for swimming (although you can rent a paddleboat). However, most visitors come to sand-board or ride the dunes.

Pisco

△D6 ⌂155 miles (250 km) S of Lima ⊞From Ica ℹMuncipaIidad (Town Hall) on main plaza

Founded in 1640, Pisco, a quiet city of farmers and fishers, was unable to withstand the earthquake that rocked the area on August 15, 2007. Three-quarters of the town was lost as historic buildings around the plaza crumbled, tens of thousands of adobe homes collapsed, and hundreds of people died. The statue of liberator José de San Martín *(p71)*, in the main plaza, was left to survey the ruins, including the 18th-century Iglesia San Clemente, which caved in during Mass, killing a number of worshippers.

Tambo Colorado

△D6 ⌂Los Libertadores Hwy, opposite Pan-American Hwy South, KM229 ⊞To Humay from Pisco via Los Libertadores; stop at KM39 ◷9am–5pm daily

Formerly a significant administrative center of the Incas, Tambo Colorado sits at the base of steep foothills in the Pisco river valley, and was home to soldiers and the upper echelons of the Incan Empire. It was a connecting point on the Inca road joining Ayacucho with the coast. It is thought that the site was the summer residence of Pachacútec, the ninth Inca. Tambo Colorado is one of the best-preserved adobe ruins in Peru. Niches in the outer walls bear traces of the red and yellow pigment used to decorate them, and alcoves are adorned with carvings of human figures.

EAT

Tambo de Tacama

A spellbinding setting – the pink hacienda of the Tacama vineyard – for gourmet Peruvian dishes. Grab a spot on the patio for traditional dance performances on weekends.

🅐D6 🏠Calle Nicanor León 140. Urb. Sr. de Luren, Ica 🌐tacama.com

---

La Olla de Juanita

Enjoy rustic criollo specialties, such as *papa a la huancaina* (potatoes with a spicy sauce) and *sopa seca* (chicken and chili-pepper soup), on a vine-lined terrace within the Tres Esquinas pisco bodega.

🅐D6 🏠Fundo Tres Esquinas, Ica 📞51 981 129 841

Los Angeles

A no-frills, great-value restaurant offering tasty criollo-style food and a wide variety of vegetarian dishes. The owner is fluent in English and French.

🅐E6 🏠Bolognesi 266, Nazca 📞51 956 345 151

La Casa Rustika

Friendly, with a good range of international and Peruvian dishes, including a renowned beef lasagna.

🅐E6 🏠Bolognesi 372, Nazca 📞998 996 754

Nazca

🅐E6 🏠285 miles (460 km) S of Lima ➡️For Nazca Lines 🚌From Lima or Ica

The discovery of the Nazca Lines *(p140)* put the town of Nazca on the map, and that is the main reason most people visit the area. The **Museo Didáctico Antonini**, however, also makes a worthwhile stop. It displays many of the finds from the nearby Cahuachi site. The collection gives an insight into all aspects of Nazca society, and includes mummies and distorted heads – the Nazca wrapped the heads of their newborns in leather or wood bands.

On the other side of town, the Planetarium inside the Hotel Nazca Lines *(p145)* has intriguing evening talks on the theories behind how and why the Nazca Lines were carved into the desert.

Another important archeological site is the Acueducto de Cantalloc. The 35 spiraling aqueducts form part of a sophisticated system of irrigation, originally built by the Nazca, but still used by local farmers today.

Some 56 miles (90 km) east on the road to Cusco, the altiplano grasslands of the **Reserva Nacional Pampa Galeras Barbara D'Achille** is home to herds of vicuñas, the relative of the llama.

Did You Know?

The world's tallest sand dune, Cerro Blanco, lies near Nazca. Even sand-boarding down it takes four minutes.

Museo Didáctico Antonini

 🏠Av de la Cultura 600 📞056 523 444 🕐9am–7pm daily

Reserva Nacional Pampa Galeras Barbara D'Achille

🏠Nazca-Cusco Rd KM 89 🚌From Nazca 📞056 522 770 🕐8am–5pm daily

---

Cahuachi

🅐E6 🏠11 miles (17 km) NE of Nazca 🕐8am–5pm daily

Cahuachi, an enormous Nazca ceremonial center, reached its zenith more than 2,000 years ago. It is dominated by a 100-ft (30-m) high central pyramid and plaza. Forty other pyramids were sculpted from the landscape with massive mud-brick adobe walls applied over them. Some 5,000 tombs have been identified but, sadly, Cahuachi has suffered from looting.

Italian archeologist Giuseppe Orefici has been excavating the site for decades and has concluded it was home to priests who conducted public ceremonies

→

Adobe pyramid at Cahuachi, a huge ceremonial center of the Nazca culture

 Repositioned skulls within the excavated graves at the Cementerio de Chauchilla

 TOP 4 SOUTHERN BEACHES

Puerto Inca
Pre-Columbian ruins make for a great hike before a swim at the crescent-shaped beach.

Chala
Have super-fresh seafood at this tumble-down fishing village.

Punta San Juan de Marcona
View sea lions, pelicans and Humboldt penguins from the cliffs.

Punta San Fernando
A rich supply of marine life and Andean condors are often visible here.

and rituals to thank the gods for water. The site's numerous treasures can be seen at the Museo Didáctico Antonini in Nazca.

Cementerio de Chauchilla

E6 **18 miles (29 km) S of Nazca** **8am-6pm daily**

Chauchilla Cemetery, naturally enough, is full of graves dating back to the Chincha period (AD 1000–1400).

At one stage mummies were scattered across the site, courtesy of tomb-raiders who fleeced the bodies of valuables and discarded textile scraps, bones, and carcasses in the desert. From an archaeologist's point of view, they effectively robbed the bodies of their identities and thus hindered researchers' ability to piece together the history of the people found here.

There are thousands of graves but only 12 have been restored; they show shrouded mummies in squatting positions with bleached skulls and long matted hair. There is also a children's-only grave.

Normally the mummies would have been well preserved by the arid sands, rich in salt and nitrates, but their exposure to the elements destroyed the mummified skin and faded the bones.

↑ The Paseo Cívico in Tacna, with its ornamental fountain and flower-roofed pavilions

Tacna

F7 **766 miles (1,233 km) S of Lima** **From Lima or Arequipa**

The attractive town of Tacna marks Peru's frontier with Chile and has a colorful history of both resistance and defeat. Founded in 1535, it became the focus of Peru's fight for independence when revolutionary Francisco Antonio de Zela unsuccessfully attempted to overthrow Spanish rule in 1811. Casa de Zela, his former home, is now a museum charting his life. In 1880, Tacna fell under Chilean control after Peru's defeat in the War of the Pacific. This history is narrated in the Museo Histórico Regional de Tacna, while northwest of the city, eight sculptures line Cerro Intiorko in tribute to those who died during the war. The Treaty of Lima, signed in 1929, finally saw Tacna become Peruvian territory once again.

This is celebrated every July 28 by the Procesión de la Bandera, when a military and civilian parade carries a Peruvian flag through the city's streets.

Unusually, Tacna has no central plaza; instead, the Paseo Cívico is the city's focal point. Its Neo-Classical fountain was designed by Gustave Eiffel – better known for the Eiffel Tower. A few blocks north, the **Museo Ferroviario** contains steam locomotives retired from use on the Tacna–Arica rail line.

Museo Ferroviario
Calle Gregorio Albarracín and Av 2 de Mayo **965 074 455** **9am–5pm daily**

Petroglifos de Miculla

G7 **14 miles (23 km) NE of Tacna** **From Tacna** **9am–5pm Tue–Sun**

Among the largest collection of their kind in South America, the Petroglifos de Miculla comprise 1,500 shapes etched into low boulders. Humans

feature prominently in the imagery, with depictions of daily activities including agriculture, hunting, dancing and conflict. Other drawings evidence rituals associated with cults of water, earth and the cosmos. They are thought to have been carved between AD 500 and 1500. There's a huge area to explore here, including two rope bridges across dry ravines.

Tarata

F7 **55 miles (89 km) N of Tacna** **From Tacna**

The attractive town of Tarata sits at 10,144 ft (3,000 m) above sea level, ringed by verdant, Andean countryside and spectacular agricultural terracing. Its chief attraction is its elegant Iglesia San

Benedicto de Abad, with delicate carvings depicting religious scenes on its facade. Construction work began in 1611, but the church was only completed 130 years later.

The town is connected with neighboring Ticaco by a stretch of the Cápac Ñan (p69), the royal Inca road. Visitors can walk past pre-Inca archeological sites, likely belonging to the Aymara and Tihuanaco cultures.

Baños Termales de Putina

F7 **63 miles (100 km) N of Tacna** **From Tacna** **4am–8:30pm Tue–Sun**

North of Tacna the highway climbs up into the mountains,

↑ Pool fed by natural hot springs at the Baños Termales de Putina

beginning its journey to Puno (p164), and these thermal baths make for a pleasant break on the route. Reached by paved Inca road, the thermal springs originate in the nearby Yucamani volcano. Rich in sodium chloride, magnesium, and zinc, the water is believed to have medicinal properties and is heated to 102°–113° F (39°–45° C). Two outdoor pools and a handful of smaller and hotter private indoor tubs are available. There are changing facilities, and families are welcome, although some of the rock-cut stairways are steep. The best time for a quiet dip is generally the mornings.

← The Petroglifos de Miculla, a treasure trove of ancient art and carvings (inset)

CROSSING TO CHILE

Peru's only international railroad is between Tacna and Arica, Chile. Built in 1856, it reopened to passengers in 2016. The cheerful yellow one-carriage train makes the 38-mile (62-km) trip twice a day. Immigration and customs formalities are dealt with at the stations at either end, usually quite swiftly, making this a relatively painless way to cross the border. Just south of Tacna station, the old railroad yards now house the Museo Ferroviario, the National Rail Museum of Peru, with steam engines, wagons, carriages, and some delightful vintage cars converted to run on rails. You can also inspect the former railroad workshops.

AREQUIPA, CANYONS, AND LAKE TITICACA

The colonial city of Arequipa sits in stark contrast to its untamed surrounds. Rock art found in this region is testimony to a civilization dating back more than 8,000 years, while lush 2,000-year-old agricultural terraces recall the ingenuity of the Collagua people.

In the 14th century, Inca leader Mayta Cápac sealed his victory over the Collagua by marrying the daughter of a local chief and building her a house made of copper. This same mineral wealth – gold, silver, lead, copper, quartz – drew the Spanish conquistadores in the 16th century. Such heritage is on full display in the Baroque churches that dominate villages such as Chucuito.

Farther east lies the sapphire expanse of Lake Titicaca, hailed in Inca mythology as the birthplace of their civilization. Ancient settlements of weavers, fishermen, and farmers still ply their trade around the shore and on near and far islands, including the famous floating isles made entirely from reeds.

AREQUIPA, CANYONS, AND LAKE TITICACA

Must Sees
1. Arequipa
2. Lake Titicaca
3. Cañón del Colca

Experience More
4. Cañón de Cotahuasi
5. Sillustani Burial Towers
6. Lampa

Amparaés

28B

Calca

Salinas de Maras

Cusco

Chinchero

Colcha

Cusipata

3S

Omacha

CENTRAL
SIERRA
p199

Cordillera de Huanzo

Huamanripa

Velille

Puquio

AYACUCHO

Chaviña

San Javier
de Alpabamba

Mina Arcata

Suycutambo

Coracora

Puyca

Sancos

Chumpi

Tomepampa

Alca

Caylloma

Pararca

Lampa

Cotahuasi

CAÑÓN DE COTAHUASI

Cordillera de Chillán

Púlio

Incuyo

Pausa

Solimana
20,744 ft
(6,323 m)

Orcopampa

AREQUIPA

Mismi
18,362 ft
(5,597 m)

Huanhuanu

Cahuacho

Coropuma
21,696 ft
(6,613 m)

Andagua

Madrigal

Chivay

Yanamachay

Salamanca

Cabanaconde

Maca

Achoma

Chichas

CAÑÓN DEL
COLCA

Chucura

Cháparra

Torrecilla

Caravelí

Cerro
Rico

Pampacolca

Tipán

Huambo

Cordillera de Chillán

Rio Yuna

Pampa Blanca

Iquipi

Huanca

Lluta

Pampa
de Arrieros

PANAMERICAN HIGHWAY

THE SOUTHERN
COAST
p136

Aplao

Huacán

Quilcapampa

30B

Atico

Pampa de Cartaderas

Corire

Pitay

Socosani

Yura

Punta Colorada

Tambillo

AREQUIPA

Ocoña

El Alto

Rodríguez Ballón
International Airport

15

Santa Rita
de Siguas

1S

30A

San Gregorio

Repartición

Camaná

Quilca

La Joya
Pampa
de la Joya

Huagri

Cachendo

AREQUIPA,
CANYONS AND
LAKE TITICACA

Punta Al Aire

Matarani

30

Chucarap

Mollendo

15A

La Curva

0 kilometers   50

0 miles   50

N

Punta de
Bombón

↑ Arequipa's cathedral and the Plaza de Armas, one of Peru's finest squares

AREQUIPA

F7 ⌂627 miles (1,009 km) SE of Lima ⤢⊠From Cusco ⊠From Puno ⊟From Puno and Lima ⓘiPeru; Plaza de Armas; 054 223 265; 9am-6pm daily

Nicknamed "the white city", Arequipa is built almost entirely from sillar, a white volcanic rock. It is Peru's second-largest city and has a long history as a hub for sheep and alpaca wool exports, which still thrive today.

① La Catedral

⌂Plaza de Armas ◷7-10am & 5-6pm Mon-Sat, 9am-1pm Sun ⊕museo catedralarequipa.org.pe

Originally constructed in 1621, the cathedral was damaged during a series of earthquakes and fire and rebuilt by

GREAT VIEW
Yanahuara

The Yanahuara district, just 10 minutes from Arequipa's city center, offers a picturesque view of the city and countryside with the majestic Misti volcano in the background.

architect Lucas Poblete in 1868. The cathedral is regarded as the most important Neo-Classical religious building in the country. Flanked by two arches, it is the only cathedral in Peru that stretches the entire length of a plaza. The main altar is made of Carrara marble, as are the 12 columns representing the 12 apostles.

② Casona Iriberry

⌂Cnr of Santa Catalina & San Agustín ☏054 204 482 ◷9am-1pm & 4-8pm daily

Built in 1793, the volcanic rock walls of the Casona Iriberry, also known as Casa Arróspide, are thought to be the thickest in Arequipa. Formerly a

private home, it is now the Cultural Centre Chávez de la Rosa, and part of the Universidad de San Agustín. Rooms, where art and photography exhibitions are held, open on to a series of charming stone patios. The top terrace has great views of the beautiful nearby cathedral.

③ Casa del Moral

⌂Calle Moral 318 ☏054 210 084 ◷8:30am-5:30pm Mon-Sat ⌂From noon on public hols

This 18th-century home is named after an ancient *mora* (mulberry) tree that, although dead, is still standing in its central patio; a new mulberry has been planted beside it. Intricate carvings, in sillar, of puma heads with snakes emerging from their mouths adorn the stone gateway, along with a crown suspended above a coat of arms held up by two angels. Inside, there are displays of furniture from colonial and republican times, Cusco School *(p179)* oil paintings, and 16th-century maps. The rooftop looks out over the towering volcanoes that surround the city.

4
Museo Histórico Municipal

📍 Plaza San Francisco 407
☎ 054 204 801 ⏰ 9am–5pm Mon–Fri

The history of Arequipa is the focus here, with photographs of the old city, maps, historical documents, and a number of archeological pieces on show. Also highlighted are Arequipa's famous residents. A series of satirical caricatures and works by famous artist Jorge Vinatea Reynoso (1900–31) are very insightful.

5
Convento de la Recoleta

📍 Jirón Recoleta 117
☎ 054 270 966 ⏰ 9am–1pm & 2–5pm Mon–Sat

Situated in the Antiquilla neighborhood, a 10-minute walk from the main plaza, this convent was founded by the Franciscans in 1648. Its enchanting four cloisters, featuring tranquil gardens and sillar columns, are an example of Arequipa's old colonial style.

Also of interest are the exhibition rooms on pre-Columbian artifacts, including ceramics and textiles, and a room dedicated to Amazonian cultures. There is also a library housing over 23,000 books from the 16th and 17 centuries.

6
Iglesia San Francisco

📍 Calle Zela ⏰ Hours vary

Despite being battered by earthquakes, the 16th-century San Francisco church is still standing. The church features an unusual brick entrance-way, and the convent contains paintings from the Cusco School *(p179)*.

EAT

Crepísimo
Savory and sweet crepes, a bar and a sun-plastered terrace.

📍 Calle Santa Catalina 208, Cercado
🌐 crepisimo.com

S/ S/ S/

Chicha
Restaurant of acclaimed chef Gastón Acurio. Sophisticated dining rooms offering regional foods, many with Arequipa's famous freshwater shrimp.

📍 Santa Catalina 210, Cercado
🌐 chicha.com.pe

S/ S/ S/

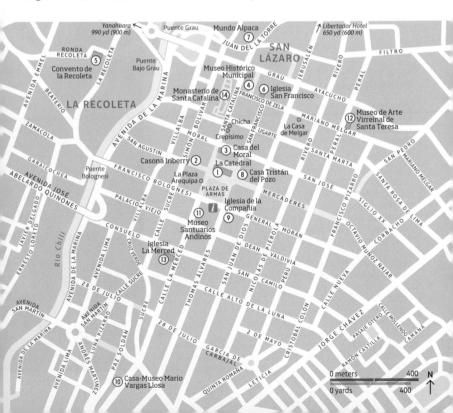

STAY

Costa del Sol Wyndham

A luxury resort 15 minutes away from the city.

 Plaza Bolívar s/n, Selva Alegre costa delsolperu.com

§/§/§/

La Plaza Arequipa

A boutique hotel, with balconies overlooking the city's main square.

 Portal de San Agustín laplazaarequipa hotel.pe

§/§/§/

La Casa de Melgar

An 18th-century house with several gardens.

 Calle Melgar 108 lacasademelgar.com

§/§/§/

Mundo Alpaca

 Juan de la Torre 101, San Lázaro 8:30am-6:30pm daily mundo alpaca.com.pe

This museum includes traditional Andean weaving demos, an area of live camelids, and the first weaving machinery used by the Michell y Cia textile firm, which was founded in 1931. There is also an art and textile gallery that is worth a visit, which includes the winning works of highly sophisticated weavers from the coast, highlands, and jungle. Also on show here are the prize-winning watercolor and oil paintings from their annual competition, the oldest in the country. The shop offers alpaca wool goods.

---

 ⑧

Casa Tristán del Pozo

 Calle San Francisco 108 ⏰9am-3pm & 4-6pm Mon-Fri (to 1pm Sat) fundacion bbva.pe/casonas-y-museos/casa-tristan-del-pozo/

This colonial home takes its name from General Domingo Tristán del Pozo who commissioned it in 1738. Built of white volcanic stone, its facade features intricately carved Baroque details above the windows and entrance. Inside, there are arched roofs and expansive patios. Today, it is home to a bank, a small museum, and an art gallery.

---

⑨

Iglesia de la Compañía

 Cnr of Calle General Morán & Álvarez Thomas 054 212 141 ⏰9am-1pm & 3-6pm daily

The Jesuit church of La Compañía is one of the city's oldest. Originally designed by Gaspar Baez in 1573, the first structure was flattened by an earthquake in 1584. Profuse mestizo ornamentation incorporating flowers, faces, and spirals, are engraved into the volcanic rock facade.

> 💬 INSIDER TIP
> ## Best Nightlife Spot
>
> Spend a leisurely evening at the rooftop bar and restaurant Déjà Vu *(Calle San Francisco 319B)* grooving to catchy music. The terrace is perfect for a pisco sundowner.

→

Iglesia de la Compañía's embellished interior, and (inset) its grand facade

---

Inside, the main altar is carved in the Churrigueresque style – Spanish Baroque with a Latin twist, involving gold leaf and cherubs with Inca faces. The cloisters now house shops.

---

⑩

Casa-Museo Mario Vargas Llosa

 (054) 283 574 ⏰8am-4pm Mon-Fri

This high-tech interactive museum is located in the home where the Nobel laureate Mario Vargas Llosa was born. A guided tour in

Spanish takes you through 17 rooms, organized chronologically, with holograms and 3D videos in spaces that recreate Vargas Llosa's world, including a fantastic bar that figures prominently in one of his novels.

Museo Santuarios Andinos de la Universidad Católica de Santa María

La Merced 110 9am-6pm Mon-Sat (to 2pm Sun) ucsm.edu.pe/museo-santuarios-andinos/

The museum's most famous exhibit is Juanita, la Dama de Ampato (the Lady of Ampato) – the Andes' first frozen female mummy, and considered one of the world's best-preserved. Along with Juanita, there are several other mummies that were discovered in Ampato. All children, they were found with textiles, gold and silver figurines, dolls, and ceramics in their mountain tombs.

Museo de Arte Virreinal de Santa Teresa

Calle Melgar 303 9am-5pm Mon-Sat museosantateresa.org

Founded in 1710 as a monastery for the Barefoot Carmelite nuns of Santa Teresa and San José, the convent only opened to the public in 2005. Over a period of 300 years, the nuns have gathered a unique collection of colonial paintings, sculptures, and decorative objects, exhibited in 13 rooms. The museum closes briefly at noon, when the nuns sing the Angelus. Although they are in a private section, their singing can be heard in the museum area. The shop sells soaps, apple cider vinegar, and cakes and biscuits, all made by the nuns.

Iglesia La Merced

Calle Merced 110 054 213 233 7-8am & 5-7pm Mon-Fri, 6am-noon & 6-7pm Sun

Construction began in 1551 and was completed in 1607. The side entrance of this sillar church features the image of the Virgin Mary with two "saints of mercy." A series of paintings portraying the Virgen de la Merced are on display. The convent has a library, too.

(14)

MONASTERIO DE SANTA CATALINA

🏠 Calle Santa Catalina 301   🕐 9am–5pm daily   Ⓦ santacatalina.org.pe

Taking up an entire block of the city, the Monastery of Santa Catalina was founded in 1579 by Doña María de Guzmán, a rich widow who became a nun. Resembling a small town, the site comprises 100 rooms, lined along six streets, three cloisters, a church, and a gallery full of superb paintings.

In its heyday the monastery housed 450 people, a third of them nuns and the rest servants. The first to join the Order of Saint Catherine of Siena were poor Creole women and women from upper-class families. The monastery underwent reform in the 1870s when Sister Josef Cadena replaced the hedonistic lifestyle with religious austerity. As a result, the servants were freed in 1871 and many of them joined the order.

The convent was opened to the public in August 1970, since tourism was thought to be the best option to raise the funds required to install electricity and running water. Today, around 15 nuns live here in an area that is off-limits to visitors.

Did You Know?

The monastery's nuns would meet in the Plaza Zocodover on Sundays to exchange handmade items.

1715–1723

▽ Claustro Mayor, the Main Cloister, is the largest in the monastery and was worked on between 1715 and 1723. It is decorated with 32 frescoes, 26 of them depicting Mary's life and 9 showing the public life of Jesus.

1748

The bell tower, Torre del Campanario, was built. The steeple has four bells facing the streets around the monastery. The oldest bell is toward the south, facing Calle Ugarte Street, and bears the inscription "Santa Catalina Ora Pronobis 1749."

Timeline

1660

△ The white *sillar* dome of the Iglesia de Santa Catalina was constructed. The long aisle is one of the highlights.

1770

Lavandería, the communal laundry, was established. Water ran through a central channel into 20 earthenware jars which served as washing troughs.

← With its terra-cotta walls, Calle Sevilla is one of the monastery's prettiest streets

CLAUSTRO DE LOS NARANJOS

The Orange Tree Cloister, an open space situated in the west of the complex, takes its name from the orange trees planted there. It is painted a striking cobalt blue and features a series of beautiful arches and columns, which are adorned with a splendid series of mural paintings. The three crosses stationed here, however, are the most important feature. Representing eternal life, they are used by nuns in the monastery to reenact the Passion of Christ (the final days of Jesus' life) on Good Friday every year. Unfortunately, the public cannot view this ancient tradition, since the monastery is closed on that day, recalling the period when the order was completely cloistered from the world.

EXPLORING MONASTERIO DE SANTA CATALINA

Claustro Mayor

The Main Cloister is bordered by five confessionals on the left side, ensuring the nuns retain a degree of privacy during their declarations. Thirty-two beautiful frescoes decorate the cloister walls. The majority of them show biblical scenes depicting the life of the Virgin Mary, while the remainder portray the life of Jesus.

Calle Córdoba

Córdoba Street, as the name implies, is inspired by the architecture of Andalusia. Terra-cotta pots filled with

↑ The three crosses and orange trees in the blue Claustro de los Naranjos

geraniums line the gleaming white walls, which trap the sun all year round.

The 18th-century wall on the right of this street is made of volcanic stones from Arequipa. These sillar blocks each measure 18 inches by 16 inches (45 cm by 40 cm). The 20th-century building on the left side of the street is out of bounds for visitors. The area forms part of the complex in which the nuns live today.

Cocina

The kitchen was probably designed as a chapel, given its high roof. The walls are blackened with soot from the coal- and wood-burning stove. The original utensils now sit unused. The Plaza Zocodover, closeby, marks the centre of the complex.

Lavandería

The communal laundry was built at a time when Arequipa's only water source was a series of small canals. The 20 huge earthenware jars, earlier used to hold grain or store wine, doubled up as wash basins.

The water for washing was channeled through a central canal, with offshoots leading into individual jars. At the bottom of each jar was a plug which was removed once the washing was finished. This helped in draining all the dirty water down to an underground canal which was connected to the river. The laundry is located at the end of a long boulevard called Calle Toledo.

Iglesia de Santa Catalina

Dating back to 1660, the Church of Santa Catalina has been reconstructed several times after a number of earthquakes in the region caused serious damage to the structure. However, the original design of the chapel has been retained.

It is made of white *sillar* (local volcanic stone). The long aisle leads to the main silver altar, which is heavily embossed with religious motifs. This altar is positioned

SOR ANA DE LOS ÁNGELES MONTEAGUDO

Santa Catalina was also home to Sister Ana of the Angels (1602–86), who was beatified by Pope John Paul II in 1985. She was educated in the monastery until she was about 11 years old, joined the order, and was eventually elected Mother Superior. It is said that an ill painter, who made the only known portrait of her *(right)*, was completely cured of all his ailments by the time he finished the painting.

←
The Plaza Zocodover, found directly at the center of the complex

 HIDDEN GEM
Sister Ana's Cell

Sister Ana, known as a miracle-worker, was buried in the monastery. Her humble cell and the utensils she used more than 300 years ago are on display in her rooms, and well worth a visit.

as the most important examples of religious art on the continent. These works are displayed in the Religious Art Gallery, which is housed in two large rooms in the shape of a cross with exposed block walls made of sillar. This space was once used as a shelter for homeless widows and single mothers. There are numerous paintings from the admired

Cusco School *(p179)* including the *Divine Shepherdess*, believed to be the work of artist Marcos Zapata. There is a depiction of St Michael, dressed in Spanish armor, complete with a feathery helmet, as well as a portrait of St Catherine, or Santa Catalina, with a description of the scene written on a panel that is held by an angel.

under an impressive dome. There is also an altar dedicated to Sister Ana of the Angels. A grand European organ takes pride of place in the high choir.

Pinacoteca

When restoration began on the monastery before it was opened to the public in the 1970s, workers uncovered a cache of religious paintings dating back to the Peruvian Viceroyalty *(p71)*. Experts restored the 400 artworks, many of which were hailed

↑ The superb collection of paintings on display in the Pinacoteca

②

LAKE TITICACA

⚑ G7 ✈ **From Lima & Arequipa** 🚌🚂 **From Cusco & Arequipa** 🚌 **From Puno; 7:30am tour recommended** ℹ **In Puno**

At an elevation of 12,500 ft (3,800 m), Lake Titicaca is the highest navigable lake in the world. South America's second-largest lake, it covers 3,210 sq miles (8,300 sq km) of Peru and Bolivia, is 120 miles (194 km) long and 50 miles (80 km) wide at its broadest point. Islands are sprinkled across the lake, and the inhabitants live traditionally, with life centered around fishing, farming, and weaving, increasingly supplemented by tourism.

①

Isla del Sol

⚑ 9 miles (14 km) from Copacabana, Bolivia
🚢 To Copacabana
🚢 From Copacabana

Famed as the birthplace of the Incas, the Island of the Sun is actually in the Bolivian waters of the lake. Close to the maze ruins of Chinkana is a sacred rock carved into the shape of a puma. Farther along are two large footprints, supposedly made when the sun came down to earth to give birth to the first Incas. A stairway leads up from the water's edge at Yumani to what is known as a fountain of youth.

Did You Know?

Ruins of an ancient temple, dating back 1,500 years, were discovered in the lake's waters in 2000.

②

Iglesia Santiago Apóstol de Pomata

⚑ 67 miles (108 km) S of Puno 🚌 **From Puno**
🕐 8am–4pm daily

This Dominican church surveys both town and lake from its hilltop position. Built in pink granite, it is known for its intricate sandstone facade, which fuses Indigenous symbols with Baroque. It is one of southern Peru's most beautiful churches. Inside are windows made from *huamanga* stone, a towering gold-leaf altar adorned with coiled columns, and Cusco School paintings (*p179*).

③

Isla de la Luna

⚑ 4 miles (7 km) from Isla del Sol 🚢

The *aqllawasi* (monastery) is the most important archeological site on the Island of the Moon. In Inca times, the island housed the "chosen women," who took part in special ceremonies dedicated to the sun. The main palace, which was rebuilt in the 1960s, has some 30 rooms centered around a courtyard.

④

Islas Uros

⚑ 4 miles (6 km) from Puno 🚢 **ℹ 977 946 569**

The Uros developed their unique floating islands

↑ Soaking up the views on the edge of Lake Titicaca

centuries ago to escape hostile cultures on the mainland. They consider themselves to be "the oldest people on earth." Legend says they existed even before the sun. Following invasions by Aymara and Inca populations, the Uros ended up at the bottom of the pre-Columbian hierarchy. They speak Aymara today and many of them live on the mainland.

The largest of the floating islands, Huacavacani, is estimated to be 160 years old, housing a meeting hall and a school. The islanders use the ubiquitous *totora* (a reed-like papyrus) for food and firewood – fires are carefully built on a layer of stone – as well as to make their boats, houses, and handicrafts. Most islanders earn a living from fishing and tourism.

⑤ Ⓜ

Isla Suasi

📍 43 miles (70 km) from Puno 🚌

The only building on this small, privately-owned island is a luxury eco lodge which mimics traditional architecture with its thatched roof and stone walls. There are also protected areas for birds and where alpacas, llamas, and vicuñas roam freely.

ISLAND HOMESTAYS

As there are no hotels on the lake, villagers on the islands of Taquile, Amantaní, and Anapia happily share their homes with visitors. Guests help in everyday tasks - harvesting, fishing, minding cattle, building houses and more. Homestays need to be booked in Puno, either by visiting the community tour operators, whose offices are down at the main jetty, or the iPerú office, which can put you in touch with the communities.

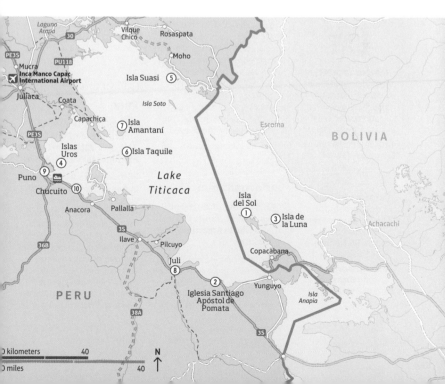

↑ One of the rustic arches dotted around Isla Taquile

crown the island's peaks. Local shamans read the future in coca tea leaves, so be sure to have a translator on hand.

⑧ Juli

🏠 **49 miles (79 km) S of Puno** 🚌🚆 **From Puno**

The Dominicans founded Juli in 1534 and turned the existing Indigenous settlement into their most important religious hub, a center for training missionaries for Bolivia and Paraguay.

The presence of four colonial churches, constructed to convert the local population, has earned the town the nickname of "Little Rome." San Juan Bautista de Letrán dates from 1570 and has dozens of Cusco School paintings depicting the life of John the Baptist and Saint Teresa.

Iglesia de San Pedro Mártir, which was completed in 1560 and remodeled in the 20th century, combines a lovely Renaissance facade with a Baroque altarpiece and paintings by Bernardo Bitti (1548–1610).

Isla Taquile

🏠 **22 miles (36 km) from Puno** 🚢

Some 350 Quechua-speaking families still live here, following the Inca creed of *Ama*

EAT

Restaurante Mojsa
Great view over Puno's main square and regional food with a sophisticated twist, including grilled alpaca.

🏠 Calle Lima 365, Puno
🌐 mojsarestaurant.com

Café Bar de la Casa del Corregidor
A relaxed atmosphere in a 17th-century colonial house. Simple, delicious dishes.

🏠 Jirón Deustua 576, Puno 🌐 casadel corregidorcafebar.com

---

suwa, Ama quella, Ama llullav (do not steal, do not be idle, do not lie). There is no police force – a reflection of their belief in honesty – and problems are solved by elected community leaders at the Sunday meetings. The people wear colorful clothes, which are only allowed to be knitted by men. Red knitted caps distinguish married men from bachelors, who don red and white. Señoritas wear multi-colored pompoms, while married women wear bright red ones on their heavy, layered skirts. With no cars, donkeys, or llamas, residents carry supplies on their backs up 545 steep steps from the jetty to the hilltop village.

---

⑦ Isla Amantaní

🏠 **25 miles (40 km) from Puno** 🚢 🛈 **Comité Central de la Isla de Amantaní: 987 451 284**

The lake's largest island has religious centers dating back to the Tiahuanacos (500 BC–AD 900). Amantaní islanders are famous for their baskets, woven from *ichu* (a native grass), and their granite carvings. Sacred Inca sites

---

⑨ Puno

🏠 **27 miles (44 km) SE of Juliaca** ✈ **From Lima & Arequipa** 🚌🚆 **From Cusco & Arequipa** 🛈 **Plaza de Armas**

Puno was a modest Indigenous settlement until Viceroy Conde de Lemos founded San Carlos de Puno as the capital of Paucarcolla province in 1668.

The Baroque-style **Catedral de Puno** on Plaza de Armas was designed by the 18th-century Peruvian architect Símon de Asto. The **Iglesia de San Juan Bautista** on Parque Pino is the sanctuary of Mamita Candelaria, Puno's patron saint.

Museo Carlos Dreyer

houses pre-Hispanic and colonial artworks collected by the German artist Carlos Dreyer, including Moche ceramics, Inca silverwork, and Paracas textiles.

The historic steamship **Yavari**, built in England in 1862, is moored on Lake Titicaca as a museum. This former gunboat took six years to reach the lake: its 1,300 pieces were transported 350 miles (560 km) by mule.

The **Museo de la Coca y Costumbres** is a small but interesting museum exhibiting the history, traditions, and uses of coca. It also offers coca leaf readings. An additional exhibition room houses a sample of the hand-embroidered costumes used in the dances for the Virgen de la Candelaria (Virgin of the Candles) festivities (p41).

The Mirador de Kuntur Wasi (House of the Condor) viewing platform offers a great view over Puno and Lake Titicaca, but be sure to check with a reliable guide before taking the road up to the platform as it is in bad shape and has become quite dangerous.

Catedral de Puno

🏛 Plaza de Armas 🕒 8am–noon & 3–6pm Mon–Fri, 8am–1pm & 3–7pm Sat

PERU'S FOLKLORIC CAPITAL

Puno melds the two ancient Andean civilizations of the Aymara from the south and the Quechua from the north with colonial influences. The result is a rich diversity of high-spirited folkloric festivals, often hailed as the best in all of Peru. The most important event is the Festival de la Virgen de la Candelaria in honor of Mamita Candelaria, Puno's patron saint.

Iglesia de San Juan Bautista

🏛 Parque Pino, Av Independencia 🕒 8:30am–1pm & 3:30–6pm Mon–Fri, 9am–noon Sat

Museo Carlos Dreyer

🏛 Calle Conde de Lemos 289 📞 51 351 019 🕒 9am–7pm daily

Yavari

🏛 Moored in the Bay of Puno, Lake Titicaca 🕒 Daily 🌐 yavari.org

Museo de la Coca y Costumbres

🏛 Calle Llave 581 📞 51 981 908 686 🕒 9am–7pm Mon–Sat, 3–7pm Sun

⑩

Chucuito

🏛 11 miles (18 km) SE of Puno 🚌 From Puno

This once important colonial town is now best known for its Templo de la Fertilidad, an archeological site with 86 stone phalluses in rows in an open-air walled-off area. There are two colonial churches, Santo Domingo and Nuestra Señora de la Asunción, with murals painted by Italian artist Bernardo Bitti. A 15-minute drive south of Chucuito takes you to the local farmers' market at Acora, where barter is still the main form of trade.

↓ Scenic view over Puno from the Mirador de Kuntur Wasi

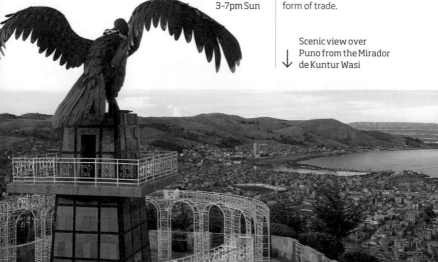

③ Ⓜ Ⓨ ▢ 🛍

CAÑÓN DEL COLCA

Ⓐ F6 Ⓐ 28 miles (42 km) W of Chivay village
🚌 From Arequipa to Chivay Ⓣ Can be hired for
2-3 days from Chivay

Nearly twice the depth of the Grand Canyon, the Colca Canyon is home to 2,000-year-old pre-Inca agricultural terraces, traditional Andean villages, and trails zigzagging down its steep valleys. The region also ranks as *the* place for spotting the national bird: the Andean condor.

Reaching a depth of 11,155 ft (3,400 m), the 62-mile (100-km) Colca and neighboring Cañón de Cotahuasi (*p168*) are among the deepest on the planet. For the most adventurous, hiking down into the canyon or up into nearby snow-tufted peaks are unmissable activities. The gushing waters of the Río Colca also offer a white-water rafting route with 300 rapids along a 25-mile (40-km) course. Along the canyon's southern edge, roadside viewpoints grant panoramic vistas of its unfathomably profound depths.

Along the Canyon's Southern Rim

A line of 14 villages trace the southern rim of the canyon, inhabited by the original Indigenous Cabana and Collagua people. In each, a main plaza is crowned by an attractive colonial church. Chivay bookends the canyon to the east, in walking distance of the mineral-rich La Calera hot springs, believed to treat rheumatism and arthritis. Continuing west, Yanque is where villagers perform the Waititi dance in the square early every morning. Some 21 miles (34 km) farther on, the Mirador Cruz del Cóndor has sweeping views into and across the canyon, while just after dawn, Andean condors glide in the thermal air currents above. The westernmost village is Cabanaconde, where the two- and three-day trails begin their descent into the canyon.

CONDORS

Considered sacred by the Inca, the Andean condor (*Vultur gryphus*) is the world's largest flying bird, measuring 4 ft (1.2 m) high with a wingspan of 10 ft (3 m). Despite weighing around 27 lbs (12 kg), it can fly for hours without using its wings, simply gliding on thermal currents and hunting carrion using its heightened sense of smell and remarkable eyesight. Once a common sight in the Andes, is now listed as "vulnerable" by the World Conservation Union due to centuries of hunting.

↑ Collagua terraces, carved out by the Collagua and Cabana people 2,000 years ago for cultivation

↑ Sun shining over the spectacular valley of Colca Canyon

↑ Relaxing at one of the five pools at La Calera hot springs

Hiking into the Canyon

From Cabanaconde, a steep path descends into the canyon, arriving at the lush, hummingbird-filled Sangalle Valley, dotted with rustic lodgings and a refreshing swimming pool – the perfect antidote to the hike down. An alternative, lesser-known route leaves from Cabanaconde toward the bubbling geysers at Chuirca. It follows the path of the Colca river to reach the hamlet of Llahuar, where hikers can stay overnight and spend an evening soothing their tired muscles in hot springs beneath a ceiling of stars. Tours can be arranged from agencies in Arequipa, although guides are cheaper directly from Cabanaconde; mules are an optional extra.

STAY

Colca Lodge & Spa
Serene, riverside setting and thermal hot pools.

⌂ Urb Selva Alegre, Cercado, Yanque
ⓦ colca-lodge.com

Ⓢ Ⓢ Ⓢ

La Casa de Santiago
Cosy guesthouse, whose hammock-slung garden overlooks the canyon. Staff organize treks into the canyon.

⌂ Grau, Cabanaconde
ⓦ lacasadesantiago.com

Ⓢ Ⓢ Ⓢ

Admiring a forest of large cacti at the Cañón de Cotahuasi

"house", thus Cotahuasi means "united house" or in this case, "united community." The canyon was an important route in Inca times, connecting the Pacific coast with Cusco. Remnants of these roads still link many of the traditional, adobe villages here. The unmistakable imprint of the Spanish conquistadores is also clear. Every settlement has a chapel and belfry, and sometimes even a bullring.

Nearby villages have their own attractions. Liucho has soothing hot springs, while the town of Pucya is a 1-mile (2-km) hike from the stone ruins of Maukallacta, built by the Wari but later used as an administrative hub by the Inca. Other sights include the Mirador Bañadero del Cóndor, where in the rainy season (Dec–Apr), condors can be spied bathing in the waters below. A 200-ft (60-m) high waterfall, the Cataratas de Sipia, near the village of the same name, is another treasure.

EXPERIENCE MORE

4

Cañón de Cotahuasi

🅰 E6 🚗 124 miles (200 km) NW of Arequipa 🚌 From Arequipa

At 11,560 ft (3,535 m), Cotahuasi is reportedly the deepest canyon in the world and twice as deep as the USA's Grand Canyon. The impressive landscape of the canyon combines sheer, shadowy cliffs rising out of riverbanks, towering snowcapped mountains, terraced citrus groves, fields of corn, stands of eucalyptus, spectacular *Puya raimondii (p211)* – the world's largest species of bromeliad – and hot springs.

In Quechua, *cota* translates as "union" and *huasi* as

5

Sillustani Burial Towers

🅰 F6 🚗 21 miles (34 km) NW of Puno ⏰ 7am–5pm daily

Standing on the shores of the pristine Laguna Umayo, Sillustani is famous for its *chullpas* (circular burial towers), some of which are more than 40 ft (12 m) high.

The Collas, who dominated the area before the Incas, buried their leaders in towers

→

Lampa's Iglesia de Santiago Apósto, with its eerie display of skeletons *(inset)*

that are wider at the top than at the base. The Lagarto and Intiwatana *chullpas* are the best examples, and whole groups are buried in one *chulpa*. The opening to the towers is always on the east side.

The insides of the tombs are said to be shaped like a woman's womb, with the corpses mummified in a fetal position. Some tombs have carvings of lizards, a symbol of life due to their ability to regrow their tails.

Blocks and a ramp used to hoist them up demonstrate the difficulty of constructing the towers.

6

Lampa

▲F6 **⌂** 50 miles (80 km) N of Puno, 22 miles (35 km) N of Juliaca **🚌** From Juliaca

Known as La Ciudad Rosada, meaning "the pink city," the dusty salmon- and maroon-tinted roofs and walls of Lampa add a welcome splash of color to the surrounding golden grass plains.

The city's other main attraction is the Iglesia de Santiago Apóstol. The church is made from river stones and lime mortar and dates back to the 1650s. Local luminary and mining engineer Enrique Torres Belón, who was responsible for the restoration of the church in the 1950s, added a marble-covered chapel and crowned it with a replica of Michelangelo's statue *La Pietà*. The Vatican provided a plaster mold of the famous statue, which, instead of being destroyed after casting as agreed, is now on display in the Town Hall.

Torres Belón, who was also the president of Peru's Congress in 1957, was buried in the chapel along with his wife and his mother.

The church also has a fine collection of beautiful colonial paintings from the famous Quito and Cusco schools (*p179*) and an elaborate carved pulpit. In a rather macabre display, hundreds of bones removed from the catacombs during restoration of the building can be seen hanging on the walls around them.

TOP 3 BARS AND CLUBS

Kamizaraky
▲G7 **⌂** Jirón Grau 158, Puno
Live rock, reggae and jazz on weekends and 1970s and 80s classics on week nights.

Museo del Pisco
▲F7 **⌂** Calle Moral 229, Arequipa **🌐** museodel pisco.org
Hip bar in a historic stone building with a cocktail menu as extensive as its name might suggest.

Déjà Vu
▲F7 **⌂** San Francisco 319B, Arequipa **☎** 054 221 904
Arequipa's top night-club, with electro and house music from the city's best DJs.

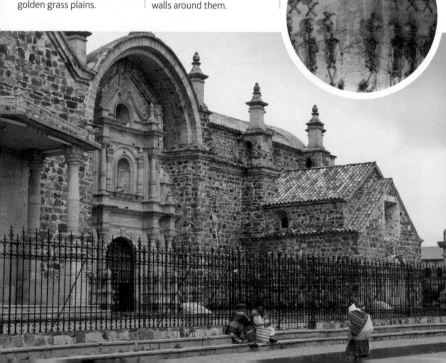

CUSCO AND THE SACRED VALLEY

For two centuries, Cusco and its environs were the homeland of the Incas. Although the area was occupied by other cultures for several centuries before the Incas arrived, including the Wari in the 8th and 9th centuries AD, it was under Inca control that Cusco reached its peak as an administrative, religious, and military hub. According to 16th-century writings, 13 Inca emperors ruled over the valley from the 12th to the 15th century. From here, they built the Inca Empire in less than a century.

In 1533, Francisco Pizarro and the Spanish arrived in Cusco and, following the crushing defeat of the Incas, founded their own city, turning pre-Hispanic structures into colonial mansions. Gradually, Cusco and its surrounds became a symbol of *mestizo*, a blend of Spanish and Andean elements, both architecturally and culturally. Once Pizarro left, the province reverted to being just another calm Andean domain until Hiram Bingham brought the ruins of Machu Picchu to international attention in 1911.

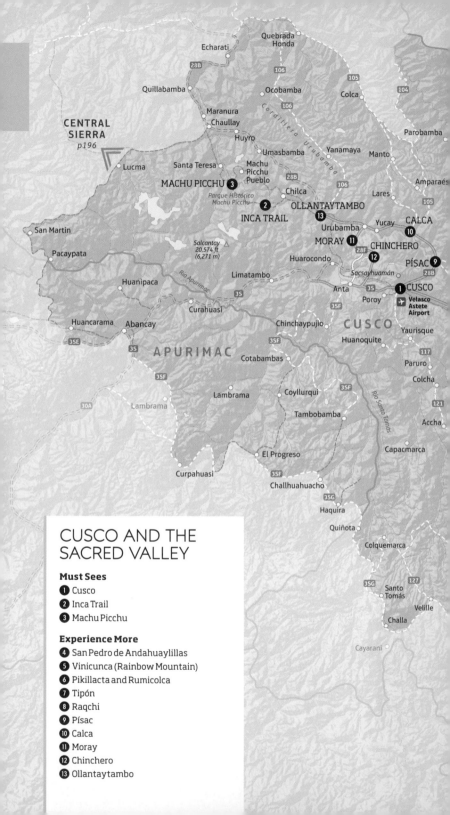

CUSCO AND THE
SACRED VALLEY

Must Sees
1 Cusco
2 Inca Trail
3 Machu Picchu

Experience More
4 San Pedro de Andahuaylillas
5 Vinicunca (Rainbow Mountain)
6 Pikillacta and Rumicolca
7 Tipón
8 Raqchi
9 Písac
10 Calca
11 Moray
12 Chinchero
13 Ollantaytambo

CENTRAL
SIERRA
p196

↑ The Spanish arches and cobbled streets of the Plaza de Armas

① 🍴 💻 🛍️

CUSCO

🅰️ **F6** 📍 **685 miles (1,102 km) SE of Lima** 🚐 🚌 ℹ️ **Oficina Ejecutiva del Comité, Av Sol 103; 8am-5:30pm Mon-Fri, 8:30am-12:30pm Sat**

Founded by the Incas and filled with Spanish arches and squares and narrow cobbled streets, the historic town of Cusco was declared a UNESCO World Heritage Site in 1983. Despite high tourist traffic as one of the best places to stop before undertaking the Inca Trail, it still retains a traditional Andean atmosphere. *Soroche*, or altitude sickness, is not uncommon here, so taking it easy for the first 24 hours is recommended.

① Plaza de Armas

In Inca times, this square was mainly used for ceremonial purposes. The stone arches of the plaza reflect a Spanish influence, along with the cathedral and the Jesuit Iglesia de La Compañía. The latter is often mistaken for La Catedral *(p178)* due to its elaborate facade.

Two flags fly in the plaza, the red-and-white Peruvian national flag and a rainbow-colored flag said to be the banner of the ancient Inca Empire, Tahuantinsuyu.

② Museo Inka

🅰️ **Cuesta del Almirante 103** 📞 **084 237 380** 🕐 **8am-6pm Mon-Fri, 9am-4pm Sat & public hols**

Built on the top of Inca foundations, the museum is also known as the Palacio del Almirante (Admiral's Palace), named after Admiral Francisco Aldrete Maldonado, who once owned the building.

The exhibition is a must for Inca enthusiasts. It comprises mummies, ceramics, textiles, jewelry, metal, and gold objects. Of particular interest is the assortment – allegedly the world's largest – of *keros* (Inca wooden drinking cups).

③   🍴 🛍️ Museo de Arte Precolombino

🅰️ **Plaza Nazarenas 231** 📞 **084 233 210** 🕐 **9am-10pm daily** 🌐 **mapcusco.pe**

The former Inca ceremonial court, Kancha Inca, was transformed into a mansion for the Spanish conquistador, Alonso Díaz, in 1580. In 2003 it was converted into the Museum of Pre-Columbian Art (MAP).

The 11 rooms are now filled with 450 masterpieces dating from 1250 BC to AD 1532. The Mochica gallery contains standout ceramic pieces. The museum also has an impressive collection of funerary ornaments.

> **The exhibition is a must for Inca enthusiasts. It comprises mummies, ceramics, textiles, jewelry, metal, and gold objects.**

INSIDER TIP
Tourist Tickets

The Boleto Turístico gains you entry into 16 sites and museums in Cusco and costs S/130. Partial tickets for fewer sites are also available. These can be bought from the information center on Av Sol.

 ④
Sacsayhuamán

🏛 1 mile (2 km) NE of Cusco ☎ 084 240 006 🚍 From Cusco, or walk ⏰ 7am–5:30pm daily

This impressive example of Inca military architecture is made up of three large terraces which overlap in a zigzag fashion. The stones are so perfectly aligned that it was said that not even a fine knife could penetrate the joints.

While designing Cusco, the Incas imagined it in the shape of a puma, with this site representing the head and its serrated walls as the teeth.

The Temple of Hanan Qospo is housed here and is dedicated to the cult of the Sun (Inti), Moon (Quilla), and other deities of the Incas.

 ⑤
Iglesia de la Compañía

🏛 Plaza de Armas ⏰ 9am–5:15pm Mon–Fri, 9–11am & 1–5:15pm Sat & Sun

Constructed in 1571 on the palace of Huayna Cápac, the eleventh Inca, La Compañía had to be rebuilt after the earthquake of 1650. Regarded as one of the best examples of colonial Baroque architecture in Peru, it features a great carved stone facade and a 69-ft- (21-m-) high cedar altar covered in gold leaf.

STAY

Tierra Viva Cuzco Plaza

Just off the Plaza Mayor, this small hotel in a colonial residence has a 17th-century courtyard of stone pillars and flagstone floor.

🏛 Calle Suecia 345 🌐 tierravivahoteles.com

 S/ S/ S/

Hotel Rumi Punku

A charming hotel, mixing Inca walls and a colonial structure with modern additions.

🏛 Calle Choquechaca 339 🌐 rumipunku.com

 S/ S/ S/

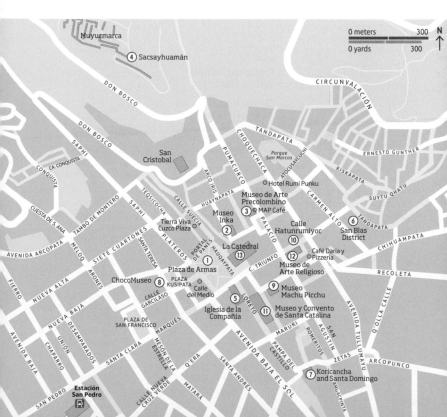

→ Art for sale in one of the courtyards in the San Blas district

San Blas District

📍 **Iglesia de San Blas**
🕐 8:30am-6pm Mon-Sat

Dotted with colonial houses featuring Inca stone walls, San Blas is also known as the craftsmen's district. Once the domain of Quechua nobility, its network of narrow streets is now home to the workshops of Cusqueño artists who practice metalwork, and stone- and woodcarving.

Iglesia de San Blas, built in 1560, is Cusco's oldest parish church. Its ornate pulpit features some fine Baroque woodcarving. The fascinating Museo de Coca, dedicated to the history of the contro-

---

🔍 **HIDDEN GEM**
Centro de Textiles Tradicionales

A 10-minute stroll from the ChocoMuseo, this exhibition showcases traditional textiles. The shop *(www.textiles cusco.org)* sells top-class work by weavers.

---

versial coca leaf *(p75)*, is also worth a visit. There is a gift shop here; be aware that coca tea is legal in Peru but not in most other countries outside South America.

Koricancha and Santo Domingo

📍 **Plaza Intipampa, cnr Av El Sol & Calle Santo Domingo** 📞 084 254 234
🕐 8:30am-5:30pm Mon-Sat, 2-5pm Sun

Koricancha, meaning the "golden enclosure," was built to honor Inti or the Sun god. It was the richest Inca temple and had gold-plated walls flecked with precious stones. The garden featured life-sized gold and silver statues of animals, local trees, and corn stalks. Mummified bodies of noble Incas were kept here for ceremonies. Unfortunately, the temple was drained of all its treasures soon after the arrival of the conquistadors.

The Iglesia and Convento de Santo Domingo were built on top of the Inca shrine.

The building brings the two cultures together. It is difficult to imagine how the temple must have looked as so little remains of it now. However, the imposing trapezoidal architecture, pebbled floor, wall niches, and holes that are thought to be either drains or speaking tubes, hint at its past glory.

---

⑧ ✏️

ChocoMuseo

📍 **Calle Garcilaso 210**
🕐 10:30am-6:30pm daily
🌐 chocomuseo.com

This museum is an ideal place for chocolate-lovers. It houses a cafeteria and a shop offering cacao from different parts of Peru. The museum has several sections on the history of cacao from the time of the Mayans, including their processing techniques, plus a section especially for children. There are different activities that can be suited to the time frame of visitors. It also holds a 2-hour chocolate factory workshop where visitors can make their own chocolate bars or truffles,

starting from Peruvian cacao beans. Register online for the workshops.

___

Museo Machu Picchu

🏛 Casa Concha, Calle Santa Catalina Ancha 320 🕙 9am-5pm Mon-Sat 🌐 museomachupicchu.com

This museum, set within an 18th-century colonial mansion, focuses on the Inca citadel that is Machu Picchu. It houses the 360 artifacts that American explorer Hiram Bingham – considered the first person to make public the existence of Machu Picchu – took back to Yale to study in 1912 and which were returned to Peru 99 years later, in 2011. These include early photographs. The two floors also display the San Antonio Abad University collection from later excavations and objects found during restoration of this museum.

___

Calle Hatunrumiyoc

This street is named after the famous 12-angled stone which is perfectly fitted into the right-hand side of the wall (visible while walking uphill). The stone was taken from the wall of the palace of Inca Roca, the sixth Inca emperor. It is now a part of the Archbishop's Palace. The wall is a brilliant example

of the Inca's skill in polygonal polished stone-masonry, which they used to construct support walls.

___

Museo y Convento de Santa Catalina

🏛 Calle Santa Catalina Angosta 401 📞 51 984 999 803 🕙 8:30am-5:30pm Mon-Sat, 2-5pm Sun (book in advance) 🌐 santacata lina.org.pe

Built over the Inca ruins of the Acllawasi (House of the Chosen Women), this convent opened in 1610. The interior includes beautifully painted arches and baroque frescoes.

The museum, which opened in 1975, is dedicated to colonial and religious art.

___

Museo de Arte Religioso

🏛 Cnr Calles Hatunrumiyoc & Herrajes 📞 084 222 781 🕙 8am-6pm daily

Housed in the Palacio Arzobispal (Archbishop's Palace), the museum displays religious paintings from the 17th and 18th centuries, including works by Diego Quispe Tito, regarded as the master of the renowned Cusco School of painters *(p179)*.

The palace features carved cedar ceilings, Moorish-

inspired doors, stained-glass windows, and a room displaying life-size models of Cusco's archbishops.

The house, which once belonged to the Marquis de San Juan de Buenavista, is built on top of the ancient Inca Roca palace.

← The acclaimed 12-sided Inca stone on Calle Hatunrumiyoc

⑬ ⚒

LA CATEDRAL

🏠 Plaza de Armas 📞 084 222 781 🕙 10am–6pm daily

Dominating Cusco's main square, La Catedral is the superb setting for over 400 works of art from the Cusco School, hailed as one of the most important painting movements in the Americas. The splendid Renaissance facade of the cathedral is in contrast with the Baroque interior, which is lavishly adorned with gold and silver.

Construction of the cathedral began in 1560 but took almost 100 years to complete. It was built on top of the palace of the eighth Inca, Viracocha, using red granite slabs from the fortress at Sacsayhuamán. Two auxiliary chapels sit on either side. To the right is El Triunfo, Cusco's first church, built on top of the main Inca armory to symbolize Spain's victory over the Incas. It has an elaborately carved altar and a crypt that contains the ashes of historian Garcilaso de la Vega. The 18th-century Jesús, Maria y José chapel is on the left, and, as the name suggests, features images of Jesus, Mary, and Joseph.

Did You Know?

Millions of guinea pigs are eaten every year in Peru – reflected in Zapata's *Last Supper* painting here.

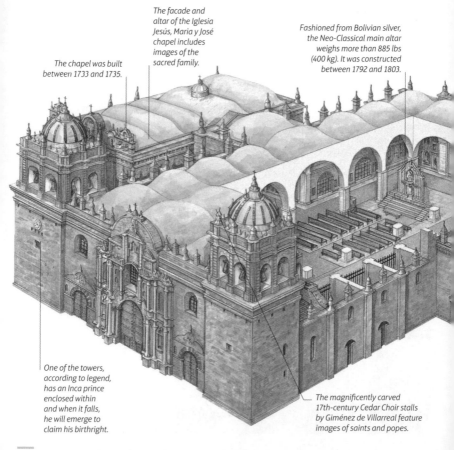

The facade and altar of the Iglesia Jesús, Maria y José chapel includes images of the sacred family.

Fashioned from Bolivian silver, the Neo-Classical main altar weighs more than 885 lbs (400 kg). It was constructed between 1792 and 1803.

The chapel was built between 1733 and 1735.

One of the towers, according to legend, has an Inca prince enclosed within and when it falls, he will emerge to claim his birthright.

The magnificently carved 17th-century Cedar Choir stalls by Giménez de Villarreal feature images of saints and popes.

↑ La Catedral's grand facade, lit by street lights at night

Painted by Marcos Zapata, the Last Supper is on display here. It has an Andean touch, with Christ and his disciples enjoying a meal of roasted guinea pig, and drinking chicha (corn beer).

↑ One of the stunning, gold Baroque-style altarpieces

The first Spanish church to be built in Cusco, its name, El Triunfo, is a constant reminder of the Spanish "triumph" over the Incas.

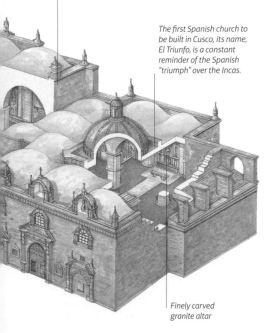

Finely carved granite altar

↑ The impressive cathedral complex, with its churches and chapels

THE CUSCO SCHOOL

The Escuela Cusqueña was a Roman Catholic art tradition initiated by the Spanish conquerors, which used paintings, such as the *Adoration Of The Magi (below),* to convert the locals to Catholicism. However, the movement was eventually used as a subtle form of cultural resistance by the Indigenous and *mestizo* artists against the colonizers.

2

INCA TRAIL

A F6

The Incas developed an extensive network of roads, covering about 15,550–18,650 miles (25,000–30,000 km), to connect their wide-ranging empire. These paths range from the Cápac Ñan (*p69*) to the Q'eswachaka Rope Bridge (*p36*). The famous Inca Trail, linking Machu Picchu with the Sacred Valley, is the best preserved of these roads. The Incas used to run along this trail, which they used to send messages across the kingdom. The present-day trail covers diverse landscapes and passes more than 30 Inca sites. Broken up into sections, it takes four days to complete.

The 24-mile (39-km) route starts at Piskacucho, near Chilca (KM82), and reaches its highest poin at Abra de Warmiwañusca, a mountain pass that leaves many a hiker panting for breath. All hikers must go as part of a group with an agency, led by a licensed guide. Reservations must be made at least six months in advance as there is a limit of 500 people a day, including both trekking staff and hikers. December to April are the wettest months; the trail can be muddy. The trail is closed in February for maintenance work.

**① **

Patallacta

A 4 miles (6 km) from KM82

Crop terraces, houses, and other edifices show Patallacta's (also known as Llactapata) significance in the region. At 9,843 ft (3,000 m) above sea level, it supplied Machu Picchu with maize, their staple crop.

The stone houses were believed to be occupied by the nobility and religious authorities, while the rest of the people lived in humble mud and cane homes.

Pulpituyuj, the large circular tower built on a huge rock, may have served as an altar or prison. Around 15 families still farm the surrounding land.

**② **

Huayllabamba

A 8 miles (13 km) from KM82

Huayllabamba is the largest and last Andean community found on this trail. At 10,040 ft (3,060 m), the village, located at the foot of a mountain, is set amid terraces where maize and potato are cultivated. On clear days, you can see the snow-covered peak of Wakaywilka (Mount Veronika) (18,640 ft/5,682 m) in the Cordillera Urubamba in the distance. Many hiking

> **INSIDER TIP**
> **Camino Sagrado de los Incas**
>
> This one-day version of the trail, from KM104, gives a flavor of the Inca Trail and offers magnificent mountain views en route to Machu Picchu. There are 250 permits available per day.

↑ Visitor hiking up one of the passes along the Inca Trail

groups camp here on the first night. This is also the last place to buy supplies such as snacks and bottled drinks.

③
Abra de Warmiwañusca

🚶 14 miles (23 km) from KM82

This mountain pass is 13,780 ft (4,200 m) above sea level and is the hardest to climb due to the lack of oxygen at this altitude. According to Inca

mythology, the Andes were formed by giants turned into stones. This pass was thought to be a reclining woman. The Incas believed they had to climb over her to get to the other side. Warmiwañusca translates as "dead woman" in Quechua, hence the name Dead Woman's Pass.

The landscape changes here to barren and cold high plains, with the wind whistling through the pass. Hikers often place a stone on an *apacheta* (mound of rocks) located at the highest points on the trail as an offering to Pachamama (Mother Earth).

④
Runkurakay

🚶 17 miles (28 km) from KM82

The ruins at Runkurakay, rediscovered by explorer

Hiram Bingham in 1915, have only a single north-facing entrance and exit. Some believe that Runkurakay was used as a marker by travelers going to and from Machu Picchu to determine how much traveling time they had left. Others suggest that it was simply a post used to guard the road. Its position on the edge of the pass offers superb views across the valley.

↑ The circular Runkurakay ruins, overlooking the valley

Huadquiña

San Miguel 9,593 ft (2,924 m)

Machu Picchu Pueblo (Aguas Calientes)

Machu Picchu

⑧ Estación de Machupicchu

CU180

Montaña Machu Picchu 10,043 ft (3,061 m)

Río Urubamba

Wiñay Wayna ⑦

Cerro Padreyoc 15,452 ft (4,710 m)

Phuyupatamarca ⑥

Cerro Runkurakay 12,106 ft (3,690 m)

Cerro Casamientuyoc 14,140 ft (4,310 m)

Estación Ollantaytambo

CU917

Sayakmarca ⑤

Patallacta ①

Piskacucho

Runkurakay ④

Abra de Warmiwañusca ③

Nevado Esquina 16,483 ft (5,024 m)

kilometers   4

miles   4

N ↑

② Huayllabamba

⑤
Sayakmarca

22 miles (35 km)
from KM82

Perched high on a ridge at a height of 11,810 ft (3,600 m) above sea level, Sayakmarca can only be reached by a narrow stairway cut into the mountain. It is carefully adapted to blend in with the natural mountain forms. The complex is thought to have been a sacred ceremonial center devoted to astronomy. Although Sayakmarca means the "inaccessible town" in Quechua, it did have a permanent supply of water and food storehouses, which indicate its importance.

Hiram Bingham named the site Cedrobamba in 1915 after discovering a cedar wood forest nearby. It was renamed in 1941 by anthropologist Paul Fejos to reflect the site more accurately.

___

⑥
Phuyupatamarca

25 miles (41 km) from
KM82

One of the best-preserved towns on the trail, it is called the "town above the clouds" because at night the clouds settle in the ravines and the complex rises majestically above them. However, at sunrise the clouds disappear.

Hiram Bingham discovered the ruins in 1915 and christened them Qorihuayrachina. As at Sayakmarca, Paul Fejos renamed them in 1941.

The curved walls and geometric terraces superbly blend with the shape of the mountains, illustrating the deep respect the Incas had for their natural environment. The ceremonial baths reflect the Inca mastery at controlling a natural force, spring water.

___

⑦
Wiñay Wayna

27 miles (44 km) from
KM82

This impressive Inca complex is situated at 8,860 ft (2,700 m) above sea level. The ruins were discovered in 1941 by

↓ Wiñay Wayna terraces, and its stonework (left)

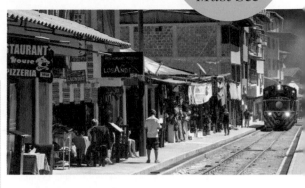

→ Train arriving in Machu Picchu Pueblo (Aguas Calientes)

Paul Fejos, but it was Peruvian archeologist Julio C. Tello who named it Wiñay Wayna in 1942. Meaning "forever young," Wiñay Wayna is also the name of a local orchid that blooms perennially.

Its location near a major access road and the striking architecture suggest that Wiñay Wayna was an important township for the Incas. The town is divided into four distinct sectors. There is the agricultural area with terraces, the religious or ritual area, the tower area, which features some of the best architecture, and the urban sector. This last one is made of rectangular single- and double-story buildings with trapezoidal windows, doors, and wall niches, as well as stairways and a series of 10 fountains that run from the top of the slope to the bottom. Significant sections of the complex illustrate the high-quality cut stone assembly of the Incas. This is the last ruin before Machu Picchu, which is just 4 miles (6 km) from here. It offers fantastic views of the beautiful valley and the surrounding mountains.

Machu Picchu Pueblo (Aguas Calientes)

🏛 5 miles (8 km) from Machu Picchu 🚉 To Cusco 🚌 To Machu Picchu 🛈 In Town Hall

Machu Picchu Pueblo is the last town for visitors going to the ruins and the end of the line for travelers arriving by train from Cusco *(p174)*. It's also known as Aguas Calientes, meaning "hot springs" in Spanish, and is popular among visitors for its natural pools.

The town's economy revolves around tourism so there are many hotels, restaurants, and countless souvenir and handicrafts stalls. Even the railroad track changes into an open market once a train leaves the station.

For hikers with aching muscles, there are **thermal baths** just out of town, including one filled with icy mountain water.

Thermal baths
🏛 End of Av Pachacutec 🕐 5am–8pm daily

GREAT VIEW
Intipunku

Signs along the Inca Trail direct hikers to the Intipunku (Sun Gate), the final section of the trail. It offers a stunning 180-degree view of Machu Picchu, especially at sunrise.

③

MACHU PICCHU

◩F5 **◭**69 miles (110 km) NW of Cusco **▣**To Machu Picchu Pueblo (Aguas Calientes), then bus or walk to Machu Picchu **◷**6am–5pm daily (last entry: 2pm) (reserve at least six months ahead) **ℹ**Av El Sol 103, Galerías Turísticas, Cusco; open 8:30am–4:30pm Mon–Sat; www.machupicchu.gob.pe

The lost city of the Incas is arguably the most famous sight in all of South America. Visitors from around the world come to admire its dramatic mountaintop setting and remarkably well preserved ruins.

The citadel is built of rock at an altitude of 7,710 ft (2,350 m), on the saddle of a mountain flanked by sheer drops to the Urubamba Valley below. Machu Picchu was never sacked by the Spanish as they failed to find it, but instead was simply abandoned and left to nature to reclaim. Comprising an upper and lower section with houses, temples, fountains, plazas, and agricultural terraces, the Inca city is linked by scores of stairways and paths, and watered by natural springs. No other civilization has managed to assemble so many colossal stone blocks so seamlessly. However, its function remains baffling. Experts speculate that it served as a place of worship, a sight for tracking stars, and the ninth Inca emperor Pachacútec's country estate.

> 💬 INSIDER TIP
> **Machu Picchu on a Budget**
>
> Take a bus from Cusco to the hydroelectric station and walk for 2–3 hours beside the railway tracks to Machu Picchu Pueblo, or catch the train halfway at Ollantaytambo. You can also take a 2–3 hour walk up to the ruins, although the bus ride is US$24 return and takes a mere 20 minutes.

↑ Exquisite Inca stonework; blocks connected flawlessly like pieces in a jigsaw, without mortar *(inset)*

VISITING MACHU PICCHU

Trains to Machu Picchu leave regularly from the station at Poroy, a 20-minute drive outside the city of Cusco, and from Ollantaytambo, halfway along the railway route. Incarail and Perurail offer several budgetary options for the scenic trip through the Urubamba Valley to Machu Picchu Pueblo (Aguas Calientes) *(p183)*. A local bus zigzags up the mountain to the historical Inca site. You can reserve online at *www.incarail.com* or *www.perurail.com*. For the best views, opt for the 24-mile hike on the Inca Trail *(p180)*, which takes four days.

A spectacular view of the ruins, terraces, and stairways, with Huayna Picchu forming the backdrop ↑

EXPLORING MACHU PICCHU

① Fountains

The Incas harnessed a natural spring located on a steep slope to the north of Machu Picchu, building a 2,457-ft (749-m) long canal to bring the water down to the city. They channeled the water through a series of 16 fountains, often referred to as the "stairway of fountains." The water collects in the cut stone base of the fountain before

going into a circular drain that delivers it to a channel leading to the next fountain.

---

② Caretaker's Hut

Perfectly positioned to allow the caretaker to observe the access points to the city's south, this has been restored with a thatched roof, similar to how it would have looked when the site was inhabited.

③ Royal Sector

The buildings here feature characteristic Inca rock lintels and abnormally spacious rooms, and lie in close proximity to the Temple of the Sun, leading experts to surmise that this is where Pachacútec, the ninth Inca emperor, lodged when he was in Machu Picchu. The entrance and exit to the Royal Palace via a single portal also signifies a high level of security. Hiram Bingham, the explorer who disclosed Machu Picchu to the world in 1911, believed that the room at the front of the inner patio was the Inca ruler's bedroom. It features 10 trapezoidal niches that would have housed significant ornaments.

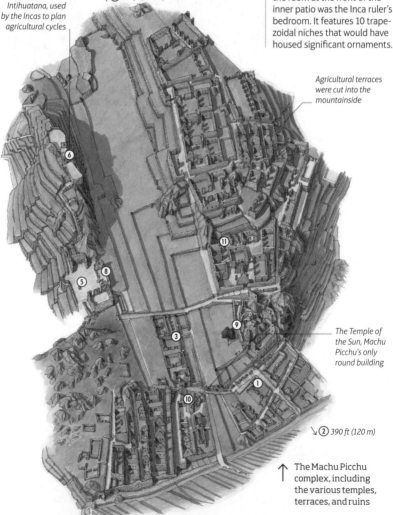

Intihuatana, used by the Incas to plan agricultural cycles

↖ ⑦ 70 ft (230 m)

Agricultural terraces were cut into the mountainside

The Temple of the Sun, Machu Picchu's only round building

↓ ② 390 ft (120 m)

↑ The Machu Picchu complex, including the various temples, terraces, and ruins

↓ ④ 328 ft (100 m)

↑ Terraces covering Machu Picchu, once used by farmers

④ Funerary Rock

Researchers believe that this rock may have been used as a sacrificial altar. Hiram Bingham, however, suggested it was a mortuary slab on which deceased Inca nobles were laid out in all weathers to mummify. Just above the rock lies the upper cemetery, where Bingham uncovered a significant number of tombs.

⑤ Sacred Plaza

The Principal Temple, the Sacristy, the House of the High Priest, the Temple of the Three Windows, and the Intihuatana make up the Sacred Plaza. The Principal Temple features fine architecture, while the Sacristy is famed for the two rocks lining the entrance: one of them is said to contain 32 angles. A stairway behind the building leads up to the Intihuatana.

⑥ Intihuatana

This stone indicates the precise dates of the solstices, equinoxes, and other astronomical periods. The June (winter) solstice was said to be the most important day of the year, when the sun is said to cast its longest shadow from the pillar. At this moment the sun is said to be "hitched" to the rock, hence its name, "hitching post to the sun." From this day onward the days become longer, meaning more time to work the land and produce food. Interestingly, the Intihuatana tilts 13 degrees to the north, which is the ancient city's latitude.

← Funerary Rock, located near the hut, with its curious engraved shapes

↑ The fascinating condor-shaped rock at the Temple of the Condor

⑦
Sacred Rock

The enigmatic carved rock, which mimics the shape of a mountain, is believed to have been used as an altar to worship the Apus, the gods of the Mountain, Water, and Fertility. Anthropologists believe that the rock mirrors the Pumasillo (Puma's Claw), a mountain peak in the Cordillera Vilcabamba, which is still revered by Andeans today. The Sacred Rock appeals to the gods whose form it recreates. It may also have been used as a sacrificial altar to appease the gods.

⑧
Temple of the Three Windows

Located on the eastern side of the Sacred Plaza, the rectangular temple has three walls and the open side faces the plaza. On the opposite

Did You Know?

In Quechua, "Machu Picchu" means "Old Mountain."

side, the wall has three trapezoidal windows, flanked by two niches. During the winter solstice, the first rays from the sun would come through these windows, filling the room with light. The windows afford sweeping views of the ruins below and across the valley.

⑨
Temple of the Condor

The temple earned its name from the two slabs which form the bird's stylized outspread wings and the head defined by the carved rock on the ground. Hiram Bingham tagged this area as the "prisons" during his expedition because of the dank subterranean dungeons and the niches above the building in which he believed prisoners were held and lashed. Modern-day historians, however, believe that the niches were altars on which mummies were placed during ceremonies devoted to the condor, one of the most important Inca deities.

⑩
Temple of the Sun

Machu Picchu's only round building has two tower windows aligned to the points

where the sun rises on the summer and winter solstices. The temple is regarded by many as having the most sublime stonework in all of Machu Picchu, and the entrance is the finest in the city. Built over a large polished rock, the walls of the temple

→ Stunning view of the mountains surrounding the Temple of the Sun

sinuously mimic its natural curve; the entire perimeter wall bends inward. It has compartments for holding offerings or idols. Archaeologists believe it served as an astral observatory, with Inca astronomers gleaning information about their crop cycles from the position of the constellations and the solstices.

Common District

The Common District, also known as Secular District or Industrial Quarter, is located above the Temple of the Condor. It was thought to have housed the workers of the realm because the construction is

$\rightarrow$

The Solstice Window at the Temple of the Sun

inferior to that of the upper section. Bingham speculated that the two circular rocks which protrude from the floor in one of the buildings were mortars used to crush grain, but as they do not show any wear and are highly polished, this seems unlikely. They may have played a role in a ritual, being filled with offerings of *chicha* or blood, or in an astrological ceremony as the sun, moon, and some stars are reflected when the mortars are filled with water. Their real purpose, however, remains a mystery to archaeologists.

CLIMBING

If you plan to climb either Huayna Picchu or Montaña Machu Picchu, make sure you book an early morning entry slot and buy a ticket that allows you to visit both the ruins and do a climb. The mountains, however, are not for the faint-hearted – Huayna Picchu is more vertical, but Montaña Machu Picchu is higher, with very steep steps. The recent addition to the climbing menu, Huchuy Picchu (Small Mountain), is a more modest goal.

INCA CULTURE AND RELIGION

At its height in the 15th and 16th centuries, the Inca Empire encompassed thousands of square miles, stretching almost the entire length of the Andes and assimilating customs from the cultures they dominated. The Incas were audacious engineers, constructing spectacular mountaintop citadels and monumental buildings. They developed elaborate farming terraces, sustaining their crops by canal and drainage systems. Their social structure was extremely rigid, with the emperor being revered as a living god. The Incas worshipped the sun, moon, earth, and mountains. Animals, such as the condor and puma, were also considered sacred.

SOCIAL HIERARCHY

Inca society was strongly hierarchical, with the Sapa Inca, the emperor, holding absolute power. Beneath him were high priests of noble blood, who led all religious ceremonies, and then regional leaders known as *curacas* whose role was largely administrative. They imposed the Inca's strict taxation system on the population.

RELIGION

The Incas revered Inti, the Sun God, who nourished the earth and controlled the harvests. The Sapa Inca, believed to be the son of the Sun God, made offerings to the sun during religious ceremonies. Festivals and ceremonies linked with the Cult of the Sun and worship of Inti were significant in the Inca calendar.

↑ Inca Emperor Atahualpa, in 1532, during the Spanish conquest

FARMING

The Incas carved up mountains into vast terraced farmlands supporting the banks of the terraces with stone walls. They cultivated corn and pota-toes, and raised llama and alpaca for food and as pack animals. Canal systems were used to divert water from rivers, sometimes many miles away, to the fields.

CULT OF THE SUN

Festivals Inti Raymi (Festival of the Sun, *p66*) was celebrated annually on June 21, the winter solstice in the Southern Hemisphere.

Ceremonies/Rituals Divination played a large part in religious life. Everything, from treating illness to determining the correct sacrifices, was performed by the high priest. Infusions of ayahuasca and coca leaves were integral to all ceremonies.

Ancestors The Inca treated their mummified dead as though they were still alive, parading them through the streets during festivals.

Keros These drinking vessels were used during ceremonies to drink *chicha* (corn beer).

Sacrifice Animal and human sacrifice was practiced periodically.

1 Inca Priest at the Inti Raymi festival celebrated in Cusco.

2 Coca leaves in a field.

3 Illustration of 16th-century Inca life.

4 Wooden *keros* (Inca Cup) depicting a face.

Did You Know?

The Incas used *quipus*, strings with a complex system of knots, as a record-keeping device.

↑ Crop terraces at Moray, where the Incas experimented with plants

The extraordinary Vinicunca (Rainbow Mountain)

EXPERIENCE MORE

4
San Pedro de Andahuaylillas

⛰F6 ⛰22 miles (36 km) S of Cusco 🚌 From Cusco ⏰8:30am–noon & 2–5pm Mon–Sat, 8:30–10am & 3–5pm Sun

The simple mud-brick facade of this 17th-century church gives no hint of the lavish treasures within that earned it the nickname the Sistine Chapel of the Americas.

These include a gold-leaf ceiling, a Baroque cedar and gold-leaf altar, and two restored 17th-century pipe organs, which are the oldest parish organs in the Americas.

5
Vinicunca (Rainbow Mountain)

⛰F6 🚌 From Cusco ⏰Apr–Aug ℹiPerú, Plaza de Armas, Cusco; 51 951 128 967; 9am–9pm daily

Surrounded by the towering peaks of the Andes, turquoise lagoons, and skies home to majestic condor, this colorful mountain is considered sacred by the locals. Vinicunca or Rainbow Mountain is a 3-hour drive from Cusco and is generally undertaken as a long day trip. The superfit can club it with the classic Ausangate Trek (p43). A far less strenuous and shorter hike at Palccoyo will reward you with similar views. It's advisable to reserve a tour in advance; several firms in Cusco offer excursions, and most provide a basic meal or refreshments. Take your own water as there are no shops in the area.

6
Pikillacta and Rumicolca

⛰F6 ⛰19 miles (30 km) S of Cusco 🚌 From Cusco ⏰7am–6pm daily

Pikillacta, meaning the City of Fleas, was one of the pre-Inca cities built at the peak of the Wari culture. It had numerous 13-ft (4-m) enclosures that formed a protective garrison.

Visitors to the large complex can see the hundreds of mud and stone two-story buildings.

Pikillacta has an almost perfect geometrical design, divided into big rectangular blocks with long, straight streets. Walls were originally covered with mud and whitened with gypsum.

A short distance away are the remains of two Inca gates called Rumicolca. Built on Wari foundations, the Inca blocks are much finer than the original Wari work. These gates acted as a checkpoint for people heading to Cusco. The gateway is one of the most impressive Inca constructions. The Boleto Turístico (p175), the tourist ticket sold in Cusco, is valid here.

7

Tipón

🅰F6 🚶16 miles (25 km)
N of Cusco 🚌From Cusco
🕐7am–6pm daily

The striking stone canals, terraces, and stairways that make up Tipón are said to be part of a royal estate built by the eighth Inca ruler, Wiracocha. According to experts, it was once a place of agricultural research and worship. Water is chaneled through traditional stone structures, underground aqueducts – some of which are still used today – and decorative waterfalls, showcasing the Incas'

impressive grasp of hydraulics. The Boleto Turístico tourist ticket is also valid here.

8

Raqchi

🅰F6 🚶73 miles (118 km)
SE of Cusco 🚌From Cusco
🕐7am–6pm daily

Located on the Cusco–Puno road, this remarkable 15th-century stone-and-mud temple of the supreme god Wiracocha still has some walls standing 39 ft (12 m) high. The complex includes housing for the nobility and circular silos that stored food.

↑ The ruins of Tipón, once a series of terraces irrigated by elaborate waterworks

EAT

El Albergue Restaurant
Tenderloin steaks of locally reared alpaca make for a Peruvian dining experience in the Sacred Valley.

🅰F6 🏠Estación de Tren, Ollantaytambo
🕐6–9:30am, noon–3:30pm, 6–8:30pm daily
🌐elalbergue.com

El Huacatay
Enjoy Peruvian food with Mediterranean influences on their splendid patio.

🅰F6 🏠Jirón Arica 620, Urubamba
📞084 201 790

Tres Keros
This atmospheric restaurant serves Peruvian classics of trout ceviche and lomo saltado.

🅰F6 🏠Av Torrechayoc s/n 🌐vallegas tronomico.com/en/3keros-en/

←
Colorful handicrafts and textiles on display at the craft market in Písac

9 Písac

F6 ⏱20 miles (32 km) N of Cusco 🚌 From Cusco

A favourite day-trip from Cusco, the town of Písac is renowned for its craft market and the **Písac Ruins,** one of the most significant Inca sites.

Inhabited since the 10th or 11th century, this became an important regional capital once the Incas arrived. It is thought the town began as a military post, then grew into a ceremonial and residential center. Agricultural terraces and steep paths lead to the hilltop fort, which has walls of polished stone. Highlights are the Templo del Sol, or Temple of the Sun; the Templo de la Luna, or Temple of the Moon, and the Intihuatana, designed to track the sun's movements. The Boleto Turístico (p75) is valid here.

Písac Ruins
🎨🎫 ⏱7am–6pm daily

> 💬 INSIDER TIP
> **Market Savvy**
>
> Visit Písac on a Sunday, when, in addition to the town's famous artisans' market, farmers from the surrounding area set up stalls selling fresh produce.

10 Calca

F6 ⏱31 miles (50 km) N of Cusco 🚌 From Cusco

Nestled in the shadow of the Pitusiray and Sawasiray mountains, Calca was once an important Inca administrative center. Today, all that remains are the maize fields and the archeological ruins of Huchu'y Qosqo (Little Cusco), just outside town. Despite its name, the adobe ruins seem to bear little resemblance to the real Cusco's streets.

Of special interest are the hot sulfur springs of Machacancha and the cold waters of Minasmoqo.

---

11 Moray

F6 ⏱31 miles (50 km) NW of Cusco 🚌 From Cusco to Urubamba, then *colectivo* from the turnoff to Moray ⏱7:30am–5pm daily

At first glimpse Moray looks like a Greek amphitheater, but researchers believe it may have been an Inca crop laboratory designed to find the best conditions for particular crop

→
The paddy field-like salt pans on hillside terraces at Salinas de Maras

varieties to thrive. There are four overlapping *muyus* (slightly elliptical terraces), each tier experiencing varying levels of sun, shade, and elevation. Built on retaining walls filled with soil, and watered by a complex irrigation system, the terraces show traces of about 250 cereals and vegetables. The Boleto Turístico (p75) can be used at this site.

The nearby **Salinas de Maras** (salt pans), dating back to pre-Columbian times, are in stark contrast. The natural salty water is channeled into 3,000 artificial pans and left to evaporate in the sun. Hundreds of people work on the site even now, using ancient techniques.

Salinas de Maras
📍10 miles (16 km) NE of Moray 🚌 *Combis* (minibuses) from Urubamba ⏱7am–5pm daily

---

12 Chinchero

F6 ⏱18 miles (28 km) NW of Cusco 🚌

Dubbed the birthplace of the rainbow, Chinchero is perched

about 12,375 ft (3,772 m) above sea level on the Anta plain, surveying the Sacred Valley. The tenth Inca, Túpac Yupanqui, reportedly built his palaces here. In the mid-16th century, Manco Inca, the puppet king appointed by the Spanish conquistador Pizarro, burned down the village, thereby cutting off his Spanish pursuers' supply lines. Viceroy Toledo established a plantation here, putting local people to work on it, and built an adobe church above the main plaza over Inca foundations.

A massive stone wall in the main plaza, featuring ten trapezoidal niches, recalls the Incas, as do extensive agricultural terraces, seats, and stairways carved into rocks just outside the village.

Quechua-speaking locals preserve the Inca customs; wearing traditional dresses, farming the terraces, and weaving. A colorful handicraft market takes place in the main plaza three days a week. Every Sunday, residents from the surrounding villages gather at the main plaza and exchange their agricultural products and handicrafts using a barter system. Much of this is likely to change since construction work has started on a new international airport. The Boleto Turístico (p175) is valid here.

Ollantaytambo

Ⓐ F6 **Ⓐ 60 miles (97 km) NW of Cusco** **Ⓐⓐ From Cusco** **Ⓒ 7am–6pm daily**

Spectacular Ollantaytambo is described as a living Inca town. The residents still strive to maintain ancient traditions such as tilling their fields with foot ploughs. The place takes its name from Ollanta, the Inca general who fell in love with Pachacútec's daughter. Significant for the greatest Inca victory over the Spanish in Peru, the town was reconquered by the Spaniards in 1537.

Originally named Qosqo Ayllu, this Inca town is divided into individual *canchas* (courtyards). Each courtyard has one entrance. A series of carved stone terraces, built to protect the valley from invaders, leads up the hillside to the fortress, Araqama Ayllu. The fort comprises the Temple of the Sun, the Royal Hall, or Mañacaray, the Princess's Baths, or Baños de la Princesa, and the Intihuatana, used to trace the sun's path.

Although unfinished, the Temple of the Sun is one of the finest examples of Inca stonework. Six pink monoliths, designed to glow as the rays of the rising sun hit the structure, fit perfectly together. The T-joints, filled with molten bronze, hold the wall in place, and traces of puma symbols can still be seen on the surface.

Traditional and lively Negritos folk parade in Huánuco

CENTRAL SIERRA

Around 12,000 years ago, hunter-gatherers occupied the caves of the scenic Ayacucho valley, at the heart of the Central Sierra. The Wari Empire (AD 600–1100) later dominated the region. Their sophisticated agricultural terracing and systems of governance influenced the Incas, whose grip on the mountainous region occurred some few hundred years after the Wari culture disintegrated. In the late 16th century, the Spanish took control of the Central Sierra, building cities such as Ayacucho and Huánuco.

A bloody and decisive battle took place just outside of Huánuco in 1824, an event that helped ensure Peruvian independence. In the 1980s and 90s, the region bore the brunt of the atrocities committed by Sendero Luminoso (Shining Path), a communist guerrilla group, and the retaliatory government-backed military; thousands of civilians were killed, with many more forced to flee to the coast. After the capture of their ringleaders in 1992, Shining Path went into decline and has now all but disappeared. Today, visitors are drawn to the area's spectacular mountainous scenery and lively traditional festivals, along with the vibrant and varied crafts scene.

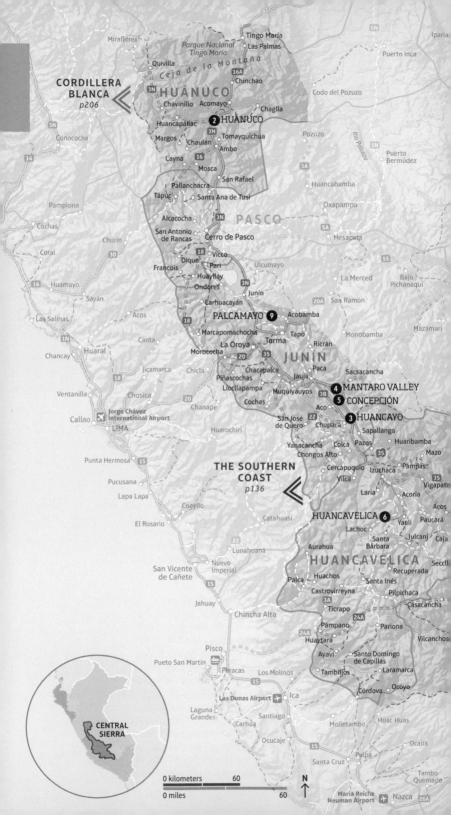

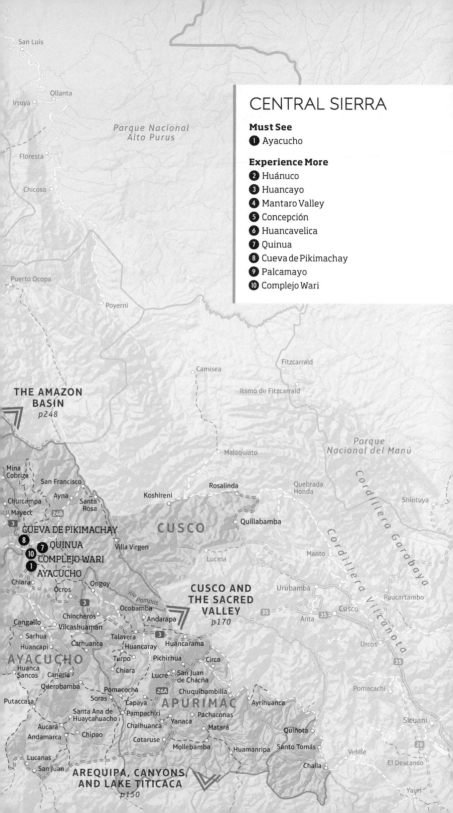

CENTRAL SIERRA

Must See
1 Ayacucho

Experience More
2 Huánuco
3 Huancayo
4 Mantaro Valley
5 Concepción
6 Huancavelica
7 Quinua
8 Cueva de Pikimachay
9 Palcamayo
10 Complejo Wari

THE AMAZON BASIN
p248

THE AMAZON
BASIN
p248

CUEVA DE PIKIMACHAY
8
7 QUINUA
10 COMPLEJO WARI
1 AYACUCHO

CUSCO

CUSCO AND
THE SACRED
VALLEY
p170

AYACUCHO

APURIMAC

AREQUIPA, CANYONS,
AND LAKE TITICACA
p150

↑ The Iglesia de Santo Domingo, overlooking Plaza de Armas

①

AYACUCHO

A E5 **A** 357 miles (575 km) SE of Lima **⊟⊟** **i** iPerú tourist office: Jirón Cusco 108; 06 631 8305; 9am-6pm Mon-Sat (to 1pm Sun)

Founded by the Spanish in 1539, Ayacucho has a rich tradition of arts and crafts. It now also plays host to the famous Holy Week celebrations, which attract visitors from all over Peru. A pleasant climate, leafy plazas and colonial architecture make strolling around it a pleasure.

①
Iglesia de Santo Domingo

A Cnr of Bellido & 9 de Diciembre **C** 9am-noon Mon-Fri

This church has a Renaissance facade which was later embellished with columns and a balcony. The Spanish Inquisition used this balcony to hang its victims. Inside, there is a fusion of Andean and Catholic influences. There is a portrait of an Inca face on the gold-leaf altar, and a hummingbird motif used for decoration. The bells were rung to declare independence from the Spanish after Peru's victory at the Battle of Ayacucho in 1824.

②
Museo de la Memoria

A Prolongación Libertad 1229, Cuadra 14 **C** 9am-1pm & 3-5pm Mon-Fri, 9am-1pm Sat **W** anfasep. org.pe/museo-de-la-memoria

This museum tells the story of violence by Shining Path (Sendero Luminoso) rebels and the brutal response by the military in the 1980-2000 internal conflict, most harshly felt in Ayacucho. Photographs, documents, artwork, and clothing are displayed in three rooms; all texts are in Spanish. It is a work in progress as mass graves continue to be found and trials of military officers await more evidence.

③
Casa-Museo Joaquín López Antay

A Jirón Cusco 424 **C** 956 695 466 **C** 3:30-7pm Mon-Sat

The home of Ayacucho's acclaimed *retablo* artisan Joaquín López Antay (1897–1987), this fascinating museum showcases many of his spectacular works. Originally carried by Spanish evangelizing priests, his portable wooden altars were adopted and adapted by Andean artists, who filled them with a decorative fusion of Andean and religious scenes. López-

---

THE SHINING PATH

This guerrilla group was founded in the 1960s *(p73)*. After assassinating unpopular government officials, they turned to the brutal murder of peasants. The military response was equally harsh, and the torture and murder of often innocent people was greatest in Ayacucho. Memories of the conflict are still vivid here.

Antay's workshop illustrates the intricate process of *retablo* making and the museum provides insights into his life. There is also a gift shop.

La Catedral

📍 **Plaza de Armas** 🕐 **10am-noon & 4-6:30pm Mon-Fri & some weekends**

Located beside the university, on the elegant Plaza de Armas, Ayacucho's 17th-century cathedral has an inauspicious pink and grey facade. The interior is more impressive, with a gilded altar and ornately carved pulpit, which is best viewed when it is illuminated during the evening service. The cathedral is the center of the famous candlelit Holy Week procession *(p41)*, when a crowd gathers here to follow an effigy of Christ around the city. There is also a Museum of Religious Art inside the church that exhibits works brought to Peru from Rome during the colonial period.

Iglesia San Francisco de Paula

📍 **Cnr of Garcilaso de la Vega & Cusco** 🕐 **10am-noon & 4-6:30pm Mon-Fri & some weekends**

This church rivals Cusco's San Blas *(p176)* as the site of Peru's finest carved pulpit. The altar here is one of the few in the city not covered in gold leaf, but is instead made from Nicaraguan cedar-wood carved with dozens of angels. The church, built in 1713, also holds a range of Flemish paintings.

---

⑥ Compañía de Jesús

📍 **28 de Julio, Arequipa & San Martín**

This Jesuit church, built in different architectural styles, has a facade of flowers sculpted in stone. Inside, the gilded altar, carved wood interior, and a good collection of colonial religious paintings and sculptures are worth seeing. Next door is the Jesuit school where Latin, music, woodcarving, and painting lessons were given to Indigenous children, before the expulsion of the Jesuits from Latin America in 1767.

---

⑦ Casa Boza y Solís-Prefecture

📍 **Portal Constitución, Plaza de Armas** 🕐 **8am-1pm & 3-5pm Mon-Fri**

This two-story mansion, built in 1748, has been turned into government offices. The interior courtyard has an original stone fountain and the upper floor is decorated with glazed Sevillian tiles. Visitors are allowed to see the cell of María Parado de Bellido, an Indigenous revolutionary figure who was incarcerated here before being executed by the Spanish in 1822.

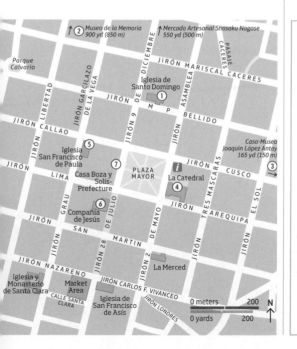

SHOP

Santa Ana
Browse the workshops and galleries of artisans working with silver, cloth, alabaster, wood, and ceramic.

📍 **Barrio Santa Ana, 1 km (0.6 miles) south of the Plaza de Armas**

Mercado Artesanal Shosaku Nagase
Five blocks north of the Plaza Mayor, this market sells ceramic churches and *retablos*.

📍 **Av Maravillas 101, Plazoleta Maria Parado de Bellido**

EXPERIENCE MORE

Huánuco

D4 **280 miles (450 km) NE of Lima** **From Lima** **General Prado 718; 513 223**

This Andean town, situated at a height of 6,214 ft (1,894 m), has the best climate in Peru. The capital of its department, Huánuco lies on the banks of the Río Huallaga. Founded by the Spanish in 1539, the town still has a few examples of fine colonial architecture. These include the cathedral, which contains some pieces from the famous Cusco School *(p179)*, Iglesia San Cristóbal, with its intricate woodcarvings, and the grand 16th-century Iglesia de San Francisco.

Just outside Huánuco lies the **Templo de Kotosh**, said to be one of Peru's oldest sites, dating from 2000–1500 BC. Although the site was redis-covered in 1935, it was not excavated until 1960, and still little is known about this ancient culture. The most important findings here are two mud moldings, each depicting a pair of crossed arms, believed to be between 4,000 and 5,000 years old. One of these is now on display at Lima's Museo Nacional de Arqueología, Antropología e Historia del Perú *(p128)*.

The site, comprising three stone-built enclosures, contains a number of replicas of the mud moldings in the temple. Local guides willingly take visitors around for a small tip.

Templo de Kotosh

3 miles (5 km) W of Huánuco **062 512 507** **9am–5pm daily**

THE LIMA TO HUANCAYO TRAIN

The 12- to 14-hour rail journey from Lima's Desamparados station to Huancayo is possibly the most spectacular in Peru. The line climbs through the lush Mantaro Valley and into the Andes through 69 tunnels and over 58 bridges. Catch your breath at Estación Galera, the second highest in the world at 15,688 ft (4,782 m). Departures leave once or twice a month (Mar–Nov) and reserving in advance is essential *(www.ferrocarrilcentral.com.pe)*.

Huancayo

E5 **224 miles (360 km) E of Lima** **From Lima** **iPerú: Pasaje Mariscal Castilla 131; 01 574 8000; 9am-6pm Mon-Fri**

Situated at a height of 10,696 ft (3,260 m) in Mantaro Valley, Huancayo is a busy, modern, commercial center. It is also the trade hub for the

nearby villages. For a good view of the town, head to the Cerrito de la Libertad, a hill a short distance from the city center. Beyond the hill stand the dramatic sandstone towers of Torre Torre.

The Huancayo region is both culturally and agriculturally one of the richest in the Andes. Every Sunday, a huge market attracts villagers from surrounding communities who come here to sell agricultural produce and local handicrafts. Huancayo is also a good base from which to visit these rural communities, each of which has its own traditional dress and style of dance. This is also the area to savor local culinary specialties such as *pachamanca* (marinated meat, potatoes, spices, and vegetables cooked in a hole dug in the ground and covered by hot stones).

Once home to the Wari culture, from around AD 600, Huancayo was absorbed into the Inca Empire in 1460. The Calle Real, which runs through the city, was part of the Cápac Ñan *(p69)* from Cusco to Cajamarca. The city was developed by the Spanish in 1572, and a few colonial buildings still remain, the most interesting of which is La Merced. It was in this church that the Peruvian constitution was approved in 1839.

↑ Drystone walls above the cloud line near Huánuco

A big visitor attraction is the Lima to Huancayo train, one of the world's highest rail journeys. An American, Henry Meiggs, was chosen to build the railroad, and between 1870 and 1908 he employed more than 10,000 workers to complete the project. Though passenger service has been disrupted many times; a limited service has now resumed.

 4

Mantaro Valley

🅰 E5 🚌 From Huancayo

The Mantaro Valley is a beautiful, verdant region of agricultural abundance, producing corn, potatoes, artichokes, and carrots. The area is dotted with small villages and the population is renowned for its distinctive craftwork, music, and dance, with numerous lively festivals taking place throughout the year.

There are few facilities here, and little English is spoken, but these communities provide a glimpse of rural Peruvian life. All the villages are accessible from Huancayo.

Many of the techniques used in the local crafts date back hundreds of years. On the eastern side of the valley, look out for beautiful woven blankets and ponchos in Hualhas and silver filigree jewelry in San Jerónimo (where market day is Wednesday).

> 🔍 HIDDEN GEM
> **Reserva Paisajística Nor Yauyos Cochas**
> This protected nature reserve, 42 miles (70 km) west of Huancayo, is well worth a day trip. It is renowned for its spectacular, virtually pristine scenery of crashing waterfalls and crystalline lagoons.

↑ The beautiful, ornate chapel of the Convento de Santa Rosa de Ocopa

 5

Concepción

🅰 E5 📍 14 miles (22 km) NW of Huancayo 🚌 From Huancayo

A sleepy village, Concepción lies in the Mantaro Valley. Just out of the village is the 18th-century Franciscan **Convento de Santa Rosa de Ocopa**, which was established as a base for training missionaries heading to the Amazon. The museum in the convent exhibits Indigenous artifacts and examples of wildlife, as well as old maps and photographs. The library has a fascinating collection of more than 25,000 volumes, some hundreds of years old. There is also a display of colonial religious art, and works by contemporary Huancayo-born artist Josué Sánchez (b.1945).

The beautiful convent, with its cloisters, stone fountains, and a picturesque garden, is a lovely place to explore. Nuns give hourly tours, in Spanish, of the premises to the interested visitors.

Convento de Santa Rosa de Ocopa

◈ 📍 4 miles (6 km) from Concepción ⏰ 9–11:15am & 3–5:15pm Wed-Mon

Huancavelica

 E5 **92 miles (147 km) S of Huancayo** **From Huancayo** **From Huancayo & Lima**

This attractive town, the capital of the department of the same name, is located in a high, remote area known for mining and agriculture. At one time a strategic Inca center, the Spanish town was founded in 1571 after the discovery of vast deposits of mercury nearby. The Spanish exploited the area's mineral wealth, bringing in enslaved people to mine for silver and mercury. Due to gradual depletion of resources, the mines were closed in the mid-1970s.

At 12,140 ft (3,700 m), the town still retains a colonial atmosphere and has some excellent examples of Spanish architecture. The churches are renowned for their intricate silver altars. Each Sunday a lively market attracts villagers from the surrounding rural communities, who come in their traditional dress.

Santa Barbara mine is a good 3-hour hike from Huancavelica, up a steep trail that reaches over 13,125 ft (4,000 m) above sea level. The walk to the mines goes over some striking terrain, past herds of alpacas and llamas. Carved into a rock face, the old entrance to one of the original 16th-century mines is still open and unguarded, but it is not advisable to enter.

Quinua

E5 **23 miles (37 km) NE of Ayacucho** **From Ayacucho**

In the rolling hills 23 miles (37 km) northeast of Ayacucho *(p200)* lies Quinua, at almost 10,827 ft (3,300 m) above sea level. This beautiful little town has an attractive cobbled plaza and is famous for its ceramic crafts. The roofs of the houses in the region are adorned with small ceramic churches, decorated with painted flowers and corn. These churches are believed to be good luck charms by the locals, and are used to ward off evil spirits.

Local artisans also produce handmade guitars, *retablos*, and comical alabaster figurines of bands of musicians or groups of gossiping women. The ceramics, made from the rich, red local clay, are on display at workshops and are also sold at the small market held every Sunday.

Just outside the village lies the site of the Battle of Ayacucho, where Spanish royalist troops were defeated, after years of struggle, on December 9, 1824 by pro-independence troops led by Antonio José de Sucre. This bloody battle brought an end to colonial rule in the country, setting the seal on independence for Peru. The battlefield is a ten-minute walk from the town, and a 132-ft- (40-m-) high white obelisk commemorates the event. There is an annual week-long festival held every December to celebrate the victory. Locals in Quinua and people all over Peru celebrate with festivities that include feasting, folk music, and dance.

Did You Know?

The manufacture of ceramics provides jobs for over 70 per cent of Quinua's working population.

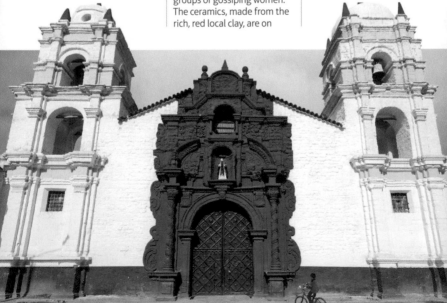

→ Exploring the ruins at Wari, capital of the empire-building Wari culture

 8

Cueva de Pikimachay

🅰E5 📍15 miles (24 km) W of Ayacucho

Situated close to Ayacucho, the cave is hewn out of limestone and is thought to date back to 20,000 BC. It holds evidence of long-term human occupation – the earliest in all of South America. These early inhabitants are thought to have been nomadic hunters and gatherers. Remains of ancient chopping implements, basalt, and blades have been found, along with bones of a giant sloth. It was not until 4,000 BC that agriculture was introduced, and people started cultivating crops such as beans, squash, and chilies.

Beyond the Cueva de Pikimachay is the Huatuscalle, a remote viewpoint that looks over the confluence of ríos Urubamba, Cachi, and Mantaro. Dramatic mountain scenery provides a stunning backdrop.

Tour operators based in Ayacucho can arrange personalized tours for visitors that take in Quinua, Cueva de Pikimachay, and the Huatuscalle.

 9

Palcamayo

🅰D5 📍82 miles (132 km) N of Huancayo 🚌From Tarma

Palcamayo is a small town situated in a green valley. The area's main attraction is the **Gruta de Huagapo**, an enormous limestone cave considered the deepest in South America. Although speleologists have explored 9,006 ft (2,745 m) of the cave, its exact depth is still unknown.

The entrance to Huagapo, which means "cave that cries" in Quechua, is through a huge hole in the mountainside from which an underground river flows. The entrance leads into a giant chamber that is 99 ft (30 m) high and 66 ft (20 m) wide. Exploring the first 984 ft (300 m) of the cave is fairly straightforward, but professional equipment, including scuba gear, is needed to go farther. The light fades and temperature drops as visitors venture deeper into the cave. Local boys act as guides, providing ropes and torches for a tip.

Gruta de Huagapo
📍2 miles (4 km) from Palcamayo
🕗8am–4pm daily

 10

Complejo Wari

🅰E5 📍14 miles (22 km) N of Ayacucho 🕗8am–5:30pm Tue–Sun

The road from Ayacucho on the way to Quinua passes the Complejo Wari. Built on a hill, at 8,100 ft (2,470 m), Wari was the capital of the first known expansionist empire in the Andes, and covers an area of approximately 4 sq miles (10 sq km). Divided into five main sections, it comprises rectangular buildings set out on a grid system, with a complex of streets, squares, tombs, paths, and irrigation channels. So far, very little restoration work has been carried out, and the site is therefore not much to look at. The site museum is usually closed but some of the artifacts from these ruins are displayed at an archeological museum in Ayacucho.

← The grand facade of Huancavelica's Iglesia Santo Domingo

CORDILLERA BLANCA

This mountainous region – named Cordillera Blanca (White Mountain Range) after its perennially snow-covered peaks – was inhabited by hunter-gatherers some 10,000 years ago; their paintings still adorn caves in the area. Between 1500–500 BC, the Chavín culture flourished in the region's fertile valley of the Callejón de Huaylas. This agro-pastoralist group dominated northern Peru, constructing the impressive ceremonial centre at Chavín de Huántar around 1200 BC; it attracted pilgrims from as far away as the Amazon. The Inca Empire spread into the area over 2,000 years later, building temples, fortresses, and roads.

In 1574, Huaraz was founded by the Spanish, who enslaved the local Indigenous population to exploit the area's mineral and agricultural wealth. Almost three hundred years after this, the city was almost destroyed by the Great Peruvian Earthquake in 1970, which killed around 70,000 people in the region. Since then, improved road links with Lima – which were part of the reconstruction work – have helped Huaraz's growing reputation as the epicentre of climbing and trekking in Peru. Its sparkling snowy mountains, stunning glacial lakes, and villages rich in traditional Andean culture now attract over 200,000 visitors a year.

CORDILLERA BLANCA

Must Sees

1 Parque Nacional Huascarán
2 Chavín de Huántar
3 Caral

Experience More

4 Caraz
5 Carhuaz
6 Campo Santo, Yungay
7 Huaraz
8 Chacas
9 Baños Termales de Monterrey
10 Cordillera Huayhuash
11 Sechín

Trujillo

LA LIBERTAD

Huacapongo

Virú

THE NORTHERN DESERT
p222

Tablones

Tambo Real

Santa
Isla Santa

Chimbote

Nepeña

Pacific Ocean

CORDILLERA BLANCA

0 kilometers   40

0 miles   40

N

PARQUE NACIONAL HUASCARÁN

🅐D4 **🅐13 miles (40 km) N of Huaraz** **🚌🚉From Huaraz** **ℹSERNANP, Federico Sal y Rosas 555, Huaraz; www.sernanp.gob.pe**

Situated in the Ancash region, the Huascarán National Park encompasses almost the entire Cordillera Blanca. Gleaming mountain peaks, jeweled turquoise lakes, and unusual fauna make this park an essential part of any visit to Peru.

Declared a UNESCO Biosphere Reserve in 1977, and a World Heritage Site in 1985, the park aims to protect the region's flora and fauna, its geological formations, and archeological remains. Locals participate in the growing adventure tourism industry, meaning that revenue is channeled to their communities.

A Climber's Paradise

With 50 towering snowcapped peaks over 18,700 ft (5,700 m), the area is attractive for hikers, climbers, and naturalists alike and is easily accessible from Huaraz (p220) or Caraz (p218). Both these lofty towns have good hotels, equipment hire shops, and mountain guides, and Huaraz has a lively pre- and post-trek scene. Regular minibuses run between major villages, and the main road is in good condition. Short trips can be organized to the surrounding mountains and lakes, such as Laguna 69 and snowcapped Chacraraju, or longer hikes, particularly the Santa Cruz Trek, for the more adventurous hikers.

> **Did You Know?**
>
> Ten mammal species, including the spectacled bear, can be found here, plus 112 species of birds.

PUYA RAIMONDII

Named after the Italian scientist Antonio Raimondi, this is the world's largest bromeliad and is found in just a few isolated Andean areas, such as the Parque Nacional Huascarán and the Cañón de Cotahuasi *(p168)*. One of the most ancient plant species in the world, it has a rosette of pliable, cactus-like leaves, and blooms once in its 100-year lifetime. The elongated cluster of flowers grows from a single main stem, which can reach 40 ft (12 m) in height.

This area is home to the highest mountain in Peru, Huascarán, at 22,205 ft (6,770 m). Freezing temperatures, glaciers, and avalanches make it a challenging climb. Alpamayo, once voted the most beautiful mountain in the world, is also found here, as is Artesonraju, believed to be the mountain in the latest Paramount Pictures logo.

Activities in the Park

High-altitude hiking is the most favored activity here, with mountain-biking and paragliding gaining in popularity. For those not as bold, Chinancocha, a splendid lake, has rowing boats for hire. Day tours from Huaraz also take you to groves of *Puya raimondii* in the park's southern end, which bloom between May and August.

←
Laguna 69, with Chacraraju mountain behind; walking through the national park *(inset)*

Punta Olímpica
Anticipate a beautiful valley, lakes, and broad views of Nevado Huascarán.

Laguna 69
A difficult 9-mile (14-km) hike starting at Yurac Corral. It takes around six hours there and back, but splendid views of the crystalline lake are ample reward.

Laguna Wilcacocha
A short but rough ascent into the Cordillera Negra, above Huaraz, with spectacular sunsets.

Quebrada Rajucolta
Prepare for a rough road leading to a valley south of Huaraz, but expect an exceptional canyon, cascades, and forests. Allow four hours to get there and back.

→
The magnificent glacier-fed Lagunas Llanganuco and surrounding mountains

SANTA CRUZ TREK

This four-day trek is one of the most popular in the Cordillera Blanca. The high-altitude trail snaking through panoramic mountain scenery passes beneath a dozen towering peaks which are over 18,700 ft (5,700 m) high.

The trail can begin from Lagunas Llanganuco. The path is well defined, and there are many long and moderate to difficult ascents along switchback trails, as well as more level walking alongside rivers and across verdant meadows.

The highest pass is Punta Unión at 15,590 ft (4,750 m). Here the cordillera opens up in front of trekkers to reveal a breathtaking 360-degree panorama of snowy peaks and glistening glacial lakes.

↑ Stopping by Taullicocha on the Santa Cruz Trek

Camping at this altitude is a chilly but spectacular affair. To wake up surrounded by towering ice-capped peaks is a once-in-a-lifetime experience. It is a suitable trek for amateur hikers, providing they are fit, properly acclimatized, and have the right equipment and clothing.

> **Here the cordillera opens up in front of trekkers to reveal a breathtaking 360-degree panorama of snowy peaks.**

400

The number
of stunning lakes
within the park.

LAGUNAS LLANGANUCO

INSIDER TIP
Altitude Sickness

Due to the high altitude in this region, make sure you bring warm clothing and drink plenty of water. It is also wise to spend up to three days acclimatizing in Huaraz before visiting the park. As a general rule, do not embark on any treks if you experience any signs of altitude sickness *(p275)*.

Situated 18 miles (28 km) east of Yungay, these two lakes sit in an awesome glacial valley 12,630 ft (3,850 m) above sea level. The peaks of Huascarán and Huandoy loom above them, covered by glaciers all year round. Surrounded by the rare Polylepis trees, the dazzling turquoise waters glow in the midday sun.

At 4,747 ft (1,450 m) long, the first lake, Chinancocha, is the most popular with visitors. You can hire rowing boats, from which you are provided with spectacular views of the surrounding mountain summits. The second lake, Orconcocha, is the smallest at the end of the valley, at 2,986 ft (910 m) in length. It offers a wide variety of flora and wildlife.

It is best to arrive in the morning as the lakes get shady later in the day and the afternoons often bring clouds and an icy wind. Pick-ups and minibuses from Yungay run throughout the day in the tourist high-season, which lasts from May through to September. The lakes are also accessible from Huaraz or Cashapampa, which is just beyond Caraz.

CHAVÍN DE HUÁNTAR

D4 **19 miles (30 km) SE of Wari; 0.6 miles (1 km) from Chavín village**
From Huaraz **From Huaraz** **8am–5pm daily**

Comprising a series of underground tunnels, temple structures, and superb wall carvings, this intricate complex is a phenomenal construction. Built and used by the oldest major culture of Peru, the Chavín de Huántar is one of the most significant prehistoric sights in the whole country.

Located in the Ancash region, halfway between the coast and the jungle, Chavín de Huántar lies at 10,335 ft (3,150 m) above sea level on the Río Mosna. Declared a World Heritage Site by UNESCO in 1985, this was the major ceremonial center for the Chavín people who inhabited the area between the 15th and 5th centuries BC. The complex, which displays a pattern of additions and renovations, has two distinct parts: an original temple with underground passageways and carved stelae, and a much larger and later extension, which comprises a mighty, pyramid-like building leading down to the main plaza. The original temple buildings sit to the right of El Castillo, the most important building in the complex.

> **Did You Know?**
>
> Trading *ch'arki* (llama jerky) was the main source of commerce for the Chavín culture.

El Castillo, in the extension of the original temple's right wing, is believed to date from 500–200 BC.

Underground tunnels, connected by ramps and stairs, are extremely well-ventilated despite there being just one doorway.

The black and white portal, Porch of Falcons, on El Castillo comprises a large carved lintel spanning the cylindrical columns.

THE CULT OF CHAVÍN (1300–400 BC)

The Chavín dominated northern Peru more than 2,000 years before the Incas. Thanks to abundant agricultural production, they had more free time to pursue artistic and religious practices. Their principal deities (anthropomorphic feline characters) were represented in stone stelae, such as this jaguar carving.

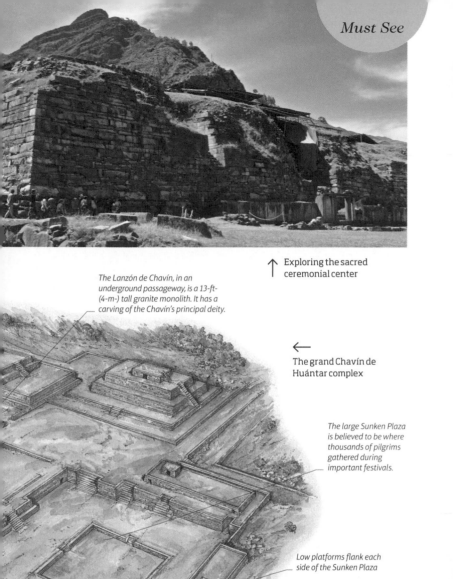

↑ Exploring the sacred ceremonial center

The Lanzón de Chavín, in an underground passageway, is a 13-ft- (4-m-) tall granite monolith. It has a carving of the Chavín's principal deity.

← The grand Chavín de Huántar complex

The large Sunken Plaza is believed to be where thousands of pilgrims gathered during important festivals.

Low platforms flank each side of the Sunken Plaza

↑ The incredible underground passageways and chambers

3

CARAL

🅐 D5 🅠 110 miles (176 km) N of Lima, off Pan-American Hwy North, KM182
🕒 9am–4pm daily 🆆 caralperu.gob.pe

Located on an arid strip of desert above the verdant Supe Valley, the UNESCO World Heritage pyramids of Caral are one of the cradles of civilization. At around 5,000 years old, this fascinating archeological site is the oldest urban center in the Americas.

Discovered in 1905, excavation work here didn't start until 1994, as archeologists wrongly believed Caral to be a more recent construction. The site encompasses an impressive range of temples, houses, and plazas that date to 2,627 BC, around the same time as when the Great Pyramid of Giza in Egypt was being built. Radiocarbon dating has proven that the advanced, pre-ceramic civilization of Caral flourished in the Americas 1,000 years earlier than believed.

The site is exceptionally well preserved due to its lack of silver and gold artifacts, which made it of little interest to looters. Research by Peruvian archeologist Ruth Shady has shown that the site was divided into two, the Sector

Alto (Upper Zone) and the Sector Bajo (Lower Zone). The former contains most of Caral's 20 stone structures, which include six pyramids with ceremonial plazas, surrounded by residential buildings.

The complexity of the buildings and their vast size suggest a culture capable of large-scale planning and decision-making processes. Archeologists believe that thousands of workers, managed by artisans and supervisors, would have been required to provide the necessary labor to construct the city. *Shicras*, woven reed bags filled with rocks, found at the site were possibly used to build the primitive but earthquake-proof foundations for buildings.

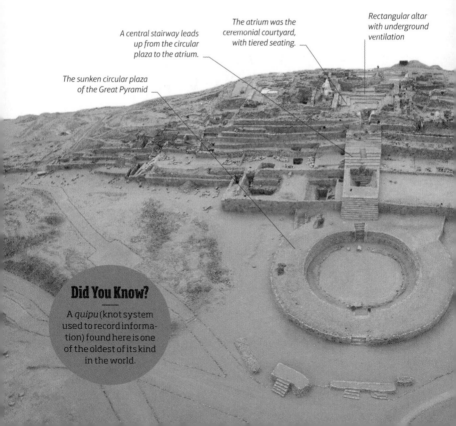

A central stairway leads up from the circular plaza to the atrium.

The atrium was the ceremonial courtyard, with tiered seating.

Rectangular altar with underground ventilation

The sunken circular plaza of the Great Pyramid

Did You Know?

A *quipu* (knot system used to record information) found here is one of the oldest of its kind in the world.

ARCHAEOLOGICAL DIGS

Digs led by archeologist Ruth Shady since 1994 have uncovered fascinating artifacts that offer an insight into life on the site. These include seed and plant fragments from species endemic to the Amazon and the Andes, indicating Caral's role as an important trade center, connecting inland and coastal communities. Rectangular religious offerings made from cotton, known as *Ojos de Dios* (God's Eyes), also indicate that cotton was the city's main crop, cultivated here and used to exchange for shellfish with fishermen on the coast.

The east wing had seven superimposed terraces with stairways and rooms.

↑ Overlooking Caral's Great Pyramid complex, with its circular plaza at the forefront

Site Highlights

Pyramid of the Circular Altar

Made of stones bonded with mortar, this pyramid was plastered and painted white, yellow, and red.

Amphitheater

▷ The sunken amphitheater was one of the main buildings of the city and was used for religious and political functions. Celebrations were held here, with 32 flutes made of condor and pelican bones, and 27 cornets fashioned from deer and llama bones, found during excavations.

Pyramid of the Gallery

▷ Containing an underground passageway painted white and with seven niches, this was thought to have been used for individual worship. Residential buildings with ceremonial altars next door were inhabited by priests.

Great Pyramid

◁ This pyramid covers an area the size of four football fields. A 30-ft- (9-m-) wide staircase climbs from its foot to an atrium, three floors above, complete with a ceremonial fireplace. The leaders could survey the city from this impressive building.

Pyramid of the Huanca

▽ This three-tier structure has a staircase leading up to a ceremonial area with a view of a large obelisk. It is thought to have had an astronomical purpose.

EXPERIENCE MORE

Caraz

🅐 D4 **🏠 42 miles (67 km) N of Huaraz, Callejón de Huaylas** 🚌 **Frequent** *colectivos* **from Huaraz & Yungay** 🛈 **Municipalidad, Plaza de Armas**

A small, pretty town at the end of the Callejón de Huaylas, Caraz has avoided total devastation from the earthquakes and avalanches that have destroyed so much of the valley. A flower-lined road leads into town, which has a leafy Plaza de Armas.

At 7,450 ft (2,270 m), Caraz is lower than nearby Huaraz (*p220*) and has a milder, much more agreeable climate. The tourism industry is developing slowly here to accommodate trekkers and climbers – it is the starting point for the panoramic Santa Cruz Trek (*p212*) and also for ascents of Mount Alpamayo.

There are a number of good places to stay and eat as well.

Not far from Caraz are the ancient ruins of Tunshukaiko – a platform structure thought to date back to the Huaraz culture, around 2000 BC. The setting, in a lush valley with the cordilleras Blanca and Negra on either side, is spectacular, although there is little to see at the site.

A road runs 20 miles (32 km) east from Caraz through an impressive canyon bordered by 3,280-ft (1,000-m) high granite walls, leading to Laguna Parón. This lake is surrounded by snowy peaks, including Mount Pirámide, at a height of 19,310 ft (5,885 m). Parón is less visited but just as spectacular as the Lagunas Llanganuco.

Carhuaz

🅐 D4 **🏠 20 miles (32 km) N of Huaraz, Callejón de Huaylas** 🚌 **Frequent** *colectivos* **from Huaraz**

This quiet little town in the northern Callejón de Huaylas has a limited tourist infrastructure, although it is a stopping point for trekkers in the Cordillera Blanca. The town lies at 8,655 ft (2,638 m) and has an attractive main square; a bustling market is held every Sunday morning with displays of agricultural produce and crafts from all over the region. Each September, for ten days, Carhuaz comes alive with dancing, drinking, music, and firework displays at the annual celebration of the Virgen de la Merced festival, thought to be the most raucous in the valley.

> **A bustling market is held every Sunday morning in Carhuaz, with displays of agricultural produce and crafts from all over the region.**

A number of good walks from Carhuaz have remained relatively unexplored as visitors favor the longer treks into the Cordillera Blanca. A pretty 5-mile (8-km) walk east from Carhuaz leads to the Baños de Pariacaca, the bubbling hot thermal waters of the natural rock pools beside a chilly river. For the brave, these are a fun place to swim.

The trail continues to the Lakes Hike, a rugged trek that passes between Laguna

 INSIDER TIP
Canyon Blast

With a pot-holed gravel surface, sheer rock-cut walls, and 35 pitch-black one-lane tunnels, the road that barrels along the Cañón del Pato (Duck Canyon) north of Caraz is considered one of the world's most dangerous. It's the ultimate pedaling challenge for adventurous mountain bikers.

→ Remains of the 1970 earthquake's destruction at Yungay

Rajupaquinan, Laguna 513, and Lagunas Auquiscocha. The longest and most spectacular hike is to a small village called Yanama. This three-day trip into the Quebrada Ulta (13,780 ft/4,200 m) features fantastic views of the towering peaks of the Parque Nacional Huascarán *(p210)*. Other major treks in Quebrada Ulta can be accessed from Chacas via a paved road through Ulta. Information on these is available at local hostels and trekking shops.

6 Campo Santo, Yungay

🅐D4 🕐7 miles (12 km) S of Caraz 🚌*Colectivos* from Caraz & Huaraz 🕐8am–6pm daily

The Callejón de Huaylas suffered immense tragedy in the last century due to a number of devastating *aluviónes*. When the high-altitude lakes of the cordillera breach as a result of earthquakes or excessive snowmelt, they send deadly cascades of water, ice, mud, and debris on to the villages below. In 1970 an enormous earthquake (measuring 7.7 on the Richter scale) rocked central Peru and the resulting *aluvión* wiped out the village of Yungay, burying around 18,000 people.

An enormous mass of ice and granite was dislodged from the west face of Mount Huascarán's north peak by the earthquake and it hurtled down toward Yungay at over 190 mph (300 kmph), burying the entire village and sparing only 400 lives. The site, known as Campo Santo or holy ground, is an expansion of where the original cemetery stood. It is open to visitors, and the thick layer of soil that covers the former village is adorned with paths and flowers. It is a poignant and evocative sight; the tip of the cathedral's spire and the tops of four palm trees are all that remain of the Plaza de Armas, and there are a number of monuments marking the sites of former homes. A large statue of Christ on a nearby hillside looks over the ruined town. It was to this point that 243 residents managed to climb and escape. Other catastrophic mudslides in 1941 and 1962 claimed around 9,000 lives.

← The snowcapped Nevado Pirámide at Laguna Parón, near Caraz

A local trader
wandering past fruit
stalls at Huaraz market

Museo Arqueológico de Ancash

📍Plaza de Armas ☎043 421
551 🕘9am-5pm Tue-Sun

8

Chacas

🅐D4 🚗73 miles (118 km) NE
of Huaraz 🚌From Huaraz

The bus journey to the rural
town of Chacas starts from
Huaraz and passes through a
tunnel beneath the pass at
Punta Olímpica (16,044 ft/
4,890 m). The town, which has
retained its original Andean-
Spanish architecture, is home
to the famous Don Bosco
School. This cooperative,
established in 1976, teaches
disadvantaged children the
art of woodcarving and
carpentry, and the profits are
used to fund medical and
agricultural projects in the
area. Beautiful carvings
created by the children can be
seen decorating many gates
and balconies in the village.

EAT & DRINK

Café Andino

A relaxed place with a
roaring fire and cosy
corners for playing
board games. Great
coffee and waffles.

🅐C4 📍Jirón Lucar y
Torre 530, Huaraz
🌐cafeandino.com

Trivio

European dishes at this
taproom-restaurant
serving local Sierra
Andina craft beer, with
occasional live music.

🅐D4 📍Parque del
Periodista, Av
Luzuriaga, Huaraz
🌐triviorestobar.com

Creperie Patrick

Savory and sweet
crepes, onion soup, and
fondues are the stars of
this restaurant with its
resident French chef.
It has a full bar.

🅐D4 📍Av Luzuriaga
422, Huaraz
📞921 176 340

7

Huaraz

🅐D4 🚗250 miles (402 km)
N of Lima 🚌From Lima
🛈iPerú, Plaza de Armas;
(043) 428 812

Huaraz makes a good base
for visitors to explore the
incredible Parque Nacional
Huascarán *(p210)* and the
Callejón de Huaylas. The town
is situated at an altitude of
10,142 ft (3,091 m), with the
colossal peaks of the Cordillera
Blanca and Negra mountain
ranges rising on either side.
The busy main street, Avenida
Luzuriaga, teems with cafés,
bars, and hiking shops. People
from nearby communities
come into town to sell local
products such as cheese,
honey, and sweets, as well
as handicrafts.

The informative **Museo
Arqueológico de Ancash**, on
the main square, is definitely
worth a visit. Spread over
three floors, it takes visitors
through the region's history
from around 10,500 BC to
AD 700. Displays include
ceramics, trepanned skulls,
carved stones, and assorted
artifacts. The delightful
garden at the back includes
over 120 monoliths, heads,
and other pieces of carved
stone from the Recuay culture.

→

Trekking up the beautiful
Peruvian Andes,
accompanied by a horse

The Mozo Danza, a ritual warrior dance, is performed in the streets during the feast of the Virgen de la Asunción.

Baños Termales de Monterrey

D4 **3 miles (5 km) N of Huaraz** *Colectivo* from Huaraz **927 965 283** **7am–5pm daily**

The hot springs of Monterrey are famous for their curative properties. The spring water's high temperature is believed to be good for digestive and other health-related problems.

> **INSIDER TIP**
> **Bathing Basics**
>
> Don't expect a tourist-style spa experience at Peru's rural thermal springs. These are local baths for the community (who often run them too); travelers are welcome, but facilities will be basic and you may have to wait in line for cubicles.

Monterrey is located at a height of 8,868 ft (2,703 m) in the Callejón de Huaylas, the beautiful valley between the Cordillera Blanca and Negra mountain ranges. About 22 miles (35 km) farther up the valley is Chancos, located at the foot of Mount Copa. It has bathing pools fed by springs and natural sauna caves, which have been adapted into private cubicles.

Cordillera Huayhuash

D4 **From Huaraz or Huánuco**

Just 19 miles (30 km) long, this remote and pristine range incorporates dramatic mountain scenery, turquoise lakes, and rolling grasslands. There are seven peaks over 19,600 ft (6,000 m), including Yerupaja, which at around 21,765 ft (6,634 m) is the second-highest mountain in Peru, and Siula Grande, at 20,853 ft (6,356 m). There are seven other peaks over 18,000 ft (5,500 m) high.

Although barely 31 miles (50 km) away, Huayhuash is very different from its more famous neighbor, the Cordillera Blanca. There are no broad valleys, mountain passes are more treacherous, and access is limited. At one time, the only trekking here

was a 12-day loop of the range from Chiquián. Today, buses carry hikers on the dirt road from Huaraz to Huallanca, where shorter, five-day trips are possible. Guides and mule handlers can be hired at either starting point. A period of prior acclimatization is essential.

Sechín

C4 **3 miles (5 km) SE of Casma** **From Casma** **9am–5pm daily**

Thought to date back to 1600 BC, the ruins at Sechín were first excavated in 1937 by Peruvian archeologist J.C. Tello. The stone frieze on the outside wall of the main temple depicts a gruesome battle scene: warriors dressed in loincloths and carrying staves or clubs standing over their victims, who are shown with severed heads and limbs. It is thought that the temples were intended to commemorate an important battle, but it is still unknown which culture constructed this ancient complex. Inside the temple, earlier mud structures are being excavated even today.

THE NORTHERN DESERT

This region was the cradle of the Moche, Sicán, and Chimú kingdoms that emerged just under two thousand years ago. All depended on fishing and agriculture, using advanced irrigation techniques to make the most of the scarce water resources along this arid coastal strip. The Moche (AD 100-800) constructed fine adobe temples, and produced splendid ceramics, and artifacts of copper and gold, such as the treasures found in the Lord of Sipán's burial chamber. Between AD 750-1375, the Sicán (or Lambayeque), thought to be descendants of the Moche, established trade routes with Ecuador and Colombia, and produced more elaborate gold, silver, and copper work. The Chimú culture built their own sophisticated cities, in particular Chan-Chan (c. AD 850), the largest adobe city in the world. The region's more recent past can be seen in Peru's third-largest city, Trujillo, which was founded by the Spanish in 1534. After surviving a major city siege by Inca forces in 1536, the city developed into an important port for the Spanish fleet. In 1820, Trujillo's place in national history was assured when it became the first Peruvian city to declare independence from Spain. These days, the region's richly flavored culinary delights and the coastal beach resorts of Máncora attract as many visitors as its historical sites.

THE NORTHERN
DESERT

Cap. FAP Pedro
Canga Rodríguez Airport
TUMBES ⑩

ZORRITOS ⑪

Cañaveral

MÁNCORA ⑧
Parque Nacional
Cerros de Amotope

Atascadero

Talara
Poechos

Negritos 1A

Sullana

Capitán FAP Guillermo Concha
Iberico International Airport 1N

Paita 2
Piura
Catacaos

La Unión 1N

Sechura

Parachique

Bayóvar

Reventazón

*Pacific
Ocean*

THE NORTHERN DESERT

Must Sees

❶ Trujillo
❷ Museo Tumbas
  Reales de Sipán

Experience More

❸ Huaca del Sol
  y de la Luna
❹ Chan Chan
❺ Huanchaco
❻ Chiclayo
❼ Complejo
  Arqueológico El Brujo
❽ Máncora
❾ Batán Grande
⑩ Tumbes
⑪ Zorritos
⑫ Túcume

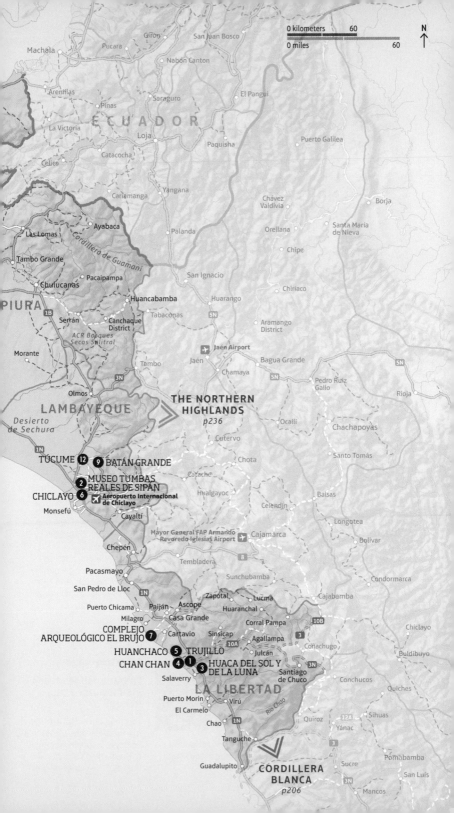

TRUJILLO

C4 **348 miles (560 km) N of Lima** **6 miles (10 km) NW** **From Lima** iPerú, Jirón Diego de Almagro 420, 044 294 561 **9am-6pm Mon-Sat (to noon Sun)**

Ranked as Peru's third-largest city, Trujillo's spring-like climate has earned it the title of "the city of eternal spring." Founded in 1534, Trujillo became the northern coast's most important area in the 16th century. Today, it is an oasis of greenery with brilliant Moche and Chimú archeological sites nearby.

① Plaza de Armas

Trujillo's main square is said to be the largest in Peru. At the center of Plaza de Armas is a giant marble and bronze monument dedicated to the figures of the Wars of Independence, designed by the German artist Edmund Moeller (1885–1957) and inaugurated in 1927. An equestrian monument of the conquistador Francisco Pizarro, who was born in Trujillo, is also worth seeing.

Every Sunday, a flag-raising ceremony accompanied by a parade is held. At certain times, enchanting *marinera (p52)* dancers perform. The famous

Peruvian Paso horses *(p229)* can also be seen striding through the plaza.

↑ Flag-raising ceremony and parade at the Plaza de Armas

② La Catedral

Cnr of Independencia & Orbegoso **976 909 049** **9am-1pm & 4-7pm Mon-Fri, 9am-1pm Sat (for guided visits only)**

On one side of the Plaza de Armas is the cathedral, also known as the Basilica Menor. First built in the mid-17th century, it was destroyed in the 1759 earthquake and then rebuilt. It features colorful Baroque sculptures and paintings from the Escuela Quiteña, a style of painting which originated in 18th-century Quito.

The cathedral also has a museum featuring a number of beautiful 18th- and 19th-century religious paintings and sculptures.

③ Casa Urquiaga

Pizarro 446 **981 064 315** **9:30am-3:30pm Mon-Fri**

This magnificently restored mansion, also known as Casa Calonge, originally belonged to Bernardino Calonge, who founded the city's first bank.

←

Bright facade of Trujillo's cathedral, overlooking Plaza de Armas

Painted royal blue with white window grills, it was bought from the Urquiaga family in 1972 and is now owned by the Banco Central de Reserva del Perú. The 18th-century mahogany desk of Simón Bolívar, who lived here after proclaiming Peru's independence in 1821, is preserved.

The building features three interior courtyards. Several Moche and Nazca ceramics, along with many Chavín and Chimú gold ornaments, are also on display in the house.

④

Iglesia la Merced

🏛 Pizarro 550 🕐 8am–noon & 4–8pm daily

This church, originally built in 1536, was destroyed in an earthquake. It was designed

and rebuilt around 1636 by Portuguese artist Alonso de Las Nieves. During the 1970 earthquake it suffered severe damage. The building, with its restored dome, features beautiful and picturesque molded figures representing scenes from the life of Saint Peter Nolasco, the French founder of the Mercedarian congregation. Other features include unusual altarpieces painted on the walls, dating from the time before free-standing altars were used, as well as a priceless Rococo pipe organ.

⑤

Casa de Orbegoso

🏛 Orbegoso 553 ☎ 044 234 950 ⓘ For art exhibitions

This elegant 18th-century mansion is no longer open to the public, except when used for art exhibitions. It was the residence of Luis José de Orbegoso y Moncada, a grand marshall and President of Peru from 1833 to 1836. His

government marked a low point in Peru's history and he disappeared from the political scene to return to his mansion in complete disgrace. The house was bought by Interbank in 1987.

⑥

Plazuela El Recreo

🏛 Jirón Francisco Pizarro 900

This small park, often used for book fairs and cultural events, is a 10-minute walk from the main square. The large fountain, made from Andean marble and surrounded by four marble statues, was moved in 1925 to its current location from the main square. A remodeling of the square included restoring the pre-Hispanic irrigation channels that used to provide water from the Río Moche, and installing reinforced glass panels so that visitors can view the water.

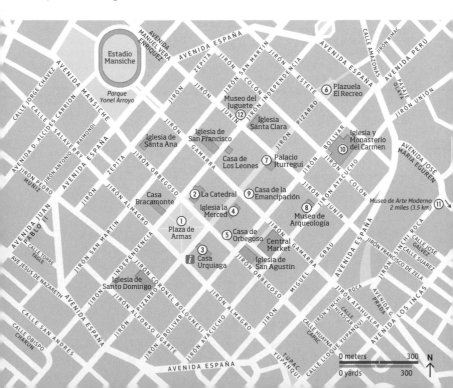

PICTURE PERFECT
Grand Mural

A spectacular mosaic mural, the longest on the continent, is at the Universidad de Trujillo. Made with millions of mosaic pieces, its colorful scenes from history and nature offer a fantastic photo opportunity. It took 16 years to complete, from drawings by artist Rafael Hastings.

⑦

Palacio Iturregui

🏠 Pizarro 688 🕐 8:30am-8pm Mon-Sat

Occupied today by the Club Central, an exclusive social center for Trujillo's upper classes, this early 19th-century Neo-Classical mansion was home to General José Manuel Iturregui y Aguilarte, father of Peruvian independence. He bought it from the Marquises of Bellavista in 1841. Situated two blocks east of the Plaza de Armas, the so-called palace has three large patios encircled by beautiful halls and galleries embellished with gold moldings on the ceilings, tall, slender interior columns, and an open roof. There is restricted access, however, with only some parts open to tourists.

Museo de Arqueología de la Universidad de Trujillo

🏠 Junín 682 📞 044 249 322 🕐 9am-5pm Mon-Sat, 9am-1pm public hols

Housed in what was once a 17th-century colonial mansion, the Museo de Arqueología de la Universidad de Trujillo is remarkable for its large and comprehensive collection of thematic exhibits covering 12,000 years of the northern coast's history. The state handed over the mansion to the university in 1995, providing a permanent exhibition space for its large archeological collection. The most impressive items on display are the Moche finds excavated from the Huaca de la Luna (p232).

⑨

Casa de la Emancipación

🏠 Pizarro 610 🕐 9am-1pm Mon-Sat 🌐 fundacionbbva.pe/casonas-y-museos/casa-de-la-emancipacion/

One of the most historically significant buildings in the city, this was where Trujillo's independence from Spanish rule was planned, declared, and spearheaded by the Marquis of Torre Tagle in 1820. Also known as Casa Rossel-Urquiaga, after the family that owned the house from 1884 to 1944, it was Peru's first seat of government and Congress.

In the mid 20th century, BBVA Banco Continental bought and restored the building as its head office. The main courtyard and entrance exhibit an austere design and the gallery contains impressive marble flooring. The plans and history of the house are displayed beside permanent exhibitions on the life of iconic poet César Vallejo (1892–1938) and Bishop Baltazar Martínez de Compañón y Bujanda (1737–97).

Iglesia y Monasterio del Carmen

🏠 Cnr of Colón & Bolívar 📞 044 233 091 🕐 9am-1pm Mon-Sat; church: 7-7:30am Sun

This church and monastery was founded in 1759, although some historians claim it was established in 1724. Occupying an entire block, this is the biggest religious complex in the city. Although severely damaged by earthquakes in 1759 and later in 1970, the complex has survived. Today,

THE PERUVIAN PASO

With Spanish horses such as the Berber and Andalusian as part of its lineage, the Peruvian Paso is an extraordinary, gentle creature. As an important Paso breeding stronghold, Trujillo hosts frequent festivals and competitions. The Paso horse has a unique and innate gait: *paso llano*, a cross between a walk and a canter. This enables the horse to cover long distances in a short period without tiring. Another virtue is *término*: a loose action in which the front legs are rolled out as the horse strides forward, giving the mount balance.

it is referred to as the "jewel of colonial art in Trujillo."

The church and monastery houses the most important collection of colonial art in Trujillo. The Pinacoteca Carmelita (Carmelite Painting Gallery) exhibits about 150 Baroque and Rococo paintings, most of which date from the 17th and 18th centuries.

The church has other great features, particularly the breathtaking central gilded altar, considered a masterpiece of the Churrigueresque style in Peru. Floral murals in soft pastel shades line each side of the single-dome nave, with exquisite altars on either side and a gold-leaf pulpit.

The monastery has two cloisters, the processional and the recreational, both with superb vaulted arches. A fair portion of the convent's art collection is kept here, but it is not open to the public.

←
Beautiful interior of a colonial-style room in the Palacio Iturregui

(11)
Museo de Arte Moderno

Av Villareal con Carretera Industrial 948 979 856
10am-5pm Mon-Sat
gerardochavez.pe/proyectos/museo-de-arte-moderno/

Primarily the work of artist and architect Gerardo Chávez (b. 1937), this museum and studio is a retrospective exhibition of his drawings, sculptures, and large-format paintings created over six decades. Chávez's work is of

→
A metal bike on display in the Museo del Juguete

great renown and has been exhibited in leading galleries and art festivals in the US, Latin America, and throughout Europe. The museum's pleasant grounds contain a number of sculptures.

(12)
Museo del Juguete

Independencia 705
044 208 181 10am-6pm Mon & Wed-Sat, 10am-1pm Sun

This museum exhibits an unusual collection of toys put together by one of the most distinguished Peruvian artists, Trujillo-born painter Gerardo Chávez. Highlights of the nearly 1,000 permanent exhibits include a unique 2,500-year-old Vicus whistle, pre-Columbian Chancay rag dolls, genuine 18th-century French bisque porcelain dolls, post-war metal cars, and battalions of tin soldiers. The museum aims to become the biggest private toy collection in Latin America. It is sponsored by Espacio Cultural Angelmira, headed by Chávez, which is located on the first floor. On the same floor, a smartly decorated café-bar offers drinks and snacks.

2 (icons)

MUSEO DE LAS TUMBAS REALES DE SIPÁN

🅰C3 🏠 Av JP Vizcardo y Guzmán s/n, Lambayeque 🚌Ⓣ From Chiclayo
📞074 283 977 🕐9am–5pm Tue–Sun

This museum is one of Latin America's biggest, with three floors and ten themed sectors. The exhibits include 1,400 objects of gold, silver, copper, bronze, precious stones, and ceramics of extraordinary beauty.

The pyramid-shaped Museum of the Royal Tombs of Sipán was inaugurated in 2002. Designed by architect Celso Prado Pastor, it is inspired by Huaca Rajada, a Moche mausoleum where the Lord of Sipán was buried 1,700 years ago. The pre-Columbian sovereign's tomb was uncovered in 1987 by archeologist Walter Alva and is arguably the richest tomb in the Americas.

Exploring Museo Tumbas de las Reales de Sipán

The visit, unusually, begins on the third floor with a video presentation of the Huaca Rajada excavations and Moche culture. Entering through the third floor enables visitors to experience seeing a tomb the way an archeologist does: working down from the top, beginning with the most recent features, digging down to ever older, more specific findings, and ending at the dream find – a royal tomb laden with riches.

↑ A selection of the museum's vast collection of pottery

Mochica ceremonial jewelry

Human-sized mannequin

←

The high priest, who watched over religious worship and rituals

Did You Know?

Peanuts were an important Mochica food staple and appear on many of their pots and jewelry.

←
The unique museum facade, designed by Celso Prado Pastor

Collection Highlights

Third floor

▽ The entrance features a dark-glass antechamber, which blocks UV rays and allows the eyes to adjust to the muted, sepulchral lighting. Highlights on this floor include a fabulous collection of ceramics depicting various aspects of Moche life such as hunting, fishing, fighting, and sexual encounters. Gods and religious ceremonies were also popular subjects, such as this image of Ai Apaec *(right)*, the main deity of the Moche people.

Second floor

▷ Much of this floor is dedicated to the Lord of Sipán Sector, where some of the most dazzling finds of the tomb are displayed. There are splendid adornments for the face and body of the Lord of Sipán, who archeologists believe was a warrior-priest of high rank, including ear ornaments and a gold peanut necklace, made from large, peanut-shaped beads *(right)*. Constructed principally of gold, silver, copper, and turquoise, this veritable treasure trove has been exhibited around the world.

First floor

▽ Finally, at the base of the museum, a precise reproduction of the Lord of Sipán's tomb is displayed in all its splendor. The Lord was flanked by two warriors, one of whom was buried with his dog. The bodies of two young females were interred at his head and feet, and a small boy was found in a niche above the burial. One of the men and the women were missing their left feet - the reason for the amputation remains a mystery.

EXPERIENCE MORE

3

Huaca del Sol y de la Luna

🅰C4 🕒5 miles (8 km) SE of Trujillo on the Pan-American Hwy, then unpaved road 🚌 🕒9am-3pm Tue-Sun 🌐huacas demoche.pe

This archeological site includes two pyramids. The imposing Huaca del Sol (Temple of the Sun) used to be 1,132 ft (345 m) long and 535 ft (160 m) wide, before it was ransacked by treasure hunters in the 17th century. Though only a third of the temple remains, it is still the largest pre-Columbian adobe structure in the Americas. The Spanish chronicler Antonio de la Calancha believed it was built by almost 200,000 workers, in around AD 500. The interior is closed to the public.

Close by is the smaller, six-level Huaca de la Luna (Temple of the Moon). It has interconnected rooms and patios with friezes of anthropomorphic figures. The Museo Huacas de Moche is on site.

4

Chan Chan

🅰C4 🕒4 miles (7 km) W of Trujillo 🚌🚊From Lima 🕒9am-6pm Mon-Sat 🌐museochanchan.pe

On the UNESCO World Heritage List since 1986, this site is considered the largest adobe city in the world and one of Trujillo's major attractions. Chan Chan was built between AD 1100 and 1300 as the capital of the Chimú Empire and residence of the Tacaynamu dynasty. This pre-Columbian metropolis once had a population of 100,000, many of whom were skilled artisans, and military personnel. The Chimú sovereigns ceded to the Incas after a siege in around 1470.

The complex is made up of nine sectors or citadels. The best preserved and most visited is Ciudadela Tschudi. A marked route leads through large sunken plazas, chambers, restored corridors, temple cloisters, residential areas, and military barracks. Most have friezes depicting sea creatures.

> Exploring the Chan Chan complex; detail of the well-preserved remains (inset)

THE PERUVIAN HAIRLESS DOG

Known as *perros sin pelo*, this ancient breed can be traced back to pre-Columbian times. Ceramic hairless dogs from the Vicus, Moche, Chimú, and Chancay cultures have been excavated along the north and central coast, offering evidence of their Peruvian origins. The Inca kept them as pets to please the Sun god and Moon goddess. The Spanish conquest nearly caused the breed's extinction, but fortunately these alert, intelligent animals survived in rural areas, where people believed in their magical forces.

Over the years, some of the structures have been damaged by floods, as well as by invaders and *huaqueros* (tomb-raiders).

Huaca El Dragón is the best-restored structure of the Chan Chan complex. It is also called Huaca Arco Iris (rainbow) after the motifs found on its inner walls dating back to the Nazca, Wari, or Tiahuanaco cultures. There is a museum on site, too.

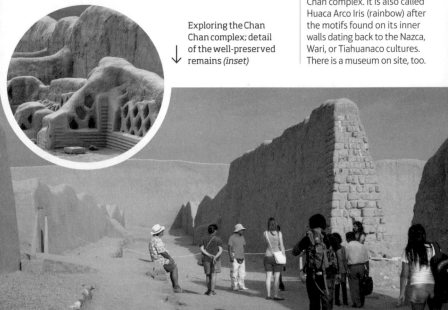

→

The "reed horse" sea rafts of Huanchaco along the coast at sunset

 ⑤ 🍴

Huanchaco

🏛C4 📍7 miles (12 km) NW of Trujillo 🚌✈ From Lima

The best beach resort near Trujillo retains some of its fishing village ambience. Although the water is too cold for swimming, it is perfect for surfers all year round. The town's 16th-century past is visible in the Baroque-style church of La Virgen del Perpetuo Socorro. The major attractions, however, are the sea rafts or *caballitos de totora*, which translates literally as "little reed horses". Locals, who still use them, are the only ones who can build these vessels, first used by the Moche some 2,500 years ago.

 ⑥ 🍴 🏛

Chiclayo

🏛C3 📍124 miles (200 km) N of Trujillo ✈ From Lima 🚌 From Lima & Trujillo

Founded in the mid-16th century as a rural village, Chiclayo today is a commercial hub and northern Peru's second-largest city after Trujillo. Major attractions here are the Neo-Classical-style cathedral, built in 1869, and the Mercado Modelo (Central Market). The market is considered one of the most interesting in Peru, offering everything from herbs and healing charms used here by *curanderos* and *brujos* (witch-doctors and healers), to mats, hats, woven straw baskets, and other products. Chiclayo serves as the most convenient starting point to visit all major archeological and historical features in the area.

About 6 miles (10 km) north of Chiclayo lies the 17th-century town of Lambayeque. It has some fine colonial houses with wooden balconies and wrought-iron, grillwork windows. Casa de la Logia o Montjoy on Calle 2 de Mayo has a 210-ft (64-m) balcony, said to be the longest in colonial America. The other big attractions here are the museums. The state-of-the-art Museo Tumbas Reales de Sipán exhibits the fabulous discovery of the Lord of Sipán's tomb (p230). The **Museo Arqueológico Nacional Brüning** has a fine collection of Sicán, Moche, Chimú, and Lambayeque archeological artifacts collected by German engineer Hans Heinrich Brüning (1848–1928).

Another museum worth a visit is **Museo Nacional de Sicán** in Ferreñafe. On display here are golden artifacts, ceramics, and other utensils; found in the tombs at Batán Grande, they rival the Sipán finds.

Museo Arqueológico Nacional Brüning

♿🚫📷 🏛Av Huamachuco, Cuadra 8, Lambayeque 📞074 282 110 🕐9am-5pm daily 🌐museos.cultura.pe/museos/museo-arqueológico-nacional-brüning

Museo Nacional de Sicán

♿🚫📷🏛 🏛Av Batán Grande, Cua dra 9, Ferreñafe 📞074 286 469 🕐9am-5pm Tue-Sun

⑦

Complejo Arqueológico El Brujo

🏛C4 📍28 miles (45 km) NW of Trujillo, off the Pan-American Hwy toward Magdalena de Cao 📞939 326 240 🕐9am-3:30pm daily

In 2006, archeologists announced the discovery of a well-preserved and tattooed 1,500-year-old mummy of a young woman. She was found in a mud-brick pyramid called Huaca Cao Viejo, part of the El Brujo Moche complex. In the tomb with La Señora de Cao (The Lady of Cao) were funeral objects such as gold sewing needles and metal jewelry, which are now on display.

↑ Distinctive Moche jar at the Complejo Arqueológico El Brujo

 8

Máncora

🅰 B2 🚗 14 miles (23 km) S of Punta Sal 🚌 From Tumbes
🌐 vivamancora.com

Máncora is without doubt the trendiest beach town in Peru. Young surfers, Western backpackers, and well-to-do Limeños all head to this town for its enchanting beaches, mainly Las Pocitas, 3 miles (5 km) to the south. It is a great surfing destination too and is renowned for its lively bars and clubs.

About 7 miles (11 km) to the east are the Baños de Barro, natural hot springs with sulfurous waters believed to have curative properties.

9

Batán Grande

🅰 C3 🚗 24 miles (38 km) NE of Chiclayo on the road to Ferreñafe 🚌 Colectivo from Chiclayo

An interesting blend of nature and history, Batán Grande consists of around 20 adobe pyramids situated in the heart of the Santuario Histórico Bosque de Pomac, an ancient forest of *algarrobo* (mesquite) trees rich in birdlife. Between 1978 and 2001, Japanese archeologist Izumi Shimada unveiled many tombs from the middle Sicán period (AD 900–1100). Some of the best gold artifacts found here are displayed at the Museo Nacional de Sicán *(p233)*. The Sicán culture (in Muchik language, *Sicán* means "Temple of the Moon") arose after the Moche fell, but the site was abandoned in the 12th century.

10

Tumbes

🅰 B2 🚗 90 miles (140 km) N of Talara 🚌 From Lima

Tumbes is a small, peaceful city originally inhabited by the Tallanes, who are related to the coastal communities of Ecuador. The Spanish conquistadores arrived here in 1527. The city was also the point of dispute in a border war with Ecuador between 1940 and 1941 that was finally won by Peru.

About 8 miles (13 km) northeast of Tumbes is the Reserva de Biósfera del Noroeste (Northwestern Biosphere Reserve), covering 702 sq miles (1,818 sq km), best accessed through a paved road along the Río Tumbes by the town of Limón.

11

Zorritos

🅰 B2 🚗 16 miles (28 km) SW of Tumbes 🚌 Colectivo from Tumbes

The area's biggest fishing village, Zorritos has great beaches. It's also home to many migratory birds, making it a favorite with bird-watchers.

About 6 miles (9 km) south of Zorritos, at KM1232 of the Pan-American Highway, is Bocapán, the main access road to the Parque Nacional Cerros de Amotape. Created in 1975, this national park

> **Young surfers, Western backpackers, and well-to-do Limeños all head to Máncora for its enchanting beaches, mainly Las Pocitas, 3 miles (5 km) to the south.**

← The superb beach at Máncora, Peru's best sandy beach

Cerro Purgatorio, a 646-ft (197-m) promontory lookout also known as Cerro La Raya, after a stingray that, as legend has it, lives within it.

Túcume is thought to have been a center of pilgrimage where there were high priests with great understanding of agro-astrology. Significant studies were conducted here by Thor Heyerdahl, an ethnographer and explorer. Heyerdahl found evidence of a pre-Columbian maritime culture, confirming theories that inspired his journey across the Pacific Ocean from Peru to Polynesia in 1947.

Evidence of the Chimú and Inca occupations of the region has been found in dedicatory offerings, burials, and ceramics. In the Huaca Larga pyramid, archeologists found the lavish burial site of a prominent Inca general. Some archeologists believe that the fire that razed central Huaca Larga coincided with the beginning of the colonial period in Peru.

The on-site Museo de Sitio Túcume exhibits the works of Heyerdahl and American archaeologist Wendell C. Bennet – the first to scientifically excavate the site in 1936.

conserves a large dry equatorial forest and protects endangered animals, including the Tumbes crocodile and South American river otter. Visitors need to get permission from the Tumbes office of the National Institute of Natural Resources, SERNANP, to enter the park.

12

Túcume

⒜ C3 ⒜ 21 miles (33 km) N of Chiclayo on the Old Pan-American Hwy to Piura ☎ 978 977 578 🚌 From Chiclayo and Lambayeque ⊙ 10am–4:30pm Tue–Sun 🖥 tucume.com

Also known as the Valley of the Pyramids, this site is located in the plains of the Lambayeque Valley and was the capital of the Lambayeque culture. The settlement was occupied by the Chimú from 1375 to 1450, until the Incas conquered the Chimú kingdom and inhabited the city until 1532.

Túcume consists of 26 major adobe pyramids about 131 ft (40 m) high and other lesser buildings constructed around

↑ Artifacts and pottery on display at Túcume's archeological museum

EAT

Fiesta Chiclayo Gourmet

Acclaimed chef Hector Solís adds contemporary flair to the traditional cuisine of Lambayeque, cooked by age-old methods.

⒜ C3 ⒜ Av Salaverry 1820, Chiclayo 🖥 restaurantfiestagourmet.com

 ⓈⓈⓈ

Big Ben

Sip a pisco sour and sample scallops or tasty *parihuela* (seafood soup) overlooking the ocean.

⒜ C4 ⒜ Av Larco 1184, Huanchaco 🖥 bigbenhuanchaco.com

ⓈⓈⓈ

Eduardo El Brujo

There's no better place to sample the regional delicacy, *conchas negras*. These black clams only grow nearby; try them as ceviche here.

⒜ B2 ⒜ Jirón Malecón Benavides 850, Tumbes ☎ 972 859 285

 ⓈⓈⓈ

La Sirena d'Juan

Savor tuna sashimi or ceviche, lobster, freshly made pastas, and excellent desserts made by Cordon Bleu-trained chef Juan Seminario. There's a good wine list, too.

⒜ B2 ⒜ Av Piura 316, Máncora ☎ 073 258 173 ⊙ 12:30–4pm & 7–11pm Wed–Mon

 ⓈⓈⓈ

THE NORTHERN HIGHLANDS

Evidence of human habitation in this area dates back to around 7000 BC, but it was the Chachapoya culture first left a lasting impression on the region. From around AD 800, these expert agriculturalists carved terraces into mountain slopes and covered lowland areas with intricately drained field systems. The spectacular ruins of the imposing citadel of Kuélap (AD 900–1100) are a testimony to Chachapoyan skill. The group's wonderful weavings were much admired by the Inca, who conquered these "warriors of the clouds", as they were known, in the late 15th century, shortly before the arrival of the Spanish. In 1532, only a year after landing in Peru, Pizarro and his troops famously captured the Inca leader Atahualpa in the regional capital of Cajamarca. Atahualpa was ransomed, but Pizarro, upon receiving the payment, did not release him; the Inca leader was executed nine months later, thereby precipitating the end of the Inca Empire. Today, visitors come to Cajamarca to see Atahualpa's El Cuarto del Rescate (Ransom Chamber) and the thermal baths where he was said to be relaxing when surprised by the Spanish, as well as to experience the city's extravagant carnival celebrations.

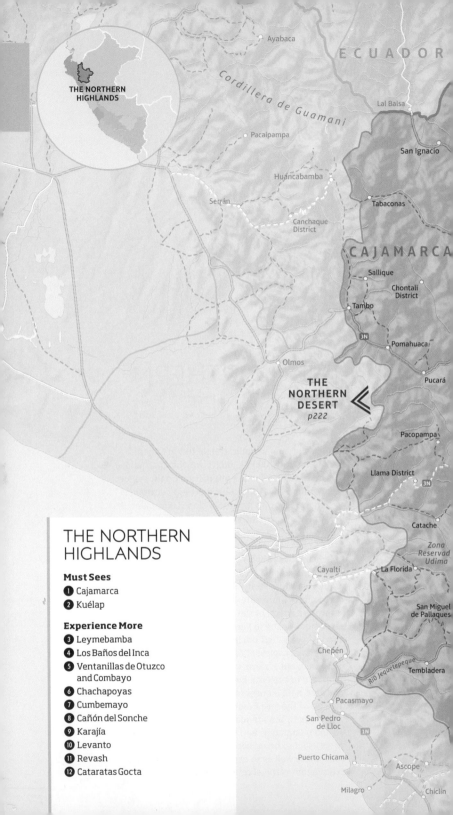

ECUADOR

Ayabaca

Cordillera de Guamani

Lal Balsa

Pacaipampa

San Ignacio

Huancabamba

Tabaconas

Serrán

Canchaque
District

CAJAMARCA

Sallique

Chontali
District

Tambo

3N

Pomahuaca

Olmos

Pucará

**THE
NORTHERN
DESERT**
p222

Pacopampa

Llama District

3N

Catache

Zona
Reservad
Udima

Cayaltí

La Florida

San Miguel
de Pallaques

Chepén

Tembladera

Río Jequetepeque

Pacasmayo

San Pedro
de Lloc

3N

Puerto Chicama

Ascope

Milagro

Chiclin

THE NORTHERN HIGHLANDS

Must Sees
1 Cajamarca
2 Kuélap

Experience More
3 Leymebamba
4 Los Baños del Inca
5 Ventanillas de Otuzco
and Combayo
6 Chachapoyas
7 Cumbemayo
8 Cañón del Sonche
9 Karajía
10 Levanto
11 Revash
12 Cataratas Gocta

THE NORTHERN
HIGHLANDS

① Ⓜ Ⓨ ▢

CAJAMARCA

🅐 C3 🏠 532 miles (856 km) N of Lima ✈ 2 miles (3 km)
🚌 From Lima & Trujillo ℹ iPerú, Jirón Cruz de Piedra 601;
51 76 365 166

Laid out in a traditional Spanish grid plan, the Andean capital of Cajamarca has been a favorite haunt of travelers since Inca times. Its colonial- and independence-era architecture rivals that of Cusco and Arequipa for elegance. Cajamarca also makes a great base from which to explore the countryside renowned for its dairy products. The best time to visit is during Peru's most raucous celebration, Carnaval.

① Ⓜ
Museo Arqueológico Horacio Urteaga

🅐 Del Batán 289 📞 076 821 546 🕘 8am-2:30pm Mon-Fri 🚫 Public hols

Run by Cajamarca University, the Archeological Museum consists of an informative run-through of archeological finds in this north Andean region, from around 3,000 years ago to the recent past. The display ranges from ceramics and textiles to black-and-white photographs, mummies, drawings of the Cumbemayo petroglyphs (p245), and a collection of carved stones. Of note are the paintings by local artist Andrés Zevallos.

② ⊗ Ⓜ
Iglesia de San Francisco

🅐 Plaza de Armas 📞 933 515 663 🕘 7am-noon & 4-8pm daily

The church and convent of San Francisco rivals Trujillo's cathedral on the Plaza de Armas with its Neo-Classical appearance. It has a fine altar, catacombs, and a religious art museum. To the right of the church is the Capilla de la Virgen de los Dolores, the city's prettiest chapel. It houses a statue of the town's patron saint, La Virgen de los Dolores, which is carried around the town during religious celebrations.

③
La Catedral

🅐 Plaza de Armas
🕘 8-11am & 6-9pm daily

On the northwest of the Plaza de Armas – with its lawns, benches, and imaginatively trimmed topiary – rises the cathedral. Begun in the 17th century, it was not consecrated until 1762. Its fine carved-stone facade is a beautiful example of the Baroque style championed in colonial Peru. The main altar is in the Churrigueresque style, covered tip-to-toe with gold leaf. The walls of the cathedral incorporate a large amount of Inca masonry.

↑ The stunning facade of the Iglesia de San Francisco, lit up at night

←

Quintessential colonial architecture near Cajamarca's Plaza de Armas

El Cuarto del Rescate

🏛 Amalia Puga 722
🕘 9:30am–2:30pm Tue–Sat
🚫 Public hols

This house (the Ransom Chamber) is the only remaining Inca building in the town, displaying its typical trapezoidal niches and doors, and some original masonry. The chamber is 39 ft (12m) long, 23 ft (7m) wide, and 10 ft (3m) high, and has plenty of historical significance. One version claims that Atahualpa, the last sovereign Inca ruler, was held captive by the Spaniards in this room. Another says that it was the room which the Inca promised to fill with gold and silver for his freedom.

El Complejo de Belén

🏛 Calle Belén 🕘 9am–1pm & 2:30–5pm Wed–Sun
🚫 Public hols ℹ️ iPerú tourist office, Jirón Cruz de Piedra 601; 076 365 166; 9am–6pm Mon–Sat (to 1pm Sun)

This colonial-era complex spreads across a group of buildings with several patios and institutions. These include the tourist office, the Institute of Culture (INC), a small medical museum, and one of Cajamarca's finest churches,

the Iglesia Belén. The church is regarded as one of Peru's best examples of the Baroque style, with its gold-leaf altars and an ornate cupola with oversized cherubs holding a centerpiece made up of flowers.

The interesting Museo Arqueólogico y Etnográfico lies across the street (at Junín y Belén) in what once served as the Women's Hospital and morgue. It houses a wide collection of objects, ceramics, and weavings from the region.

Cerro Santa Apolonia

🏛 SW of Plaza de Armas 🚌

This hill is a great spot for getting a feel of the city and can be explored via a series of splendid walks through gardens with native plants. Located here are the remains of Chavín- and Inca-era stone carvings. One of the rocks, known as the Silla del Inca (the Seat of the Inca), is shaped like a throne.

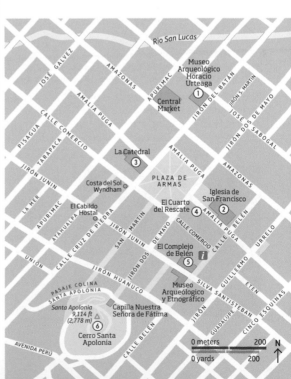

Did You Know?

Kuélap is thought to have contained three times more stone than the Great Pyramid at Giza in Egypt.

→

One of hundreds of round stone houses throughout the site

2 ✍ Ⓜ

KUÉLAP

🅰 C3 🏠 58 miles (93 km) S of Chachapoyas 📞 939 392 347 🚌 From Chachapoyas to Tingo, then a four-hour hike 🚠 From Nuevo Tingo 🕐 8am–5pm daily

The imposing fortress of Kuélap is the main attraction of the Chachapoyas region. It ranks among the finest and most impressive ruins in Peru, occupying a perfect vantage point, set on a dramatic ridge high above the Río Utcubamba, amid verdant, rolling countryside.

↑ Beautiful bromeliads and orchids growing on one of the ruined walls

Reclaimed by the surrounding forest for more than 300 years, it wasn't until 1843 that this site was rediscovered by a local judge, and it wasn't truly explored until the late 19th and early 20th centuries. Ceramics discovered in Kuélap indicate that the area had been inhabited since AD 500, but the majority of construction occurred between AD 900 and 1100. The result is a fortress bigger than any other single structure in Peru. The complex had an outer wall protecting over 400 circular houses, thought to have been home to about 3,500 people. It also had terraces, outlying settlements, and burial areas outside the main walls. When the Incas arrived in around 1470, they found Kuélap, full of formidable

Chachapoyan warriors, a difficult place to conquer. They were unable to take control of the fort and only five Inca buildings have been found here.

Exploring Kuélap

The funnel-shaped entrance, one of three main entrances into the fortress, becomes narrower as you go farther in, until eventually it is wide enough for only one person.

El Tintero is the most visited structure within the walls and means "inkwell" because of its shape. Early surveys attributed a variety of functions to this building, ranging from a water reservoir to a jail – even a torture chamber and a cemetery. However, studies now suggest that the building had astronomical functions, since the small entrance lines up with the sun at the most favorable times for planting crops.

The 23-ft (7-m) high lookout tower, Torreón, at the north end of Pueblo Alto, is one of the main features at the ruins and provide views in every direction. Here, archeologists found an arsenal of broken stone axe heads and, piled on the floor, 2,500 stones of a perfect size to fit in the slingshots that defenders would have used.

↑ The mysterious inverted-cone-shaped structure, El Tintero, on the southern side of the citadel

THE CHACHAPOYA PEOPLE

The name Chachapoya is commonly believed to come from the conflation of two Quechua words, *sacha* and *puyu*, together translating as forest-cloud. The Chachapoya people were famous for their shamans, and were known as great sorcerers and herbalists. The people were skilled agriculturalists, and renowned for their weaving. The finds displayed at the Museo Leymebamba *(p244)* testify to the range of techniques, such as plain weaves, brocades, and embroidery, used on a single textile.

EXPERIENCE MORE

Leymebamba

D3 **50 miles (80 km) SE of Chachapoyas**

The attractive market town of Leymebamba, about a 10-hour drive from Cajamarca, is not covered by most travel itineraries of Peru. However, the surrounding countryside is wonderful for exploring on foot or horseback. Just south of the town, the **Museo Leymebamba** houses the amazing archeological finds from the nearby Laguna de los Cóndores. Among the 5,000 artifacts on display are some 150 exceptionally well-preserved mummies, plus an ethnographic display on life in the region. The museum also has a colorful orchid garden, planted with more than 100 native species of this plant. Just across the road, a small café serves excellent snacks and has feeders that attract 17 species of hummingbirds. The town has a handful of lodgings or can be visited on a day trip from Chachapoyas.

Museo Leymebamba

 Av Austria, San Miguel **10am–4:30pm daily** **peru.travel/en/attractions/leymebamba-museum**

Los Baños del Inca

C3 **3 miles (5 km) E of Cajamarca** **6am–6:30pm daily**

A pleasant way to spend an afternoon is to wallow in the thermal baths at the Baños del Inca, just a short taxi or bus ride from Cajamarca. The baths date back to pre-Inca times. It is believed that the last Inca, Atahualpa, and his army had camped at the baths when Spanish conquistador Pizarro arrived – hence the name.

The resort is popular on weekends, when you can expect to share the bath with dozens of strangers. There are a few pools at varying temperatures and prices. The complex has a modest restaurant and hotel, and is equipped with a sauna.

Ventanillas de Otuzco and Combayo

C3 **Otuzco: 5 miles (8 km) NE of Cajamarca** **From Cajamarca** **8am–6pm daily**

One of the oldest cemeteries in Peru, the Ventanillas de Otuzco date back about 3,500 years. The necropolis comprises a series of burial niches carved into the volcanic rock of the cliff, some of which are decorated with carvings. The chieftains of Cajamarca were buried in these niches. From a distance, they look like windows, hence the Spanish name *ventanillas* (little windows).

A collection of these niches can be found at Combayo, also 18 miles (30 km) southeast of Cajamarca. Both the sites can be visited on a tour from Cajamarca. Otuzco is a 90-minute walk from Los Baños del Inca.

> **LA LAGUNA DE LOS CÓNDORES**
>
> Hidden away in cloud forest, the spellbinding Laguna de los Cóndores is also known as the Laguna de las Momias (Lake of the Mummies). In 1997, hundreds of mummies, overlooked by the Spanish, were recovered from cliff tombs surrounding the lake. They now reside in Leymebamba's museum. It's a demanding 12-hour trail to the tombs, which climbs to 12,139 ft (3,700 m) before descending to the lake shore. A three-day trip can be organized with agencies in Chachapoyas or Leymebamba.

6

Chachapoyas

C3 **204 miles (329 km) NE of Cajamarca** **From Lima** **From Cajamarca**

Though it is an unremarkable place in itself, good transportation links make Chachapoyas the gateway to northern Peru's finest archeological sites. Its pretty central square hosts a bronze bust of independence leader Toribio Rodríguez de Mendoza and is flanked by colonial buildings. One houses the Museo el Reino de las Nubes, which introduces local sights, including a scale model of Kuélap (p242). For a fine overview of the city, the Mirador de Luya Urco in the northwest affords panoramas across the rooftops.

The city is the ideal base from which to visit nearby ruins attributed to the Chachapoya, or "Cloud People," an unusually fair-skinned race that excelled in building mountain-top fortresses and buried their dead in cliffside mausoleums. They were absorbed into the Inca Empire sometime in the 15th century.

↑ Hikers at one of the austere, monk-like rock formations at Cumbemayo

7

Cumbemayo

C3 **13 miles (20 km) SW of Cajamarca**

The mountainous region of Cumbemayo, southwest of Cajamarca (p240), is famous for a canal and aqueduct carved from rock and pieced together by deft stonemasons with great skill. The structure is thought to be about 2,000 years old and perhaps had ritual as well as practical significance, considering the great effort that went into its

construction. It originally carried water from the Atlantic watershed over to the Pacific side through an intricate system of tunnels and canals, some of which are still in use.

To one side of the aqueduct is a rock, shaped like a face, into which an artificial cave has been carved. Inside the cave, with the aid of a torch one can make out 3,000-year-old petroglyphs which have feline features. This is a hallmark of the Chavín (p69) style, which dominated this part of Peru at that time.

Don't miss the odd natural rock formation known as the Bosque de Piedras (Stone Forest), clearly visible from the Cajamarca–Cumbemayo road. Here, limestone rock masses have eroded, forming tapered shapes which are reminiscent of the human form, giving them their Spanish name, los frailones (the big monks).

←

The fascinating "little windows," or ventanillas, at Otuzco

EAT

Café Fusiones

Sandwiches, salads and desserts using regional organic products are on offer in a colorful and cosy setting. Organic local coffee is roasted and ground on site.

C3 **Jirón Ortiz Arriet 779, Chachapoyas** **cafefusiones.com**

Kentikafé

This outdoor café serves up delicious cakes, but the real attraction are the hummingbirds that come to sip from feeders in the trees.

D3 **Av Austria s/n, Leymebamba** **971 118 273**

THE SPATULETAIL

Endemic to this region of Peru, the marvelous spatuletail is a rare hummingbird species. It uses its four tail feathers, two of which end in dark blue disks, in dazzling courtship dances. Its coloring is exquisite, with a blue cap of feathers and a turquoise throat. Illegal huntings to obtain the male's heart which is considered an aphrodisiac, have caused a dramatic decline in their population.

Cañón del Sonche

D3 · 5 miles (8 km) N of Chachapoyas · From Chachapoyas

Around 5 miles (8 km) north of Chachapoyas (p245), a viewing platform (for which there is a small entrance charge) perches on the edge of the 3,156-ft (962-m) Cañón del Sonche. Verdant, folded valley sides plunge into this dramatic canyon, where the Sonche river has carved a 7-mile (11.5-km) route between the mountains.

When the skies are clear, it's possible to see Gocta Falls in the distance north, while turkey vultures glide in the skies above. In the rainy season (December–April) the canyon is transformed, with waterfalls cascading down from the mountains and into the valley. At sunset, the diminishing light brings a delicate, other-worldly hue to the scenery.

Karajía

C3 · 30 miles (48 km) SW of Chachapoyas, near Luya · From Chachapoyas

Oversized, colorfully painted vertical sarcophagi made of earth, wood, and straw, and decorated with faces, were the final resting places of important members of the famous Chachapoyan culture. Many of these coffins have been discovered and the ones found at Karajía are the easiest to visit from Chachapoyas. The site is reached by minibuses from Chachapoyas to Luya, from where it is a 3-hour hike. Tours from Chachapoyas are also available. Karajía is a 45-minute walk from Cruzpata.

Cavernas Quiocta, near Lamud, a town about an hour and a half's drive from Karajía, can be combined with a visit to Karajía. This series of caves contains Inca remains, pools, and geological formations. Visitors need to ask for a guide in Lamud and should visit between 8am and 5pm.

Levanto

D3 · 14 miles (22 km) S of Chachapoyas

An original and unrestored Inca road joins Chachapoyas with Levanto, which is situated at a height of 9,488 ft (2,892 m).

It was first settled by the Spanish in 1532, and remains a small village with only a few remnants of its colonial past.

A few miles away is the site of Yalape (built 1100–1300) which has classic circular buildings adorned with geometric friezes, and the remains of an irrigation system. This is part of the second-largest known Chachapoyan fortress after Kuélap, with other sites nearby.

Most visitors make it a day trip, arriving by the morning bus uphill from Chachapoyas and returning along the Inca road downhill on foot.

HIDDEN GEM
Huaylla Belén

A few hours' drive from Chachapoyas, a winding river known as the "Silver Serpent," filled with rainbow trout, snakes through verdant meadows in the Huaylla Belén Valley. This picturesque spot is ideal for relaxed picnicking or fly fishing. Several operators offer guided fishing trips.

→
The cliff mausoleums of Revash, looking like miniature clay houses

11

Revash

D3 37 miles (60 km) S of Chachapoyas, near Santo Tomás

Named for the Revash culture, contemporary with the Chachapoyans (*p242*), this site is famed for its *chullpas* (funerary chambers). These small, multi-hued buildings perch precariously on ledges high up on the limestone cliffs. They are made from mud and stone walls, then plastered over and painted, and topped with peculiar gabled roofs. The *chullpas* have been looted, but a dozen burials and funerary offerings were discovered by archeologists. A variety of pictographs can be seen on the cliff behind the structures.

There are daily minibuses from Chachapoyas to Santo Tomás, the nearest town to the Revash site. Visitors should disembark at the Santo Tomás turnoff. Allow three hours for the steep climb up to the ruins. Near Santo Tomás is the village of Yerbuena, which has a busy Sunday market.

12

Cataratas Gocta

C/D3 Near San Pablo

In 2002 it was discovered that this huge waterfall, hidden in the cloud forest and known only to the locals, was one of the highest in the world. Stefan Ziemendorff, a German hydro-engineer, saw the falls on the Río Cocahuayco and his preliminary measurements of its height were an astounding 2,531 ft (771 m). Though this is a two-tiered fall, the tiers are close enough for the World Waterfall Database to consider them to be one. It rates them among the top ten in the world.

Gocta is on the east of the main Chachapoyas–Pedro Ruíz road. Taxis from either town can be taken for San Pablo, where informal guides take visitors on a trail which lasts 1–2 hours to a view of the upper falls. En route, good views of both tiers are available. To see the falls from the bottom, it is necessary to backtrack and take another taxi to the smaller hamlet of Cocachimba, and then to walk about three hours each way through the cloud forest.

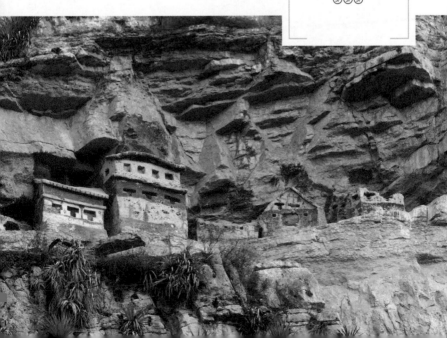

THE AMAZON BASIN

The incredibly ecologically diverse Amazonian rainforest is home to more species of animals than any other area on earth. However, little is known about the history of its original human inhabitants. At the height of the Inca Empire, the upper Amazon Basin was incorporated into Antisuyo (the empire's eastern quarter) and scarlet macaw feathers and jungle fruits were traded for metal tools. After the conquest, the Spaniards concentrated on the coastal and highland regions. Their greatest impact was in the unintended introduction of diseases, such as smallpox and influenza, to which citizens had no resistance.

In the 16th century, colonial outposts were established in places such as Moyobamba, but the Amazon was not permanently occupied until a few missions were built in the 18th century. With the 1880s rubber boom, the population exploded. Four decades later, the boom collapsed and the once-opulent towns survived by logging, exploitation of jungle crops, and export of animals for zoos.

The discovery of oil in the 1960s fueled another population boom, soon followed by a nascent tourism industry. Slowly, cities such as Iquitos, Pucallpa, and Puerto Maldonado gained renewed importance, and *ribereños* (river-dwellers) began to clear forests for agriculture.

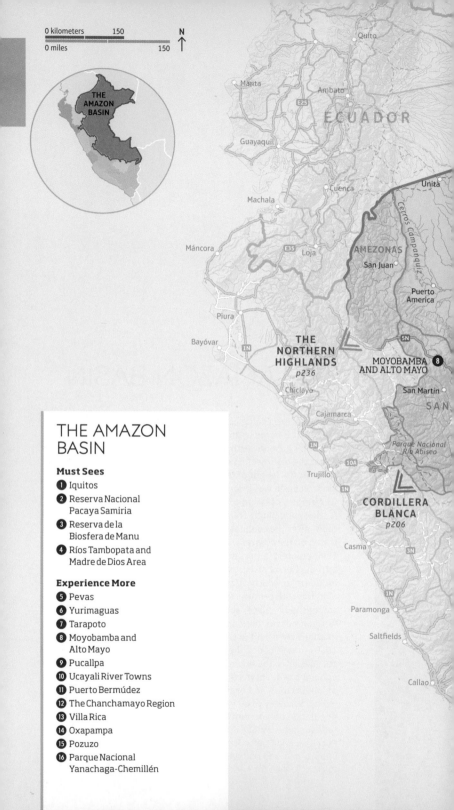

THE AMAZON BASIN

Must Sees

1. Iquitos
2. Reserva Nacional Pacaya Samiria
3. Reserva de la Biosfera de Manu
4. Ríos Tambopata and Madre de Dios Area

Experience More

5. Pevas
6. Yurimaguas
7. Tarapoto
8. Moyobamba and Alto Mayo
9. Pucallpa
10. Ucayali River Towns
11. Puerto Bermúdez
12. The Chanchamayo Region
13. Villa Rica
14. Oxapampa
15. Pozuzo
16. Parque Nacional Yanachaga-Chemillén

↑ The renowned floating wooden houses in Iquitos

 ❶

IQUITOS

▲E2 **△373 miles (600 km) NE of Pucallpa** **✈From Panama only** **✈From Lima** **⛴From Pucallpa or Yurimaguas** **ⓘPlaza de Armas, Napo 161; www.iquitos-peru.com**

On the banks of the majestic Río Amazonas, the atmospheric city of Iquitos is the undisputed capital of the Peruvian Amazon. Founded as a Jesuit mission in 1797, the tiny river port was transformed by the rubber boom of the 1880s into a thriving town, with a lovely waterfront, markets, and architectural gems.

 ①

Malecón Tarapacá

One block off the main square, Iquitos' waterfront boulevard is the perfect place to unwind, whether browsing the stalls at the Centro Artesenal Anaconda for crafts, or sipping a cocktail in an outdoor bar at sunset.

💬 INSIDER TIP
Reaching Iquitos

This is the largest city in the world that is inaccessible by road; you can either fly from Lima or take a boat from Pucallpa or Yurimaguas.

②

Museo de las Culturas Indígenas Amazónicas

⌂Malecón Tarapacá 332 **☎065 235 809** **🕙10am-6pm Thu-Tue** **🌐fund amazonia.org**

Showcasing the varied traditions and rituals of 40 of the Peruvian Amazon's Indigenous peoples, this fascinating anthropological museum contains a wealth of information and artifacts,

 →
Sculpture from the Museo de las Culturas Indígenas Amazónicas

from extravagant ceremonial headdresses and jewelry to ancient weaponry and musical instruments.

③

Museo Barco Histórico "Ayapua"

⌂Moored by Plaza Ramón Castilla **🕙10am-6pm Thu-Tue** **🌐fundamazonia.org**

Built in Germany in 1906, and lovingly restored, this steam-ship-turned-museum offers insights into

Iquitos' boom era. It explores the extravagance of the notorious rubber barons, such as Fitzcarrald *(p259)*, fed by the exploitation of the Amazon's natural resources and populations.

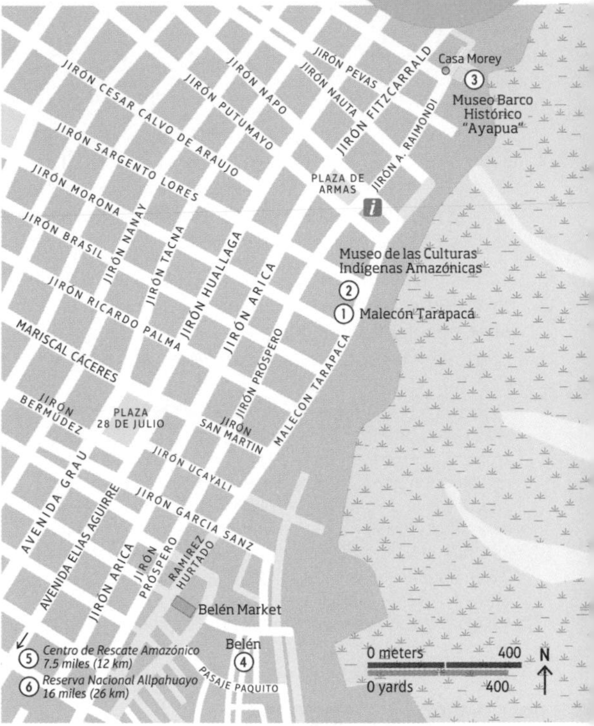

4 Belén

South of the city center, the vast, sprawling market of Belén is the beating heart of Iquitos and is famous for its huge variety of jungle produce. Whether you explore on your own, or sign up for a guided tour, Pasaje Paquito, a narrow alleyway filled with stalls selling unique jungle remedies, is not to be missed. Below the market, the famous wooden houses of Belén barrio perch on stilts or float on balsa rafts when the river waters are high.

5 Centro de Rescate Amazónico

Carretera Iquitos-Nauta, 2.8 miles (4.5 km) SW of Iquitos 991 476 519 9am-3pm Tue-Sun

Working with a US aquarium, this Amazonian rescue center predominantly rehabilitates orphaned manatees. The guided tour (usually in Spanish) lasts one hour and tells you all you need to know about the rescue, rehabilitation and release program of these extraordinary-looking and elusive aquatic mammals.

The vast, sprawling market of Belén is the beating heart of Iquitos and is famous for its huge variety of jungle produce.

STAY

Casa Morey

This historic mansion features period furniture and modern comforts. Reserve an upstairs suite with French windows and a spectacular river view.

Plaza Ramón Castilla
casamorey.com

S/ S/ S/

6 Reserva Nacional Allpahuayo-Mishana

Carretera Iquitos-Nauta, 16 miles (26 km) S of Iquitos From Iquitos 956 750 555 8am-5pm daily

Known in particular for its rare white-sand forests, or *varillales*, this relatively diminutive (in Amazonian terms) yet biodiverse reserve lies a short ride outside Iquitos. It has an interpretive center and a short trail, popular with bird-watchers, drawn by over 500 bird species, five of which are endemic to the reserve. Another interpretive path, close the reserve's scientific research center, takes you on an informative tour of native Amazonian fruit trees and medicinal plants. During the high-water months (usually Dec–May), local eco-tourism operators can take you along the flooded blackwater channels of the Río Nanay, offering opportunities to swim in creeks or stay overnight in rustic lodgings with guided night walks that bring you close to the sights and sounds of the reserve's nocturnal creatures.

2 🔄 🔄

RESERVA NACIONAL PACAYA SAMIRIA

🔺E3 ⌂190 miles (306 km) SW of Iquitos 🚤 ℹSERNANP, Calle Jorge Chávez 930, Iquitos; 065 223 555

Sandwiched between the Ucayali and Marañón tributaries to the Amazon, this reserve is Peru's second-largest protected area and its largest expanse of seasonally flooded jungle. Laced with several rivers, countless creeks, and mirror-like lagoons, these black-water wetlands are extremely picturesque.

To really savor the experience at this reserve, staying several days is a must, with options ranging from a romantic river-boat cruise to a rustic lodge with daily forays into the reserve by motorized dugout. The reserve teems with wildlife, from anacondas and river turtles to 13 species of monkeys. Farther away from human habitation, elusive large mammals such as tapirs, pumas, and jaguars can even make an appearance. When water levels are low, guided night-hikes reveal a world of shy nocturnal creatures, including spiders, frogs, and snakes. Village visits are great opportunities to buy locally made crafts and experience shamanic rituals. For the truly adventurous, the Indigenous Cocama-Cocamilla of Lagunas offer unique jungle tours, paddling tourists in dugout canoes. While sleeping on makeshift beds and washing in the river is not for everyone, the silence of the forest, broken only by squawking macaws, is magical.

←

Beautiful Peruvian night monkeys in the tangled treetops

←

Traveling by boat on the Río Samiria, one of three river basins within the reserve

Did You Know?

The large Amazon or pink river dolphins *(Inia geoffrensis)*, found in the lagoons here, get pinker with age.

↑ The large Río Marañón, which borders the reserve in the north

3 ⊛ ⊛

RESERVA DE LA BIÓSFERA DE MANU

🅰 G5 ✈🚌 From Cusco 🚤 From Boca Manu 🅸 Av Cinco Los Chachacomos, F2-4, Larapa Grande, San Jerónimo, Cusco; www.visitmanu.com

This stunning UNESCO World Heritage Site covers an impressive 7,700 sq miles (20,000 sq km) of the Manu Basin. Manu Biosphere Reserve drops from 13,120 ft (4,000 m) above sea level north of Cusco, through remote cloud forests containing some of the most diverse bird populations on earth, to lowland rainforests which are home to a proliferation of jungle flora and fauna.

The reserve has three zones. Over 80 per cent lies in the "intangible zone", which is the abode of Indigenous peoples who have almost no contact with the outside world; travelers are prohibited. The "multiple-use" zone is where the one road from the highlands enters, and has several villages. The "reserved zone" is the relatively flat rainforest of the Río Manu, and traveling into this zone is possible only by boat. It allows tourism, and camping on beaches is permitted with authorized guides. Canopy platforms and towers are also available for visitors. Meandering in huge curves, the river in this zone sometimes leaves behind oxbow lakes known as *cochas*, which are the haunt of the rare giant river otters and some spectacular waterbirds.

The wide-ranging elevations of the cloud forest create ideal environments for birds, and new ornithological species are frequently recorded here. Mixed feeding flocks of dozens of bird species are a highlight, and hikers on steep trails are regularly rewarded with sightings of woolly monkeys and brown capuchins.

TOP 4 WILDLIFE TO SPOT

Toucans
These striking birds live in the forest canopy and are mainly fruit eaters.

Giant Katydids
Resembling a leaf, these are one of the thousands of insect species in the reserve.

Woolly Monkeys
This group inhabit the cloud forest and have a prehensile tail which can be used to hold objects.

Hoatzins and Horned Screamers
Both known for their ornate head plumes, these birds are commonly found around oxbow lakes.

↑ A haven of tropical forest reflected in a beautiful lake at the Reserva de la Biósfera de Manu

1 Río Manu flows across the reserve, which is home to a vast variety of flora and fauna. The meandering oxbow lakes are home to hoatzins and giant river otters.

2 Over a dozen monkey species roam the forests here. Woolly monkeys *(left)* live in groups.

3 The paradise tanager, found in the reserve's cloud forest, is a beautiful bright bird known for its seven-colored plumage.

④ ⑱

RÍOS TAMBOPATA AND MADRE DE DIOS AREA

🅰 G5 🏠 37 miles (60 km) SW of Puerto Maldonado ✈ From Lima 🚌 From Cusco

The beautiful rivers, pristine lakes, and primary rainforests of southeastern Peru are teeming with wildlife, making this the most biodiverse area of Peru's Amazon. Offering the highest concentration of jungle lodges, staffed by naturalist guides and reached only by river, this region is a must for those seeking wildlife adventures.

The stunning Río Madre de Dios flows from the highlands near the Reserva de la Biosfera de Manu into Bolivia. Most of the land south of this river is protected by national parks. The vibrant frontier city of Puerto Maldonado sits at the confluence of the Madre de Dios and Tambopata rivers, and is the best base for visiting the area. After the rubber boom, this town turned to logging, rainforest agriculture, and gold panning. Reserva Nacional de Tambopata provides excellent access to the rainforest. It attracts over 630 species of birds and 1,200 species of butterflies.

Stunning sky above the Madre de Dios region; Lago Sandoval *(inset)* ↑

1 Views of the ubiquitous corrugated-metal roofed buildings can be seen from a 98-ft- (30-m-) high tower in Puerto Maldonado.

2 Riverside mud cliffs with abnormally high salt content attract hundreds of parrots and macaws, who nibble on the clay to obtain minerals.

3 Lago Sandoval, just off the Río Madre de Dios, is home to the endangered giant river otter.

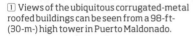

Did You Know?

The banks of the Río Tambopata are home to capybaras, the world's largest rodents.

THE SHIPIBO-CONIBO

One of Peru's 40 Indigenous peoples of the Amazon, the Shipibo-Conibo are renowned for their shamanic knowledge of medicinal plants and use of ayahuasca *(p260)*. This knowledge is reflected in the geometric designs (known as *kené*) on their ceramics, textiles, and bodies. Many Shipibo live in Ucayalí Valley, where they are under threat from illegal logging, drug trafficking, and agricultural expansion.

→ Ceramic jug

EXPERIENCE MORE

Pevas

F2 **90 miles (145 km) downriver from Iquitos** **From Iquitos**

The oldest town on the Peruvian Amazon, Pevas is made up of wooden structures, many with thatched roofs. Founded by missionaries in 1735, the town, sadly, has no buildings left from that era. It is known for not having cars, banks, or a post office. Most of the friendly inhabitants are mestizos or belong to the Bora, Huitoto, Yagua, or Ocainas groups.

The most famous resident of the town is artist Francisco Grippa, whose works can be seen in the towering hilltop studio and gallery where he lives. Visitors are always given a warm welcome and, uniquely, served beer and bananas.

Yurimaguas

D3 **240 miles (390 km) SW of Iquitos** **From Tarapoto**

Founded by a Jesuit priest in 1710, this town derives its name from two Indigenous groups, the Yoras and the Omaguas. These groups no longer exist, though there are reports that some Omaguas still live in the more remote jungle regions.

Yurimaguas remained a tiny outpost until the rubber boom, and the tilework from its early days can be seen along the east end of Avenida Arica. It became the main port on the Río Huallaga, popularly known as the Pearl of Huallaga, and today, life here continues to revolve around the colorful river port. However, the frenetic 20th-century growth seen in Iquitos and Pucallpa has passed the town by. Despite being closer to Iquitos, Yurimaguas has been the forgotten option, while Pucallpa has long been considered the best route from Lima to the Amazon. Highways now connect Yurimaguas with Tarapoto and locals hope that the town will develop.

> ## Did You Know?
>
> Yurimaguas is the last town on the Huallaga that can be reached by road; after that, it's boat or plane.

> ### AYAHUASCA
>
> Ceremonies involving drinking ayahuasca tea – a vine used in spiritual medicine and a powerful hallucinogen – have become big tourist business, offered by some lodges, who bring in a local shaman, or in specialist retreats. Most participants report positive experiences but unpleasant purging (usually vomiting) is common as the plant rids the body of chemicals such as salt; details about the shaman, venue, and ceremony need careful research.

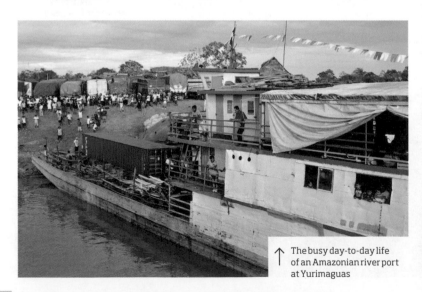

↑ The busy day-to-day life of an Amazonian river port at Yurimaguas

7

Tarapoto

⛰D3 ⏱72 miles (116 km)
SE of Moyobamba
🚌🚐From Moyobamba or
Chiclayo ℹJirón Ramírez
Hurtado; 042 526 188;
8–11am daily

The bustling town of Tarapoto is the largest and fastest-growing city in the region of San Martín. Located at a height of 1,181 ft (360 m), it is a place for fishing, swimming, and relaxing, with some of the finest waterfalls in Peru. The Río Mayo, 19 miles (30 km) away, offers white-water rafting from June to October.

Tarapoteños enjoy a good party, and their festivals feature street dances, folk music, costumed processions, and plenty of food. Among their many sought-after local drinks is *uvachado*, which is a potent brew made by soaking grapes in a cocktail of sugar-cane alcohol, cinnamon, and honey for a month.

The famous Quechua-speaking hillside town of Lamas is located 18 miles (28 km) northwest from Tarapoto. Still recovering from the devastation of the 2005 earthquake, the village welcomes travelers interested in experiencing the traditional dance, music, and folklore, seeing the thatch and mud-wall architecture, or buying arts and crafts. Guided tours are available from Tarapoto.

Of the many lakes in this area, the Laguna Sauce is the most popular, with hotels and camping

→

Intricate carving
from one of
Tarapoto's colorful
craft centers

↑ Crossing a footbridge
above the Alto Mayo
at Moyobamba

facilities, swimming, boating, and angling. Getting there is half the fun as taxis and minibuses have to cross the Río Huallaga on a balsa raft on the 32-mile (52-km) drive.

8

Moyobamba and Alto Mayo

⛰D3 ⏱99 miles (160 km)
E of Chachapoyas 🚐From
Chachapoyas 🌐moyo
bamba.com

Located on the edge of the Amazon Basin, this area was likely first inhabited by the Chachapoyas people, before the Spaniards established the small town of Moyobamba in the 1540s. Despite destructive earthquakes in the 1990s and 2000s, it has recovered well and provides good access to the high subtropical jungle. The locals call it the City of Orchids.

Moyobamba is the oldest city in this region and, according to some, Túpac Yupanqui *(p195)* made this area a base from which the Incas

made incursions into the surrounding areas. The name Moyobamba derives from the Quechua word *muyupampa*, which means a "circular plain."

Located on the upper Río Mayo basin, Moyobamba's main visitor attractions are essentially water-related. The Baños Termales San Mateo, fed by natural hot springs, are popular with the locals. They are located just to the south of town and can be reached on foot or by a *motocarro* (a motorcycle rickshaw). Just an hour's drive from Moyobamba are the Cataratas del Gera, the most popular among the many falls in the region.

STAY

Ulcumano Ecolodge
A handful of idyllic, simple cabins set in fabulous cloud forest.

⛰D5 📍Sector La Suiza
Chontabamba,
6 miles (10 km) SW
of Oxapampa
🌐ulcumano
ecolodge.com.

💲💲💲

Carolina Egg Gasthaus
Relaxing B&B in a flower-filled garden.

⛰D5 📍Av San Martín
1085, Oxapampa
🌐carolinaegg.com

💲💲💲

Albergue Frau María Egg
Wooden chalets surrounded by lush greenery. Expect superb breakfasts.

⛰D4 📍Av Los
Colonos, Pozuzo
🌐pozuzo.com

💲💲💲

↑ Sunrise on the river, the dream of many Amazonian travelers

⑨ Pucallpa

Ⓐ E4 ⬤ 178 miles (288 km) NE of Lima ✈ From Lima & Iquitos ⛴ From Lima ⛴ From Iquitos

A late-blooming city in the Peruvian Amazon, Pucallpa is now among its fastest growing; in 1900, it had a population of just 200. The highway from Lima came in 1930, changing Pucallpa into a major logging center. Exploration for oil, gas, and gold has further boosted the city's economy, making

>
> HIDDEN GEM
> ### Maroti Shobo Craft Center
>
> This excellent women's craft cooperative in Puerto Callao, roughly 30 miles (50 km) south of Pucallpa, sells pieces made by Shipibo women from around 40 villages. Items are primarily patterned textiles but beautiful ceramics and jewelry are also sold. Open 8am–5pm daily.

Pucallpa the most important port on the Río Ucayali.

Not attractive in the traditional sense, Pucallpa is a city of modern buildings encircled by mud streets. Most travelers use it as a base or pitstop. For artistically inclined visitors, however, an essential destination here is the gallery in the **Casa-museo de Agustín Rivas**, a famous local woodcarver, whose pieces grace many public buildings in the town. Another is **"Usko-Ayar" Escuela de Pintura Amazónica**, where shaman and painter Pablo Amaringo teaches, works, and exhibits his esoteric pieces inspired by ayahuasca *(p260)* visions in the rainforest.

Just 6 miles (10 km) northeast of downtown Pucallpa is Yarinacocha, a lake which offers some pleasant recreational opportunities, including boat trips to look for dolphins or to visit the Chullachaqui botanical garden, where sloths and green iguanas may be seen. There are Shipobo villages to visit, too. Visitors arrive at the lakeside village of Puerto Callao, which has basic hotels and restaurants.

Casa-museo de Agustín Rivas

Ⓢ Ⓖ Ⓐ Tarapaca 861
☎ 061 571 834 ⏱ 10:30am–1pm, 3–5pm Mon–Fri, 10:30am–noon Sat

"Usko-Ayar" Escuela de Pintura Amazónica

Ⓖ Ⓐ Sánchez Cerro 465
⏱ 10am–5pm Mon–Fri

---

⑩ Ucayali River Towns

Ⓐ E4–E2 Ⓐ Btwn Pucallpa & Iquitos ⛴ From Iquitos or Pucallpa

For decades, the main waterway linking Iquitos *(p252)* with the rest of Peru has been along the Río Ucayali from Pucallpa. Two- and three-decked riverboats ply the river between Pucallpa and Iquitos, delivering everything from motorcycles to medical equipment to the villages and small towns in between. The riverboats also provide passenger transportation to locals, most of whom hang their own hammocks on the second or third deck, while stuffy cabins with bunk beds are also available for extra charge. Basic on-board meals are also provided on these boats. The boats stop frequently at the many small villages along the river. The trip from Pucallpa to Iquitos, with the current, takes around four days, while the return, against the current, can take as long as six (faster *expreso* boats take one or two days).

The main towns on the route are Contamana and Requena, both of which have basic hotel and restaurant facilities. Contamana, located 267 miles (430 km) from Iquitos, is known for its hot springs and a macaw clay lick that can be reached by car via a 14-mile (22-km) dirt road.

Requena, a growing town, lies about 100 miles (160 km) from Iquitos. It has a small cathedral and is close to Laguna Avispa, which is 5 miles (8 km) by boat. This is a popular spot with the locals for fishing, both with lines and nets, and swimming in the calm, warm lake waters. Bird-watchers enjoy the small lake, not for any rare species, but for chances to observe some of the best-known Amazonian birds in their natural sur-roundings. Watching long-toed jacanas running speedily over the tops of the water lilies and other aquatic vegetation is a beautiful sight for any bird-lover. Female jacanas mate with several partners, moving on after each laying and leaving the males to take on the majority of hatching duties, a rare feature among birds.

 Puerto Bermúdez

E4 **160 miles (255 km)** **S of Pucallpa** **From La Merced or from Pucallpa via Constitución** **Mincetur, Av Capitán Larry; 065 792 558**

Well off the beaten track, and inaccessible after heavy rains, this sleepy jungle town's claim to fame is that it lies in the geographical centre of Peru. Much of the surrounding forest has been cleared for cacao, plantain, and yucca plantations, but the scenic Río Pichis affords opportunities for relaxing boat trips, and visits to picturesque local waterfalls. Tourism is in its infancy here, and lodgings and other visitor facilities are basic. Even so, rewarding day trips can be organized to the scenic forested Reserva Nacional del Sira, home to Asháninka and Yanesha communities, and brimming with spectacular orchids and stunning birdlife.

EAT & DRINK

Vater Otto
Cosy drinking den with a wide range of craft and imported German beers, spirits galore, and a lively vibe. The drinks are inexpensive and the bartenders are friendly. There's also a sibling bar by the main plaza.

D5 **Jr Bolívar 514, Oxapampa** **986 995 841**

Restaurante Típico Prusia
Pozuzo's Austro-German heritage has permeated the cuisine here. This restaurant is famous for its wurst and smoked pork, accompanied by fried plantain. Occasional Tyrolean dancing performances are put on here throughout the year.

D4 **Av Cristóbal Johann 110, Prusia, Pozuzo** **064 631 251**

Parrillada Orlando's
Expect sizzling meat from the grill accom-panied by piles of *patacones* (deep fried squashed plantain) and hearty salads at this no-nonsense local favorite. Its pitchers of Camu Camu are equally popular.

Jirón Aguaytia s/n, Pucallpa **937 657 573**

↑ Hammocks strung on a Ucayali riverboat deck, a cooler and cheaper option than a cabin

The Chanchamayo Region

D5 📍193 miles (310 km) NE of Lima

As the road crests a barren Andean pass some 193 miles (310 km) northeast of Lima, it swoops down into the warm, lush Chanchamayo Valley, filled with fruit orchards and coffee plantations. The delicious coffee and fruit juices slip down nicely in the restaurants and cafés of La Merced – the valley's main town and center – and nearby San Ramón.

La Merced, with its good transportation links, is the gateway to adventure. About 34 miles (55 km) south of the town is one of Peru's most-visited waterfalls, the Catarata Bayoz. The spectacular falls form tiers of swimming holes, perfect for cooling off in the lush, humid jungle. Farther along this road is the frontier-town Satipo, in the ancestral heartland of the beleaguered Asháninka people (*p74*). Visitors are welcome in several of their remote communities.

North of La Merced, on the high road, are the idiosyncratic Peruvian-Tyrolean communities of Oxapampa and Pozuzo; along the low unpaved road is the town of Villa Rica.

Villa Rica

E5 📍 33 miles (53 km) N of La Merced 🚌From La Merced or Oxapampa

A giant coffeepot in the Plaza de Armas greets arrivals in Villa Rica. Last of the Austro-German settlements in this region, established in 1928, this is coffee central – the country's best beans are produced in fincas in the neighboring Pichis and Palcazu valleys. Some, such as Finca Santa Rosa, can be visited on a tour. The annual Feria de Café (July/August) is heaven for coffee connoisseurs, with a full program of gastronomic, artisanal, and cultural entertainment.

Oxapampa

D5 📍49 miles (78 km) N of La Merced 🚌From La Merced or Lima

This provincial capital owes much of its clean, ordered streets to its Tyrolean roots. The same goes for the interesting architecture, as the town is dotted with wooden gabled houses, with wide eaves and decorative, carved balconies.

The Iglesia Santa Rosa, on the main square, is also an impressive wooden structure.

Tropical warmth tempered by fresh mountain air makes the climate here extremely pleasant. Surrounded by the cloud-forested hills of the *selva alta* – the "high jungle" – this town makes a great base for forays into the Parque Nacional Yanachaga-Chemillén, while thrill-seekers should consider the roller-coaster mountain-bike ride to Pozuzo. For music-lovers, Oxapampa is synonymous with Selvámonos (*p67*), a feel-good, family-friendly festival of cultural activities, street partying, and alternative music.

Did You Know?

Elementary school uniform in Pozuzo draws its inspiration from traditional Tyrolean dress.

Pozuzo

🅐D4 🚩50 miles (80 km) N of Oxapampa 🚌From Oxapampa

A serpentine descent down an unmade road from Oxapampa leads you to tiny Pozuzo, set in a lush, steep-sided valley streaked with waterfalls. Pozuzo's Austro-German roots make a visit to this tidy jungle community distinctly surreal. Founded in 1857 by Tyrolean settlers at the invitation of the Peruvian government, Pozuzo has evolved a hybrid Peruvian-Tyrolean culture, where yucca and plantain accompany schnitzel and wurst; German-style beer is served in tankards at the local microbrewery; and dancers clad in lederhosen and dirndls dance the polka. More of this history is on display in the museum. For nature lovers, riverside walks and the chance to see the outlandish courtship displays of cocks-of-the-rock (*Rupicola peruviensis*, the national bird of Peru) are additional attractions.

Parque Nacional Yanachaga-Chemillén

🅐E4 🚩19 miles (30 km) N of Oxapampa 🅸SERNANP, Prolongación Pozuzo 156, Oxapampa; www.sernanp. gob.pe

This little-known national park is one of the country's most varied, bordered by Yanesha and Ashaninka communities.

←
Enjoying the cooling spray at the Catarata Bayoz, Chanchamayo

Extending over 470 sq miles (1,220 sq km), the reserve protects a fabulous species-rich landscape, ranging from cloud-forest-clad mountains cleft by deep canyons, to scrubland and low-lying tropical forest. Four separate entrances get you close to different habitats and abundant wildlife. Three of these areas are within easy reach of Oxapampa and have lovely, simple camping spots or bunkhouses. The Huampal sector, near Pozuzo, offers a view of the impressive Cañón de Hunacabamba and bountiful birdlife, including the exhibitionist cock-of-the-rock and the torrent duck, a white-water diving specialist. An enjoyable hiking trail features in the San Alberto area, while the San Daniel zone has beautiful orchids fringing a reed-lined lake. However, the more inaccessible eastern Paujil sector is the biggest gem: steamy rainforest surrounding a biological station, laced with lovely rivers, and a lake harboring giant river otters. Getting here requires many hours by road and boat and an adventurous spirit but the ample rewards include possible sightings of tapir at a nearby clay lick, monkeys swinging nimbly through the treetops, and caiman sunning themselves on sandbanks.

 INSIDER TIP
Asháninka Village Visits

Be wary of the brief, often exploitative and voyeuristic visits to Ashaninka communities included in many tours from La Merced. If you want to spend time in a community (some offer homestays), contact the Asociación Regional de Pueblos Indígenas de Selva Central (ARPISC; *www.aidesep.org.pe/ node/12*) in Satipo.

NEED TO KNOW

Before You Go.............................268

Getting Around..........................270

Practical Information....................274

BEFORE YOU GO

Things change, so plan ahead to make the most of your trip. Be prepared for all eventualities by considering the following points before you travel.

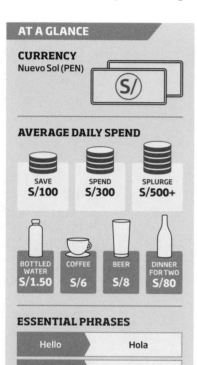

AT A GLANCE

CURRENCY
Nuevo Sol (PEN)

AVERAGE DAILY SPEND

SAVE	SPEND	SPLURGE
S/100	S/300	S/500+

BOTTLED WATER	COFFEE	BEER	DINNER FOR TWO
S/1.50	S/6	S/8	S/80

ESSENTIAL PHRASES

Hello	Hola
Please	Por favor
Thank you	Gracias
Excuse me	Con permiso
I don't understand	No entiendo

ELECTRICITY SUPPLY
Standard voltage is 220v. Power sockets are mainly type C, fitting two-pin, round, pronged plugs, or type A, flat-pronged plugs. Some fit both types.

Passports and Visas

For entry requirements, including visas, consult your nearest Peruvian embassy or check the country's official tourism website, **Iperù**. Citizens of the UK, US, Canada, Australia, New Zealand, and the EU are generally granted a 90-day stay upon arrival. A passport valid for at least six months from the date of departure is required.
Iperù
🅆 peru.travel/en

Government Advice

Now more than ever, it is important to consult both your and the Peruvian government's advice before travelling. The **UK Foreign, Commonwealth and Development Office**, **US State Department**, **Australian Department of Foreign Affairs and Trade**, and **Iperù** website provide up-to-date travel safety information.
AUS
🅆 smartraveller.gov.au
UK
🅆 gov.uk/foreign-travel-advice
US
🅆 travel.state.gov

Customs Information

You can find information on the laws relating to goods and currency taken in or out of Peru on either the **Iperù** or **LimaEasy** websites.
LImaEasy
🅆 limaeasy.com/peru-guide/legal-stuff/what-you-can-and-can-t-bring-into-peru

Insurance

We recommend taking out a comprehensive insurance policy covering theft, loss of belongings, medical care, cancellations and delays, and dangerous activities such as mountain climbing, and read the small print carefully. The policy should include medical evacuation as serious emergencies may require transfer to Lima or a flight home. Be ready to pay upfront and claim on insurance after, as most hospitals adopt a pay-first policy.

Vaccinations

Visit your doctor at least six weeks before travel to discuss vaccinations. No vaccinations are officially required but travelers planning on visiting the jungle are advised to get a yellow fever vaccination. Malaria is prevalent in the eastern sections of the jungle; discuss necessary prophylactics with your doctor before traveling. For information regarding COVID-19 vaccination requirements, consult government advice (p268).

Money

The unit of currency in Peru is the Nuevo Sol, although US dollars are widely accepted at high-end hotels, travel agencies, and restaurants. Banks are the safest places to exchange money but rates are better at *casas de cambio* (foreign currency exchanges) or street money changers; never change large sums of money at the last two. Credit cards and contactless payments are widely accepted in cities, and ATMs are found in major towns and cities. Carry small change for bus and taxi fares.

Tip wait staff 10 per cent, hotel porters S/3-5 per bag, and tour guides S/15–S/20 per day.

Booking Accommodations

Most lodgings across Peru are available to reserve online. In many parts of the jungle and remoter sections of the Andes, however, accomodations need to be reserved via telephone or upon arrival. The 18 per cent IGV tax (which doesn't apply to those staying fewer than 59 days) shouldn't be included in rates but confirm this before paying.

Peak season (July to August) sees prices rise, particularly in Cusco, where advance reservations are recommended. The coast is popular during summer (December to February); rates increase and prior reservations are essential.

Travelers with Specific Requirements

While facilities for travelers with specific requirements are improving, they are still inadequate. Wheelchair ramps and disabled toilets are rare and bus travel can be complicated. Only high-end hotels have more accessible rooms. The following tour agencies make arrangements:

Accessible Journeys
w disabilitytravel.com
Apumayo
w apumayo.com
Latinamerica for All
w latinamericaforall.com

Language

Spanish and Quechua are Peru's official languages, with Spanish the most widely used. Aymara is also recognized, along with 48 other Indigenous languages. English is used and understood by workers in tourism. Outside large cities, expect only a basic (if any) knowledge of English – a small grasp of Spanish will go a long way.

Opening Hours

> **COVID-19** Increased rates of infection may result in temporary opening hours and/or closures. Always check ahead before visiting museums, attractions and hospitality venues.

Lunchtime Some museums close for lunch.
Sunday Banks and some museums are closed, with shops open for limited hours.
Public holidays All banks, information offices, and most tourist attractions close.

PUBLIC HOLIDAYS

Jan 1	New Year's Day
Mar/Apr	Jueves Santo
Mar/Apr	Viernes Santo
May 1	Labor Day
Jun 29	Feast of Saints Peter and Paul
Jul 28-29	Independence Day
Aug 30	St. Rose of Lima Day
Oct 8	Anniversary of the Battle of Angamos
Nov 1-2	All Saints' Day
Dec 8	Immaculate Conception
Dec 9	Battle of Ayacucho
Dec 25	Christmas Day

GETTING AROUND

Whether you are visiting for a week or a more lengthy adventure, discover how best to reach your destination and travel like a pro.

AT A GLANCE

TRANSPORTATION COSTS

LIMA

S/2.50

Metropolitana bus fare

CUSCO

S/29

10-hour bus from Arequipa

IQUITOS

S/140

15-hour speedboat from Yurimaguas

TOP TIP
Avoid on-the-spot fines – be sure to stamp your ticket to validate your journey.

SPEED LIMIT

HIGHWAY

60
mph
(100 km/h)

MAJOR ROAD

50
mph
(80 km/h)

URBAN AREAS

37
mph
(60 km/h)

SMALL STREETS

25
mph
(40 km/h)

Arriving by Air

The only international gateway into Peru is Jorge Chávez International Airport in Lima. It receives direct flights from Panama City in Panama and Miami in the US – the main hubs for Latin America – as well as Houston and Atlanta in the US. Air Canada also offers direct flights from several Canadian cities. From Europe, most flights depart from Madrid, although KLM runs direct flights from Amsterdam.

The table opposite has details of transportation from the city center to Lima Airport and vice versa. Unofficial taxis charge a cheaper fare but it's much safer to take a cab through the airport's official **Taxi Green** service, the **Airport Express Lima** transfer service, or the **Quick Llama** shuttle.
Airport Express Lima
⬚ airportexpresslima.com
Taxi Green
⬚ taxigreen.com.pe
Quick Llama
⬚ quickllama.com

Arriving by Land

Visitors can enter Peru overland through Ecuador, Bolivia, or Chile. There are three border crossings for vehicles – from Huaquillas in Ecuador to Aguas Verdes in Peru, from Arica in Chile to Tacna in Peru, and from Desaguadero in Bolivia to Desaguadero in Peru. From Bolivia, there is also a frequent bus service from La Paz and Copacabana to Puno, and on to Cusco. From Chile, most buses travel from Arica to Tacna, although the reopened railway line between the two cities is an alternative. From Tacna, connecting buses continue on to Arequipa or Lima. All buses should stop on both sides of the border and wait for passengers to complete the necessary passport formalities.

Arriving by Boat

Peru is an important stop on the itineraries of several international cruise lines, which stop off in the port of Callao, near Lima. A selection of companies also stop off in the port of Salaverry in Trujillo for visits to the nearby Mochica temples.

Public Transportation	Journey time	Fare
Taxi	40 mins	S/55
Bus	1hr 10 mins	S/26

For the most adventurous, Peru can be reached by boat along the Amazon River coming from Manaus, Brazil. Vessels are slow boats, with the journey to Iquitos in Peru taking four days; bring a hammock, food, and water, and plenty of insect repellent. The smaller ports of Tabatinga in Brazil and Leticia in Colombia are also connected by speedboat to Santa Rosa in Peru at a tri-border. These ports can be reached by air from Bogotá (Colombia) or Manaus (Brazil).

Transportation Around Peru

With a nation reliant on public transportation, infrastructure between large cities is steadily improving in Peru, although road conditions in remote coastal areas and into the Andes leave a lot to be desired. Long-distance buses and domestic-flight routes are the most expedient methods of traversing the country. Within cities and smaller urban areas, organized networks of colectivo combis (minibuses), colectivo cars (shared taxis), and even tuk-tuks in jungle regions provide transportation. Few train routes remain, although those that do are often taken for the scenery – and have tourist prices to match. Transport around the Amazon region is primarily by boat, with options including motorized dugouts, larger cargo boats, or quicker passenger speed boats.

Domestic Air Travel

In a country with such rugged terrain, internal flights offer a convenient alternative to long bus journeys. However, flights can be canceled or delayed at short notice due to unpredictable and extreme weather conditions (especially during the rainy season from December to March) or other unavoidable situations, so always reconfirm flight timings. Air travel is also generally more expensive than the bus, although not excessively so if purchased several weeks in advance.

Lima acts as the central hub for air travel. It is possible to fly directly from Cusco to Arequipa and Puerto Maldonado, but for most other places you have to fly via Lima. Flights from the capital to larger destinations run several times a day.

LATAM is the largest and most expensive of the main airlines and operates the most extensive network of regular flights. These include Lima to Arequipa, Cusco, Iquitos, Pucallpa, Ayacucho, Juliaca, Trujillo, and Tumbes. The smaller and cheaper domestic airline **Star Perú** has flights from Lima to various Amazonian destinations, including Puerto Maldonado, Pucallpa, Tarapoto, and Iquitos. New Chilean low-cost carrier **Sky Airlines** flies to around a dozen destinations, including Cusco and Arequipa.

LATAM
W latam.com
Star Perú
W starperu.com
Sky Airline
W skyairline.com

Train Travel

All of Peru's surviving railway services are in the highland regions south of Lima. Train is the main way most visitors travel from Cusco to Machu Picchu Pueblo (Aguas Calientes), the station for Machu Picchu. You can also leave for the ruins from Ollantaytambo in the Sacred Valley. **PeruRail** and **Inca Rail** offer competing services. Expect to pay S/233 for the cheapest option and up to S/1,400 for the most luxurious option.

There are also services between Cusco and Puno. One or two times monthly between March and November, the **Ferrocarril Central Andino** operates trains between Lima and Huancay along the second-highest railroad in the world, from where it's possible to connect with the Huancayo to Huancavelica line. Reserve at least a week in advance, and earlier in high season.

Ferrocarril Central Andino
W ferrocarrilcentral.com.pe
Inca Rail
W incarail.com
PeruRail
W perurail.com

Boats and Ferries

Peru has no coastal ferry services. In the jungle, it is possible to take affordable *lanchas* (cargo boats), which connect cities such as Iquitos with Pucallpa and Yurimaguas. To travel on them, you'll need to bring a hammock or rent a private cabin. You can also find upmarket river cruises from Iquitos, which explore the national reserves of Allpahuauyo-Mishana and Pacaya Samiria, accessible only by boat. On Lake Titicaca, vessels shuttle passengers between Puno's port and the islands, but there is no regular service to Bolivia.

Long-Distance Buses

Intercity luxury bus services are often the way to go for covering long distances, with the majority operating overnight services. Companies such as **Cruz del Sur**, **Movil Tours**, **Oltursa**, and **TEPSA** are more comfortable, much safer, and more reliable than other services. These deluxe buses offer fully reclining bed-like seats, direct non-stop travel, air conditioning, movies, reading lamps, and on-board toilets.

Always check departures carefully; buses tend to leave from the central terminal of the city, although this isn't the case in Lima, where most companies have their own depots. While most arterial routes through Peru are paved, roads in rural, mountainous, and jungle areas

can be jarringly poorly maintained – and the buses are in a similar state.

On all journeys, be sure to bring all valuable items on board with you and keep them attached to your person, as theft can be an issue. Traveling overnight was once considered too dangerous for foreign visitors; although this is no longer the case along the coast, overnight journeys should be avoided in the more remote and mountainous regions, where the chances of accidents or robberies are increased.

The larger, more modern companies sell tickets and publish bus timetables online. You can always reserve in person at their office, or directly at the bus terminal, but it is often easiest to book online. Reservations should be made well in advance during peak travel periods, such as May to November, Easter (Semana Santa), Christmas, and the national Fiestas Patrias (July 28 and 29). Fare prices are significantly higher during these times.

Cruz del Sur
W cruzdelsur.com.pe
Movil Tours
W moviltours.com.pe
Oltursa
W oltursa.pe
TEPSA
W tepsa.com.pe

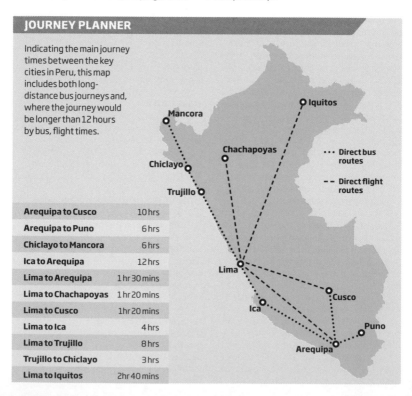

JOURNEY PLANNER

Indicating the main journey times between the key cities in Peru, this map includes both long-distance bus journeys and, where the journey would be longer than 12 hours by bus, flight times.

··· Direct bus routes

-- Direct flight routes

Arequipa to Cusco	10 hrs
Arequipa to Puno	6 hrs
Chiclayo to Mancora	6 hrs
Ica to Arequipa	12 hrs
Lima to Arequipa	1 hr 30 mins
Lima to Chachapoyas	1 hr 20 mins
Lima to Cusco	1 hr 20 mins
Lima to Ica	4 hrs
Lima to Trujillo	8 hrs
Trujillo to Chiclayo	3 hrs
Lima to Iquitos	2 hr 40 mins

Colectivos

The cheapest way to get around major Peruvian cities is via *colectivo* minibuses (also known as *combis*) and *colectivo* cars (shared taxis). Both also run rural routes between cities and towns, offering an often faster means of getting between the two than by bus. Fixed routes are indicated by signs on the windscreens of the *colectivo* minibuses. Conductors call out street names as the minibus hurtles along the road, cramming in as many passengers as possible. *Colectivo* cars fit up to seven passengers and *colectivo* minibuses anywhere from 12 upwards. However, these vehicles have an appalling safety record and you're often better off with a taxi.

Taxis

While taxis can be flagged down in the streets, it is far safer to reserve one by phone. **Easytaxi** and **Taxi Real** are friendly and safe services to use. Taxi hailing apps are not recommended in Peru, as drivers are known to game the system and scam passengers – with little chance of redress.

Short journeys within cities outside Lima rarely cost more than S/10. Since taxis do not have meters, be sure to agree a price in advance and confirm that it is in Nuevo Sol – not dollars. Prices increase by about 35 per cent after midnight.

Easytaxi
W easytaxi.com/pe
Taxi Real
W taxireal.com

Mototaxis

In provincial towns, motorcycle rickshaws, known as *mototaxis* or *motocarros*, are common. They are not the safest means of transport, nor the most comfortable. A more convenient alternative is to contact your hotel or tour agency to hire a car and driver, or a taxi by the hour or day.

Traveling by Car

Traveling at your own pace in a car is one of the most flexible ways to explore Peru. However, poor road conditions and aggressive drivers are just a few of the hazards. Car theft is also an issue.

Car rental is available with international companies in Lima, while in more rural areas, you'll likely find more informal local companies. Make sure you understand the rental agreement and all costs involved before signing. Four-wheel drive vehicles are best for remote rural areas, with motorcycle rental usually limited to jungle towns. An International Driving Permit is not legally required, but can be helpful in proving the authenticity of your driving license.

Outside of cities, fuel stations can be scarce, so fill up at every possible opportunity. Fuel is expensive, with costs rising according to the grade, diesel being the cheapest.

Rules of the Road

When driving in Lima on its multi-lane highways, jampacked with aggressive, honking traffic, it can often feel like road rules don't exist, and it's very wise to avoid driving in the capital where possible. On narrow, rural roads, be aware of other drivers attempting risky overtaking maneuvers and always be ready to drop back out of harm's way. Use your horn when driving around blind bends on mountainous or other rural roads.

Avoid driving at night, where possible, due to the increased likelihood of an accident or robbery, particularly on highland roads. Police checkpoints along highways usually present no problems, and it's sensible to carry a photograph of your passport and an original driving license to present if requested. Keep drinking water, food, warm clothes, and a spare tire inside your vehicle in case of emergency.

Cycling

Cycling is increasingly popular in Peru, especially mountain biking and bikepacking, with bike hire and repair shops ubiquitous in major towns and cities as a result. Good spots for mountain biking include the Colca Canyon, while a popular route for bikepackers is Peru's Great Divide, an off-road trail through the Cordillera mountains. Alternatively, tour operators in places such as Cusco, Arequipa, and Huaraz offer some great day or multi-day guided biking adventures through spectacular scenery. The independent cyclist should consult **Bikemap**, which offers dozens of routes across Peru.

Lima's best places to cycle include the route along the Miraflores clifftops and along Avenida Arequipa, from Miraflores to the city centre, on Sunday mornings, when it is closed to traffic.

Bikemap
W bikemap.net

Walking

In most towns and cities the main sights are concentrated in the historical centers, which are easy and safe to explore on foot. Lima is not as pedestrian-friendly as other places, but it does have several walkable areas, including the historical center, Barranco, and Miraflores; transport is necessary between different areas.

Outside of the urban centres – and especially in the Andes – longer walks or hikes are guaranteed to be trip highlights. The most well-known areas for trekking are around Cusco, including the Inca Trail, the Cañón del Colca (reachable from Arequipa), and in the Cordillera Blanca (accessible from Huaraz). Rainforest walks in the Amazon are usually shorter affairs, focused on wildlife viewing and learning about tropical eco-systems.

PRACTICAL
INFORMATION

A little local know-how goes a long way in Peru. Here you will find all the essential advice and information you will need during your stay.

AT A GLANCE

EMERGENCY NUMBERS

AMBULANCE	POLICE
106	**105**

FIRE SERVICE

116

TIME ZONE
GMT-5;
no daylight saving.

TAP WATER
Tap water is not safe to drink. Instead, use water purification tablets, a water filter or sterilization device, or buy bottled water.

WEBSITES AND APPS

Iperù
The official government tourism website has plenty of detailed information about destinations and is very receptive to emails *(www.peru.travel)*.

SpanishDict Translator
This handy app includes a Spanish-English dictionary (with audio pronunciations for dictionary entries) and a translator function.

Personal Security

Crime – particularly theft and pickpocketing – is an issue for visitors so always be alert to your surroundings. Robbery is most common in the main tourist cities, on long-distance bus routes, and at bus terminals. Always use ATMs during the day when there are more people around and avoid walking alone in deserted areas at night. Carry copies of important documents, such as your passport, all the time and be aware of scams involving fake police officers – never accompany one into a car.

If something does get stolen, English-speaking tourist police offices exist in a number of cities, where you can register for a *denuncia* (a document required by your insurance company).

As a strictly Catholic society with a macho culture, the country's attitudes toward homosexuality remain hostile, despite a number of laws protecting LGBTQ+ rights: homosexuality itself was legalized in 1924; laws prohibiting discrimination based upon sexual orientation were introduced in 2017; and trans people were permitted a national identity card in accordance with their chosen gender identity in 2021. Public displays of affection by same-sex couples should be avoided. There is, however, an established gay scene in the Miraflores and Barranco districts of Lima.

It is safe for women to travel alone but Peruvian men can be persistent in their attention. Wearing a wedding ring or traveling in a group can be a disincentive.

Health

Peru's health-care system is fairly good, with several public hospitals in Lima, and top-notch, English-speaking private clinics such as **Clínica Anglo Americana**. There are also good English-speaking private hospitals and clinics in Cusco and Arequipa, including **Clínica Peruano-Suiza** (Cusco) and **Clínica Arequipa**. Elsewhere healthcare facilities are more variable and often non-existent in rural areas. A list of recommended hospitals can be found on the Iperù tourism website *(p268)*.

Malaria is becoming increasingly common in jungle regions; cover up and use repellent in the evenings. Zika, mainly transmitted by mosquito bite, is also a risk, and pregnant women are advised against traveling to Peru. There is no vaccination, so follow measures for avoiding mosquito bites.

Stomach upsets caused by unfamiliarity with the food or contaminated water are common. Pharmacies are well-stocked and open long hours in all major towns and cities, but communicating can be a trial without Spanish, so remember to bring basic medicines from home.

Altitude sickness, with symptoms including shortness of breath, fatigue, headaches, and nausea, may affect visitors to highland areas. Rest, drinking lots of water, and avoiding intense exercise can help alleviate symptoms, as can drinking coca-leaf tea. If any symptoms develop, descend to a lower altitude and seek medical advice at once. At altitude, the sun can also be very strong and so a high SPF sunscreen is definitely recommended.

Clínica Anglo Americana
W clinicaangloamericana.pe
Clínica Arequipa
W clinicarequipa.com.pe
Clínica Peruano-Suiza
W cps.com.pe/en

Smoking, Alcohol, and Drugs

Smoking is banned in public places, including on all public transportation.

Peru has a strict limit of 0.05 per cent BAC (blood alcohol content) for drivers. This is roughly equivalent to a small beer.

Possession of, or trafficking in, illegal drugs is considered an extremely serious offense, with lengthy imprisonment; there is no bail for drug-trafficking offenses.

ID

There is no legal requirement to carry a copy of your ID, though it is strongly recommended to keep a photocopy of your passport on you at all times. You may be required to show ID when making credit card payments. For entrance to Machu Picchu, you must show your original passport.

Local Customs

Peruvians are polite and fairly conservative. A hand-shake is exchanged at the start and end of a meeting. People who know each other greet with a single kiss. Personal space is not a respected commodity – buses and streets are crowded.

Modest clothing, including below-the-knee shorts and t-shirts that cover your shoulders, is advised. Wearing revealing clothes or shorts in a church is considered disrespectful; both men and women should cover their shoulders and legs. Be respectful when taking photographs at religious sites, too.

The use of "gringo" toward foreign travelers is not an insult. Avoid using the words "Indian" to describe Peruvian people; "Indigenous" is the correct term to use.

Cell Phones and Wi-Fi

Travelers with GSM cell phones usually have reception in all cities and large towns. It is also possible to buy a local sim card cheaply from vendors around the country for in-country calls and inexpensive internet browsing. Most hotels, hostels, and cafés offer free Wi-Fi to customers.

Post

The Peruvian mail service is run by the privately owned Serpost, with branches in all major cities and towns. International letters and postcards usually take a few weeks to reach their destination. A *certificado* (registered mail) service is also available. The fastest way to send important documents or packages is via courier.

Taxes and Refunds

An 18 per cent sales tax (IGV) is often added to hotel stays. However, foreigners spending less than 59 days in Peru are not required to pay this charge; producing your passport is enough to get it removed. Tax refunds for departing visitors exist, but they are hard to acquire.

Discount Cards

It's worth bringing a student ID card, as these can lead to discounts of up to 50 per cent in museums and historical sites across the country.

INDEX

Page numbers in **bold** refer to main entries.

A

Abra de Warmiwañusca **181**
Accommodations
    reservations 269
    see also Homestays; Hotels
Achiote 75
Adoration of the Magi (Cusco School) 179
Adventure sports **46-7**
Afro-Peruvian music 53
Aguilar, María Luisa 72
Air travel 270, 271
Alcohol 51, 275
Almagro, Diego de 70
Altitude sickness 51, **213**, 275
Alto Mayo **261**
Amaringo, Pablo 82
Amazon Basin, The 21, 43, **248-65**
    hotels 253, 254, 261
    map 250-51
    restaurants and bars 59, 263
    river adventures **64-5**
Amazonian people 74-5
Amazon rainforest **43**
Amazon River 43
    adventure sports 46, 47
    boat trips 10, 47, 64-5, 271
Amphitheater (Caral) **217**
Ancient monuments **60-61**
    Batán Grande **234**
    Cahuachi **146-7**
    Caral **216-17**
    Cementerio de Chauchilla **147**
    Chan Chan 11, **232**
    Chavín de Huántar **214-15**
    Chinchero **194-5**
    Choquequirao **39**
    Combayo **244**
    Complejo Arqueológico El Brujo **233**
    Complejo Wari (near Ayachuco) **205**
    Cumbemayo canal and aqueduct **245**
    El Cuarto del Rescate (Ransom Chamber) (Cajamarca) **241**
    Huaca del Sol y de la Luna 61, **232**
    Huaca Huallamarca (Lima) **112-13**
    Huaca Pucllana (Lima) **108-9**

Ancient monuments (cont.)
    Intipunku **183**
    Karajía **246**
    Koricancha (Cusco) **176**
    Kuélap 60, **242-3**
    Machu Picchu 10, 37, 171, 180, **184-9**
    Moray 190-91, **194**
    Nazca Lines 11, 60, 61, **140-41**
    Ollantaytambo **195**
    Pachacámac (Lima) **133**
    Palpa Lines 61, **140**
    Paracas Necropolis 142
    Patallacta **180**
    Petroglifos de Miculla **148-9**
    Phuyupatamarca **182**
    Pikillacta and Rumicolca **192**
    Písac Ruins **194**
    Raqchi **193**
    Revash **247**
    Runkurakay **181**
    Sacsayhuamán (Cusco) **175**
    Sayakmarca **182**
    Sechín **221**
    Sillustani Burial Towers **168-9**
    Tambo Colorado 61, **145**
    Templo de Kotosh (Huánuco) 202
    Tipón **193**
    Túcume **235**
    Ventanillas de Otuzco **244**
    Wiñay Wayna **182-3**
    see also Castles and fortifications; Museums and galleries; Pyramids; Temples
Andean people 74
Apps 274
Archeology **60-61**
    archeological digs **217**
Architecture, Lima's colonial **86-7**
Arequipa 151, **154-61**
    hotels 156
    map 155
    restaurants 155
Arequipa, Canyons, and Lake Titicaca 17, **150-69**
    hotels 156, 163, 167, 168
    itinerary 28-9
    map 152-3
    restaurants 155, 164

Art
    Cusco School **179**
    Lima for Art Lovers **82-3**
Asháninka people 74, 263, 264, **265**
Atahualpa 69, 70, 190
Austro-German settlers 59, 264-5
Avenida Sáenz Peña (Lima) 124
Ayacucho 41, 197, **200-201**
    map 201
Ayacucho, Battle of 204
Ayahuasca 75, 191, **260**
Aymara people 74

B

Bahia de Paracas 143
Bajada de los Baños (Lima) 124
Baños Termales de Putina **149**
Baños Termales de Monterrey **220-21**
Barranco (Lima) 85, **116-25**
Bars and clubs
    Amazon Basin 263
    Arequipa and Puno 169
    Cusco 177
    Lima 84, 85, 121
    peñas 13, **84**
Batán Grande 223, **234**
Beaches **54-5**
    Lima 120, 132
    Northern Desert 233, 234
    Southern Coast 147
Beer 50
Belaúnde, Fernando 72
Belén (Iquitos) **253**
Bingham, Hiram 39, 181, 182
Birdwatching 10, **56-7**
Boat travel 270-71, 272
    Amazon Basin 10, 47
    Islas Ballestras 142, 143, 144
    Reserva de la Biósfera de Manu 256
    Reserva Nacional Pacaya Samiria 254
    Ríos Tambopata and Madre de Dios 258-9
    Río Ucayali 262-3
Bolívar, Símon 71, 128
Bolivia 72, 270
Border crossings 270

Bosque El Olivar (Lima) **113**
Bungee jumping 46
Bus travel 270, 272
Butterflies 63

C

Cahuachi **146-7**
Cajamarca 237, **240-41**
  Carnaval 40
  hotels 241
  map 241
Calca **194**
Calendar of events **66-7**
Calle Córdoba (Monasterio de
  Santa Catalina, Arequipa)
  160
Calle Hatunrumiyoc (Cusco) **177**
Callejón de Huaylas 207, 218,
  219, 220, 221
Camino Sagrado de los Incas **180**
Campo Santo, Yungay **219**
Cañón de Cotahuasi 13, 47, **168**
Cañón del Colca 13, 46, 57, **166-7**
Cañón del Pato **218**
Cañón del Sonche **246**
Canopy walkways 56
Cápac Ñan (Royal Road) **37, 69**,
  180
Caral 68, **216-17**
Caraz **218**
Caretaker's Hut (Machu Picchu)
  186
Carhuaz **218-19**
Carnaval (Cajamarca) **40**
Car travel 273
Casa Andina Observatory **39**
Casa Boza y Solís-Prefecture
  (Ayacucho) **201**
Casa de Aliaga (Lima) 86, **97**, 102
Casa del la Emancipación
  (Trujillo) **228**
Casa del Moral (Arequipa) **154**
Casa de Orbegoso (Trujillo) **227**
Casa-Museo Joaquín López
  Antay **200**
Casa-Museo Mario Vargas Llosa
  (Arequipa) **156-7**
Casa Ricardo Palma (Lima) **111**
Casa Tristán del Pozo (Arequipa)
  156
Casa Urquiaga (Trujillo) **226-7**
Casona Iriberry (Arequipa) **154**
Castles and fortifications
  Fortaleza del Real Felipe
    (Lima) **130**
  Kuélap **242-3**
  Yalape fortress 246
Catarata de Yumbilla
  (Chachapoyas) **42**

Cataratas Gocta 246, **247**
Cathedrals see Churches and
  cathedrals
Caves
  Cavernas Quiocta (near
    Lamud) 246
  Cueva de Pikimachay 68,
    205
  Gruta de Huagapo
    (Palcamayo) 205
Cell phones 275
Cementerio de Chauchilla 60,
  147
Central Sierra 19, **196-205**
  hotels 205
  map 198-9
Centro de Rescate Amazónico
  (Iquitos) **253**
Centro de Textiles Tradicionales
  de Cusco 44, 176
Ceramics 45
  Chavín 129
Cerro Santa Apolonia
  (Cajamarca) **241**
Cerros de Amotape, Parque
  Nacional de 234-5
Ceviche **49**
Chacas **220**
Chachapoyan civilization 237,
  243, 245, 246
Chachapoyas 42, **245**
Chala 147
Chanchamayo Region **264**
Chan Chan 11, **232**
Charles I, Emperor 70, 94
Charles IV of Spain 71
Chávez, Gerardo 82, 229
Chavín, Cult of 28, 29, 68, 69,
  214
Chavín de Huántar 129, 207,
  214-15
Chicama 55
Chicha 50
Chiclayo **233**
Chile 72, 270
  visiting **149**
Chimú Kingdom 69, 223, 232, 235
Chinatown (Lima) **100**
Chinchero **194-5**
Choco Museo (Cusco) **176-7**
Choquequirao **39**
Chucuito 58, **165**
Churches and cathedrals
  Catedral de Puno 164, 165
  Compañía de Jesús
    (Ayacucho) **201**
  Iglesia de la Compañía
    (Arequipa) **156**
  Iglesia de la Compañía (Cusco)
    175

Churches and cathedrals (cont.)
  Iglesia de la Merced (Lima) 103
  Iglesia de San Francisco
    (Cajamarca) **240**
  Iglesia de San Juan Batista
    (Puno) 164, 165
  Iglesia de San Pedro (Lima)
    87, **98**
  Iglesia de Santa Catalina
    (Monasterio de Santa
    Catalina, Arequipa) **160-61**
  Iglesia de Santo Domingo
    (Ayacucho) **200**
  Iglesia La Merced (Arequipa)
    157
  Iglesia la Merced (Trujillo) **227**
  Iglesia San Francisco
    (Arequipa) **155**
  Iglesia San Francisco de Paula
    (Ayacucho) **201**
  Iglesia Santiago Apóstol de
    Pomata (Lake Titicaca) **162**
  Iglesia Santisima Cruz (Lima)
    125
  Iglesia y Monasterio del
    Carmen (Trujillo) **228-9**
  La Catedral (Arequipa) **154**
  La Catedral (Ayacucho) **201**
  La Catedral (Cajamarca) **240**
  La Catedral (Cusco) **178-9**
  La Catedral (Lima) **96**, 103
  La Catedral (Trujillo) **226**
  La Ermita (Lima) **120-21**, 124
  Las Nazarenas (Lima)
    100-101
  San Francisco (Lima) 87, **92-5**
  San Pedro de Andahuaylillas
    192
  Santo Domingo (Cusco) **176**
  Santo Domingo (Lima) **98**
Circuito Mágico del Agua (Lima)
  84, **95**
Claustro los Naranjos
  (Monasterio de Santa
  Catalina, Arequipa) 159
Claustro Mayor (Monasterio de
  Santa Catalina, Arequipa)
  159, 160
Climate 42
Cloud forest 57
Coca 51, 75
Cocina (Monasterio de Santa
  Catalina, Arequipa) **160**
Coffee 51, 264
Colectivos 273
Collagua people 151, 166
Collas 168
Colonial architecture (Lima)
  86-7
Combayo **244**

Common District (Machu Picchu) **189**
Compañía de Jesús (Ayacucho) **201**
Complejo Arqueológico El Brujo **233**
Concepción **203**
Condors **166**
Conquering Kingdoms 69
Conquistadors 70, 71
Contamena 263
Convents *see* Monasteries and convents
Cordillera Blanca 19, **206-21**
    hotels 219
    map 208-9
    restaurants 220
Cordillera Huayhuash **221**
Cordillera Negra 207
Cordillera Vilcabamba 38
COVID-19 269
Craft beer 50
Crafts **44-5**
    Maroti Shobo Craft Center (Puerto Callao) **262**
    see also Shopping
Crime 274
Criolla 53
Cruises 64, 271
Cruz del Cóndor 57
Cueva de Pikimachay 68, **205**
Cult of the Sun **191**
Culture
    Inca **190-91**
    Indigenous people 12
Cumbemayo **245**
Currency 268
Cusco 69, 70, 171, **174-9**
    hotels 175
    map 175
    restaurants and bars 177
Cusco and the Sacred Valley 18, **170-95**
    hotels 47, 175, 187
    itinerary 30-31
    restaurants 177, 193
    shopping 195
Cusco School **179**
Customs information 268
Cycling 39, 46, 59, 142, 218, 273

D

Dance **52-3**, 84, 85
Delfín, Victor **123**
    El Beso 82-3, 115
De Szyslzo, Fernando 82
Discount cards 275
Dress code 275

Drugs 275
Dugout canoes 65

E

Early Horizon 69
Earthquakes
    Cordillera Blanca 207
    Lima **101**
Easter 41
Ecuador 70, 234, 270
El Beso (Delfín) 82-3, 115
El Candelabro geoglyph 142, 143
El Chaco (Paracas) **144**, 145
El Complejo de Belén (Cajamarca) **241**
El Cuarto del Rescate (Ransom Chamber) (Cajamarca) **241**
El Dorado 70
Electricity supply 268
El Frontón (Lima) **130**
Emergency numbers 274
Entertainment
    Arequipa 156
    Lima 84-5, 113
Estadio Nacional (Lima) **95**
Etiquette 275

F

Farming, Inca 190
Fejos, Paul 182, 183
Ferries 272
Festivals and events 11, **40-41**, **66-7**
    Inca 191
Fiesta de la Virgen de la Candelaria **41**
Fishing 246
Flights, sightseeing 141
Folklore (Puno) **165**
Food and drink 11
    ceviche **49**
    festivals 41, 49
    Peru for Foodies **48-9**
    Peru's Home Brews **50-51**
    pisco 12, **50**
    walking food tours 97
Fortaleza del Real Felipe (Lima) **130**
Fountains (Machu Picchu) **186**
Fujimori, Alberto 73
Funerary Rock (Machu Picchu) **187**

G

Garcia, Alan 73
Geoglyphs 137, 140-41, 142, 143
Gourds, painted 45

Graffiti (Lima) 120
Granda, Chabuca 123
Gran Teatro Nacional del Perú (Lima) 85
Guano 137, 144
Guerrilla war 73
Guinea pigs **94**
Guzmán, Abimael 73

H

Hastings, Raphael 228
Health 274-5
    insurance 268
    vaccinations 269
Heyerdahl, Thor 235
Hiking and trekking 46
    Andes 12
    Ausangate 43
    Cañón del Colca 46, **167**
    Cápac Ñan 37
    Carhuaz 218-19
    Choquequirao **39**
    Cordillera Blanca 46, 207
    Cordillera Huayhuash 58, 221
    Inca Trail **180-83**, 184
    Inca treks **38-9**
    Jungle Trek **39**
    Lares Trek **38**
    Machu Picchu Montaña **189**
    Parque Nacional Huascarán 210-13
    Salkantay Trek **38**
    Vinicunca (Rainbow Mountain) 43, **192**
Historic buildings
    Biblioteca Municipal (Lima) 125
    Casa Boza y Solís-Prefecture (Ayacucho) **201**
    Casa de Aliaga (Lima) 86, **97**, 102
    Casa del la Emancipación (Trujillo) **228**
    Casa del Moral (Arequipa) **154**
    Casa de Orbegoso (Trujillo) **227**
    Casa de Osambela (Lima) 86
    Casa de Pilatos (Lima) 86
    Casa Riva-Agüero (Lima) 203
    Casa Tristán del Pozo (Arequipa) **156**
    Casa Urquiaga (Trujillo) **226-7**
    Casona Iriberry (Arequipa) 154
    El Complejo de Belén (Cajamarca) **241**
    Quinta del Virrey Pezuela (Lima) **128-9**

History **68-73**
Hogar de un Suspiro (Rivera) 83
Homestays (Lake Titicaca) 58, 74, 163
Horse riding 47
Hospitals 274
Hotels
   Amazon Basin 253, 254, 261
   Arequipa, Canyons, and Lake Titicaca 156, 163, 167, 168
   Central Sierra 205
   Cordillera Blanca 219
   Cusco and the Sacred Valley 47, 175, 187
   jungle lodges 13
   Lima 113
   Northern Highlands 241, 247
   remote retreats 59
   Southern Coast 145
Huaca del Sol y de la Luna 61, **232**
Huaca Huallamarca (Lima) **112-13**
Huaca Pucllana (Lima) **108-9**
Huancaco **233**
Huancavelica **204**
Huancayo **202-3**
Huánuco 197, **202**
Huaraz 207, **220**
Huáscar 69, 70
Huascarán, Parque Nacional **210-13**
Huayllabamba **180-81**
Huaylla Belén Valley **246**
Huayna Cápac 69, 70
Huayno 52
Humala, Ollanta 73

I

Ica **144-5**, 146
ID 275
Iglesia see Churches and cathedrals
Inca **69**
   Cápac Ñan (Royal Road) **37**, **69**, 180
   culture and religion **190-91**
   experience Inca Peru **36-7**
   Inca Trail 37, **180-83**, 184
   Inca treks **38-9**
   Museo Inka (Cusco) 37, **174**
   Museo Nacional de Arqueología, Antropología e Historia del Perú (Lima) 128-9
   Spanish conquest and rule 70-71
   see also Ancient monuments; Museums and galleries

Inca Trail 37, **180-83**, 184
Indigenous people **74-5**
   homestays 58, 163
Insurance 268
Internet access 275
Inti Raymi 41
Intihuatana (Machu Picchu) **187**
Intipunku **183**
Inti (Sun God) 190
Iquitos **252-3**, 262
   hotels 253
   map 253
Isla Amantaní (Lake Titicaca) 58, 163, **164**
Isla Ballestas 57, 143, **144**
Isla de la Luna (Lake Titicaca) **162**
Isla del Sol (Lake Titicaca) **162**
Isla Suasi **163**
Islas Uros (Lake Titicaca) 74, **163**
Isla Taquile (Lake Titicaca) 58, 163, **164**
Itineraries **22-35**
   2 Weeks Across Peru 22-5
   3 Days in Lima 80-81
   4 Days on the Southern Coast 26-7
   5 Days in Canyon Country 28-9
   5 Days in Cusco and the Sacred Valley 30-31
   10 Days in Northern Peru 32-5

J

Jaguars 62
Jesuits 71
Jewelry 45
Juli **164**
Jungle Trek **39**

K

Karajía **246**
Kayaking 47
Koricancha (Cusco) **176**
Kuczynski, Pedro Pablo 73
Kuélap 60, **242-3**

L

La Catedral (Cusco) **178-9**
La Catedral (Lima) **96**, 103
La Ermita (Lima) **120-21**, 124, 125
Laguna 69 210, 211, 212
Laguna Avispa 263
Laguna de las Momias **244**
Laguna Parón 218
Lagunas Llanganuco **213**
Laguna Wilcacocha 212
Lagunillas 143
Lake Titicaca 47, 74, 151, **162-5**
   map 163
La Marina Lighthouse (Lima) 114
Lamas 261
Lambayeque culture 235
La Merced 264, 265
Lampa **169**
Lanchas (cargo boats) 49, 65, 272
Landscape **42-3**
Language 269
   essential phrases 268
   Indigenous people 74
   phrase book 284-6
Larco Hoyle, Rafael **131**
Larcomar (Lima) 85, **110**, 115
Lares Trek **38**
Las Nazarenas (Lima) **100-101**
Las Pocitas 54, 55, 234
Last Supper (Zapata) 94, 178, 179
Lavandería (Monasterio de Santa Catalina, Arequipa) **160**
Leguía, Augusto 72
Levanto **246**
Leymebamba **244**
Ley Seca (Dry Law) 51
LGBTQ+ safety 274
Lima 16, 70, **76-133**
   airport 271
   Barranco 116-25
   bars 84, 85, 121
   beaches 120, 132
   Beyond the Center 126-33
   Central Lima 88-103
   colonial architecture 86-7
   earthquakes 101
   food scene 48
   hotels 113
   itinerary 80-81
   map 78-9
   map: Barranco 118-19
   map: Beyond the Center 127
   map: Central Lima 90-91
   map: Miraflores and San Isidro 106-7
   Miraflores and San Isidro (Lima) 104-15
   nightlife 13, 84-5
   restaurants 100, 111, 122, 130
   walks 102-3, 114-15, 124-5
Llachón 58
Llamas 63
Local customs 275

Los Baños del Inca **244**
Lugar de la Memoria (LUM) (Lima) **113**

M

Machu Picchu 10, 37, 171, 180, **184–9**
ID at 275
Machu Picchu Montaña **189**
Machu Picchu Pueblo (Aguas Calientes) 39, **183**
Mail services 275
Malaria 274
Malecón de Miraflores (Lima) **114–15**
Malecón Tarapacá (Iquitos) **252**
Manco Cápac 69
Máncora 54, 55, **234**
Mantaro Valley **203**
Manu Basin **254–5**
Maps
  Amazon Basin 250–51
  Arequipa 155
  Arequipa, Canyons, and Lake Titicaca 152–3
  Ayacucho 201
  Cajamarca 241
  Central Sierra 198–9
  Cordillera Blanca 208–9
  Cusco 175
  Iquitos 253
  journey planner 272
  Lake Titicaca 163
  Lima 78–9
  Lima: Barranco 118–19
  Lima: Beyond the Center 127
  Lima: Central Lima 90–91
  Lima: Miraflores and San Isidro 106–7
  Northern Desert 224–5
  Northern Highlands 238–9
  Peru 14–15
  Southern Coast 138–9
  Trujillo 227
Marañon river 254
Marinera 52
Markets
  Andean food markets 36
  Belén (Iquitos) **253**
  Central Market (Lima) **97**
  for crafts 45
  Písac 36, 194
Maroti Shobo Craft Center (Puerto Callao) **262**
Maté de coca 51
MATE - Museo Mario Testino (Lima) **122**
Military dictatorship 72

Miraflores Clifftops (Lima) **110–11**
Miraflores and San Isidro (Lima) 85, **104–15**
Mistura (Lima) 41, 49
Moche culture 69, 128, 223, 233, 234
Museo de las Tumbas Reales de Sipán 230–31
Monasteries and convents
  Convento de la Recoleta (Arequipa) **155**
  Convento de los Descalzos (Lima) **99**
  Convento de Santa Catalina (Cusco) **177**
  Convento de Santa Rosa de Ocopa (Concepción) 203
  Convent of Santa Teresa and San Jose (Arequipa) 157
  Iglesia y Monasterio del Carmen (Trujillo) **228–9**
  Monasterio de Santa Catalina (Arequipa) **158–61**
  San Francisco (Lima) **92–5**
Money 269
Monkeys 63
Moray 190–91, **194**
Mototaxis 273
Mountain-biking 39, 46, 59, 218
Mount Alpamayo 211, 218
Mount Huascarán 211, 219
Mount Pirámide 218, 219
Mount Veronica 180
Mount Yerapaja 221
Movimiento Revolucionario Túpac Amaru (MRTA) 73
Moyobamba 249, **261**
Mummies 146, 157, 233, 244
  Cementerio de Chuachilia 60, **147**
  Huaca Pucllana (Lima) 109
  Inca culture and religion 191
  Paracas culture 129
Mundo Alpaca (Arequipa) 45, **156**
Murals 83, 228
Museums and galleries
  80m2 Livia Benavides (Lima) 124
  Casa-museo de Augustín Rivas (Pucallpa) **262**
  Casa-Museo Joaquin López Antay **200**
  Casa-Museo Mario Vargas Llosa (Arequipa) **156–7**
  Casa Ricardo Palma (Lima) **111**
  ChocoMuseo (Cusco) **176–7**

Museums and galleries (cont.)
  Lugar de la Memoria (LUM) (Lima) **113**
  MATE - Museo Mario Testino (Lima) **122**
  Mundo Alpaca (Arequipa) 45, **156**
  Museo Amano (Lima) **112**
  Museo Andrés de Castillo (Lima) **197**
  Museo Arqueológico de Ancash 220
  Museo Arqueológico Horacio Urteaga (Cajamarca) **240**
  Museo Arqueológico y Etnográfico (Cajamarca) **241**
  Museo Arqueológico Nacional Brüning (Chiclayo) 233
  Museo Arqueológico Rafael Larco Herrera (Lima) 37, 61, **131**
  Museo Barco Histórico "Ayapua" (Iquitos) **252–3**
  Museo Carlos Dreyer (Puno) 164–5
  Museo de Arqueologia de la Universidad de Trujillo **229**
  Museo de Arte de Lima 92, **99**
  Museo de Arte Contemporáneo (Lima) 83, **122**
  Museo de Arte Italiano (Lima) **101**
  Museo de Arte Moderno (Trujillo) 82, **229**
  Museo de Arte Precolombino (Cusco) 61, **174**
  Museo de Arte Religioso (Cusco) **177**
  Museo de Arte Religioso de la Catedral (Lima) 103
  Museo de Arte Virreinal de Santa Teresa (Arequipa) **157**
  Museo de la Coca y Costumbres (Puno) 165
  Museo de la Electricidad (Lima) **120**
  Museo de la Memoria (Ayacucho) **200**
  Museo de las Culturas Indígenas Amazónicas (Iquitos) **252**
  Museo del Automóvil Colección Nicolini (Lima) **132–3**
  Museo del Banco Central de la Reserva (Lima) 103

Museums and galleries (cont.)
Museo del Juguete (Trujillo) **229**
Museo de Oro del Perú (Lima) **132**
Museo de Sitio Bodega y Quadra (Lima) **96-7**
Museo de Sitio Submarino Abtao (Lima) **130-31**
Museo Didáctico Antonini (Nazca) 146
Museo Ferroviario (Tacna) **148**
Museo Histórico Municipal (Arequipa) **155**
Museo Inka (Cusco) 37, **174**
Museo Leymebamba 244
Museo Machu Picchu (Cusco) 37, **177**
Museo Nacional de Arqueologia, Antropologia e Historia del Perú (Lima) 37, 61, **128-9**, 202
Museo Nacional de la Cultura Peruana (Lima) **101**
Museo Nacional de Sicán (Chiclayo) 233
Museo Naval de Perú (Lima) **130**
Museo Pedro de Osma (Lima) **123**
Museo Regional Adolfo Bermúdez Jenkins (Ica) 60, 145
Museo Santuarios Andinos de la Universidad Católica de Santa María (Arequipa) **157**
Museo de las Tumbas Reales de Sipán 60, **230-31**, 233
Museo y Convento de Santa Catalina (Cusco) **177**
Pinacoteca (Monasterio de Santa Catalina, Arequipa) **161**
Revolver Galería (Lima) 83
"Usko Ayar" Escuela de Pintura Amazónica (Pucallpa) 262
Wu Galería 83
Yavari (Puno) 165
Music **52-3**
festivals 41
nightlife 84

N

National parks and nature reserves
Chaparrí Reserva Ecológica 56
Owlet Lodge 57
Pantanos de Villa 133

National parks and nature reserves (cont.)
Parque Nacional Cerros de Amotape 234-5
Parque Nacional Huascarán **210-13**
Parque Nacional Yanachaga-Chemillén **265**
Reserva de Biósfera del Noroeste 234
Reserva de la Biósfera de Manu **256-7**
Reserva Huembo 57
Reserva Nacional Allpahuayo-Mishana **253**
Reserva Nacional Pampa Galeras Barbara D'Achille **146**
Reserva Nacional del Sira 263
Reserva Nacional de Paracas **142-3**
Reserva Nacional de Tambopata 258
Reserva Nacional Pacaya Samiria **254-5**
Reserva Paisajística Nor Yauyos Cochas **203**
Nature reserves see National parks and nature reserves
Nazca 140, 141, 145, **146**
Nazca Lines 11, 60, 61, **140-41**
Nazca people 69, 128, 137, 146
Nevado Salkantay 38
Nightlife
Arequipa 156
Lima 13, **84-5**
Northern Desert, The 20, **222-35**
itinerary 32-5
map 224-5
restaurants 235
Northern Highlands, The 20, **236-47**
hotels 241, 247
itinerary 32-5
map 238-9
restaurants 245

O

Odebrecht scandal 73
Off the beaten track **58-9**
Oil industry 249, 262
Ollantaytambo **195**
Opening hours 269
Oxapampa 41, 59, **264-5**

P

Pachacámac (Lima) **133**
Pachacútec 69, 184

Paddington Bear statue (Lima) 114, 115
Palaces
Palacio Arzobispal (Lima) 103
Palacio de Gobierno (Lima) **97**, 102
Palacio de Torre Tagle (Lima) 86, 103
Palacio Iturregui (Trujillo) **228**
Palcamayo **205**
Palpa Lines 61, **140**
Pantanos de Villa **133**
Paracas civilization 61, 129, 137, 140
Paragliding 46
Parks and gardens
Bosque El Olivar (Lima) **113**
Parque Antonio Raimondi (Lima) 115
Parque del Amor (Lima) 82-3, 111, 115
Parque de la Muralla (Lima) **98**
Parque El Libro (Lima) 114
Parque Kennedy (Lima) **110**
Parque Miguel Grau (Lima) 114
Parque Municipal (Lima) **122-3**
Parque San Marcelino Champagnat (Lima) 115
Plazuela El Recreo (Trujillo) **227**
see also National parks and nature reserves
Parque Nacional see National parks and nature reserves
Passports 268
Patallacta **180**
Peñas 13, **84**
Peruvian War of Independence 71, 129
Petroglifos 148-9
Petroglifos de Miculla **148-9**
Pevas **260**
Phrase book 284-6
Phuyupatamarca **182**
Picanterías 49
Pikillacta **192**
Pinacoteca (Monasterio de Santa Catalina, Arequipa) **161**
Písac **194**
Pisacacucho 180
Pisco **145**
Pisco (drink) 12, **50**
Pizarro, Francisco 70, 89, 96, 97, 171

Plants 75
Plaza de Armas (Cusco) **174**
Plaza de Armas (Trujillo) **226**
Plaza Mayor (Lima) **102–3**
Plaza San Martín (Lima) **100**
Plazuela El Recreo (Trujillo) **227**
Postal services 275
Pozuzo 59, **265**
Prices
  average daily spend 268
  transportation 270
Public holidays 269
Public transportation 271
  prices 270
Pucallpa 249, **262**
Pucusana 132
Puente de los Suspiros (Lima)
  121, 124, 125
Puerto Bermúdez **263**
Puerto Inca 147
Puerto Maldonado 249, 259
Puka Wamani (de Szyslzo) 82
Puno 41, 162, **164–5**
Punta Arquillo 143
Punta Hermosa 132
Punta Olimpica 212, 220
Punta Rocas 132
Punta Sal 54
Punta San Fernando 147
Punta San Juan de Marcona
  147
Puya raimondii **211**
Pyramids
  Batán Grande **234**
  Cahuachi **146–7**
  Chavín de Huántar 214
  Great Pyramid (Caral) **217**
  Huaca del Sol y de la Luna 61,
    232
  Huaca Huallamarca (Lima)
    112–13
  Huaca Pucllana (Lima)
    108–9
  Pachacámac **133**
  Pyramid of the Circular Altar
    (Caral) **217**
  Pyramid of the Gallery (Caral)
    217
  Pyramid of the Huanca (Caral)
    217
  Túcume **235**
  see also Ancient monuments

Q

Q'eswachaka Rope Bridge **36**
Quebrada Rajucolta 212
Quechua 12, 74
Quinta del Virrey Pezuela (Lima)
  128–9

Quinua **204**
Quipus 191, 216

R

Rail travel 271
  Lima to Huancayo train **202**,
    203
Rainforest, Amazon **43**, 56
Raqchi **193**
Reasons to Love Peru **10–13**
Refunds, IGV 275
Reiche, Maria 140
Religion, Inca **190–91**
Requena 263
Reserva de la Biósfera de Manu
  256–7, 258
Reserva Nacional Allpahuayo-
  Mishana **253**
Reserva Nacional del Sira 263
Reserva Nacional de Paracas
  142–3
Reserva Nacional de Tambopata
  258
Reserva Nacional Pacaya
  Samiria **254–5**
Reserva Paisajistica Nor Yauyos
  Cochas **203**
Restaurants
  Amazon Basin 59, 263
  Arequipa, Canyons, and Lake
    Titicaca 155, 164
  Cordillera Blanca 220
  Cusco and the Sacred Valley
    177, 193
  Lima 100, 111, 122, 130
  Northern Desert 235
  Northern Highlands 245
  picanterías 49
  Southern Coast 146
Revash **247**
Río Amazonas 252
Río Madre de Dios 56, 65, **258–9**
Ríos Tambopata and Madre de
  Dios Area **258–9**
Río Ucayali 254, 259, 262
  Ucayali River Towns **262–3**
Río Utcubamba 242
Ritual ceremonies **109**
Rivera, Jade, Hogar de un
  Suspiro 83
Riverboat cruises 64
Road travel 270, 273
Rock-climbing 47
Royal Sector (Machu Picchu)
  186
Rubber 259, 260
Rules of the road 270, 273
Rumicolca **192**
Runkurakay **181**

S

Sacred Plaza (Machu Picchu)
  187
Sacred Rock (Machu Picchu)
  188
Sacred Valley *see* Cusco and
  the Sacred Valley
Sacrifices 109, 191
Safety
  government advice 268
  personal security 274
Saint *see* San; Santa; Santo
Salinas de Maras **194**
Salkantay Trek **38**
San Bartolo 132
San Blas District (Cusco) **176**
San Francisco (Lima) 87,
  92–5
San Isidro (Lima) *see* Miraflores
  and San Isidro
San Martín, José de 71, 100,
  128, 143
San Pedro de Andahuaylillas
  192
San Pedro (Lima) 87, **98**
Santa Cruz Trek 210, **212**
Santa Rosa de Lima **99**
Santo Domingo (Cusco) **176**
Santo Domingo (Lima) **98**
Sapa Inca 190
Sayakmarca **182**
Scuba diving 55
Sea-kayaking 54
Seasons 42
Sechín **221**
Sechura Desert 223
Selvámonos (Oxapampa) 41
Semana Santa **41**
Sendero Luminoso (Shining
  Path) 72, 73, 197, **200**
Señor de Wari **61**
Shady, Ruth 216, 217
Shamans 75, 260
Shipibo-Conibo **259**
Shopping
  Amazon Basin 262
  Ayacucho 201
  Cusco and the Sacred Valley
    176, 195
  Lima 125
  see also Crafts
Sicán Kingdom 69, 223
Sillustani Burial Towers **168–9**
Simpson, Joe 221
Sipán, Lord of 230–31, 233
Smoking 275
Sor Ana de los Angeles
  Monteagudo **160**, 161

Southern Coast, The 17, **136–49**
  beaches 147
  hotels 145
  itinerary 26-7
  map 138-9
  restaurants 146
Spanish conquest and rule 70-71
Spatuletails **246**
Specific requirements, travelers
  with 269
Spectacled bears 62
Speed limits 270
Street art 82, 83
Sucre, Antonio José de 204
Sun protection 275
Supay pa Wasin Tusuq (Scissors
  Dance) 53
Surfing 55

T

Tacna **148**
Tahuantinsuyu 69
Tambo Colorado 61, **145**
Tambopata River **258-9**
Tap water 274
Tarapoto **261**
Tarata **149**
Taxes 275
Taxis 273
Teatro Municipal (Lima) 85
Telephones 275
Tello, Julio C. 129, 183
Temples
  Huaca del Sol y de la Luna 61,
    232
  Koricancha (Cusco) **176**
  Raqchi **193**
  Temple of the Condor (Machu
    Picchu) **188**
  Templo de Kotosh (Huánuco)
    202
  Temple of the Sun (Machu
    Picchu) **188-9**
  Temple of the Sun
    (Ollantaytambo) 195
  Temple of the Three Windows
    (Machu Picchu) **188**
  see also Ancient monuments;
    Pyramids
Testino, Mario 122
Textiles 44, 45, 176
Theater 85
Thermal springs
  Baños de Pariacaca 218
  Baños Termales de
    Monterrey **220-21**
  Baños Termales de Putina **149**
  Baños Termales San Mateo
    261

Thermal springs (cont.)
  Calca 194
  Llucho 168
  Los Baños del Inca **244**
  Machu Picchu Pueblo
    (Aguas Calientes) 39, **183**
Time zone 274
Tipón **193**
Titicaca, Lake see Lake Titicaca
Toledo, Alejandro 73
Toledo, Francisco de 71
Trains see Rail travel
Travel
  city transportation 273
  getting around **270-73**
  journey planner map 272
  safety advice 268
  to Machu Picchu 184
Trekking see Hiking and trekking
Tres Cruces **42**
Trujillo 223, **226-9**
  map 227
Túcume **235**
Tumbes **234**
Túpac Amaru II 71

V

Vaccinations 269
Valverde, Vicente de 198
Vargas Llosa, Mario 156-7
Velasco Alvarado, General Juan
  72
Ventanillas de Otuzco **244**
Vicuñas 44, 63
Villa Rica **264**
Vinicunca 43, **192**
Viracocha 178
Virgen del Carmen 41
Visas 286
Vizcarra, Martín 73

W

Walking 273
  A Long Walk: Malecón de
    Miraflores (Lima) 114-15
  A Short Walk: Barranco (Lima)
    124-5
  A Short Walk: Plaza Mayor
    (Lima) 102-3
Wari culture 69, 171, 197
  Complejo Wari **205**
  Huaca Pucllana (Lima) 108-9
  Museo Nacional de
    Arqueologia, Antropologia
    e Historia del Perú (Lima)
    128, 129
  Pikillacta and Rumicolca **192**
  Señor de Wari **61**

War of the Pacific 72
Waterfalls
  Catarata Bayoz 42, 264
  Catarata de Yumbilla
    (Chachapoyas) **42**
  Cataratas Gocta 42, 246,
    247
Websites 274
White-water rafting 47, 261
Wi-Fi 275
Wildlife **62-3**
  Amazon river dolphins 255
  birdwatching 10, **56-7**
  Centro de Rescate Amazónico
    (Iquitos) **253**
  condors 57, **166**
  Islas Ballestas 57, 144
  Pantanos de Villa **133**
  Parque Nacional Huascarán
    210
  Peruvian hairless dog
    232
  Peruvian Paso **229**
  photography 65
  Reserva de la Biósfera de
    Manu 256-7
  Reserva Nacional de Paracas
    142-3
  Reserva Nacional Pacaya
    Samiria 254
  Reserva Nacional Pampa
    Galeras Barbara D'Achille
    146
  spatuletails **246**
  Whale watching 55
  see also National parks and
    nature reserves
Wiñay Wayna **182-3**
Windsurfing 54
Wine, Ica 145
Women travelers 274
Woodwork 45

Y

Yanachaga-Chemillén, Parque
  Nacional **265**
Yanahuara district (Arequipa)
  154
Yavari (Puno) 165
Ychsma culture 108
Yurimaguas **260**

Z

Zapata, Marcos, *Last Supper*
  94, 178, 179
Ziplines 46
Zorritos 54, **234-5**
Zubarán, Francisco 92

PHRASE BOOK

In Peru, there are three main different forms of pronunciation of Spanish: variations from the Andes, from the coast (Lima being its center), and a combination of the two which has emerged during the last 50 years due to internal immigration.

In the variation from the Andes, sometimes the **e** and **o** become **i** and **u**; thus, **ayer** would be pronounced 'a-yeer' and **por** is 'poor'. There is often a distinction between **ll** and **y**, where the pronunciation would be like the English **y** for **yes** and **j** for **job** respectively. It is also common that **r** and **rr** are pronounced similarly.

In the variation from the coast, there is a clear distinction between **r** and **rr**. Sometimes the **s** becomes **h** before another consonant as in **pescado** 'pehkado'. In addition, the **ll** and **y** are pronounced the same, such as in the English **j** for job. Finally, the **d** at the end of the word may become **t** or may be omitted; for example, **usted** would be pronounced 'oosteh'.

In the variation which combines Andean and coastal pronunciations, there is always a clear distinction between **r** and **rr**. In this variation, the **ll** and **y** are also pronounced as in the English **j** for job. in addition, the sounds **b, d, g,** and **y** may become nonexistent between vowels; for example, **cansado** would be pronounced 'kansa-o'. Finally, the **s** may become **h** before another consonant as in **fresco** 'frehko'.

SOME SPECIAL PERUVIAN WORDS

¡A la firme!	*a la feermeh*	Sure!
agua de caño	*agwa deh kan-yo*	tap water
bravazo	*brabaso*	wonderful
brevete	*brebeteh*	driving license
carro	*karro*	car
chamba	*chamba*	job; work
chelear	*cheleh-ar*	to drink beer
chévere	*chebaireh*	cool, great
chibolo	*cheebolo*	young person
chorear	*choreh-ar*	to steal
coco	*koko*	dollar
del carajo	*del karaho*	excellent, very good
estar con la bicicleta	*estar kon la beeseekleta*	to have diarrhea
estar hasta la coronilla	*estar asta la koronee-ya*	to be fed up
feria	*fair-ya*	market
hacer cholito a alguien	*asair choleeto a algen*	to deceive someone
los tombos	*los tombos*	the police
pan comido	*pan komeedo*	it is easy
pata	*pata*	pal, mate
pueblo jóven	*pweblo hohven*	shanty town
rubia	*rroob-ya*	beer

EMERGENCIES

Help!	**¡Ayuda!**	*ah-yoo-dah*
Stop!	**¡Pare!**	*pareh*
Call a doctor	**Llamen un médico**	*yamen oon medeeko*
Call an ambulance	**Llamen a una ambulancia**	*yamen a oona amboolans-ya*
Police!	**¡Policía!**	*poleesee-a*
I've been robbed	**Me robaron**	*meh rrobaron*
Call the police	**Llamen a la policía**	*yamen a la poleesee-a*
Where is the nearest hospital?	**¿Dónde queda el hospital más cercano?**	*dondeh keda el ospeetal mas sairkano?*

Could you help me?	**¿Me puede ayudar?**	*meh pwedeh a-yoodar?*
They stole my...	**Me robaron mi...**	*meh rrobaron mee...*

COMMUNICATION ESSENTIALS

Yes	**Sí**	*see*
No	**No**	*no*
Please	**Por favor**	*por fabor*
Excuse me	**Disculpe**	*deeskoolpeh*
I'm sorry	**Lo siento**	*lo s-yento*
Thanks	**Gracias**	*gras-yas*
Hello!	**¡Hola!**	*houla*
Good day	**Buen día**	*bwen dee-a*
Good afternoon	**Buenas tardes**	*bwenas tardes*
Good evening	**Buenas noches**	*bwenas noches*
Night	**Noche**	*nocheh*
Morning	**Mañana**	*man-yana*
Tomorrow	**Mañana**	*man-yana*
Yesterday	**Ayer**	*a-yair*
Here	**Acá**	*aka*
How?	**¿Cómo?**	*komo*
When?	**¿Cuándo?**	*kwando*
Where?	**¿Dónde?**	*dondeh*
Why?	**¿Por qué?**	*por keh*
How are you?	**¿Qué tal?**	*keh tal*
Very well, thank you	**Muy bien, gracias**	*mwee byen gras-yas*
Pleased to meet you	**Encantado /mucho gusto**	*enkantado/ moocho goosto*
It's a pleasure!	**¡Es un placer!**	*Es oon plahcer*
Goodbye, so long	**Adiós, hasta luego**	*ad-yos, asta lwego*

USEFUL PHRASES

That's fine	**Está bien**	*esta b-yen*
Fine!	**¡Qué bien!**	*keh b-yen*
How long?	**¿Cuánto falta?**	*kwanto falta?*
Do you speak a little English?	**¿Habla un poco de inglés?**	*abla oon pako deh eengles?*
I don't understand	**No entiendo**	*no ent-yendo*
Could you speak more slowly?	**¿Puede hablar más despacio?**	*pwedeh ablar mas despas-yo?*
I agree/OK	**De acuerdo/ bueno**	*deh akwairdo/ bweno*
Certainly!	**¡Claro que sí!**	*klaro keh see*
Let's go!	**¡Vámonos!**	*bamonos*
How do I get to...?	**¿Cómo se llega a...?**	*komo se yega a...?*
Which way to...?	**¿Por dónde se va a...?**	*por dondeh seh ba a...?*

USEFUL WORDS

large	**grande**	*grandeh*
small	**pequeño**	*peken-yo*
hot	**caliente**	*kal-yenteh*
cold	**frío**	*free-o*
good	**bueno**	*bweno*
bad	**malo**	*malo*
so-so	**más o menos**	*mas o menos*
mediocre	**regular**	*regoolar*
sufficient	**suficiente**	*soofees-yenteh*
well/fine	**bien**	*b-yen*
open	**abierto**	*ab-yairto*
closed	**cerrado**	*serrado*
entrance	**entrada**	*entrada*
exit	**salida**	*saleeda*
full	**lleno**	*yeno*
empty	**vacío**	*basee-o*
right	**derecha**	*dairecha*
left	**izquierda**	*eesk-yairda*
straight on	**(todo) recto**	*rrekto*

under	**debajo**	*debaho*
over	**arriba**	*arreeba*
quickly	**pronto**	*pronto*
early	**temprano**	*temprano*
late	**tarde**	*tardeh*
now	**ahora**	*a-ora*
soon	**ahorita**	*a-oreeta*
more	**más**	*mas*
less	**menos**	*menos*
little	**poco**	*poko*
much	**mucho**	*moocho*
very	**muy**	*mwee*
too much	**demasiado**	*demas-yado*
in front of	**delante**	*delanteh*
opposite	**enfrente**	*enfrenteh*
behind	**detrás**	*detras*
first floor	**primer piso**	*preemair peeso*
ground floor	**sotano piso**	*soutano peeso*
lift	**ascensor**	*asensor*
bathroom	**baño**	*ban-yo*
women	**mujeres**	*moohaires*
men	**hombres**	*ombres*
toilet paper	**papel higiénico**	*papel eeh-yeneeko*
camera	**cámara**	*kamara*
batteries	**pilas**	*peelas*
passport	**pasaporte**	*pasaporteh*
visa	**visa**	*beesa*
tourist card	**tarjeta turistica**	*tarheta tooreesteeka*

HEALTH

I don't feel well	**Me siento mal**	*meh s-yento mal*
I have a stomach ache/ headache	**Me duele el estómago/ la cabeza**	*meh dweleh el estomago la kabesa*
I have altitude sickness	**Tengo mal de altura**	*tengo mal deh altoora*
He/she is ill	**Está enfermo/a**	*esta enfairmo/a*
I need to rest	**Necesito descansar**	*neseseeto deskansar*
drug store	**farmacia**	*farmas-ya*

POST OFFICE AND BANK

bank	**banco**	*banko*
I'm looking for a bureau de change	**Busco una casa de cambio**	*boosko oona kasa deh kamb-yo*
What is the dollar rate?	**¿A cómo está el dolar?**	*a komo esta el dolar?*
I want to send a letter	**Quiero enviar una carta**	*k-yairo emb-yar oona karta*
postcard	**postal**	*postal*
stamp	**estampilla**	*estampee-ya*
draw out money	**sacar dinero**	*sakar deenairo*

SHOPPING

I would like/ want	**Me gustaría/ quiero...**	*meh goostaree-a/ k-yairo...*
Do you have any...?	**¿Tiene...?**	*t-yeneh...?*
expensive	**caro**	*karo*
How much is it?	**¿Cuánto cuesta?**	*kwanto kwesta?*
What time do you open/ close?	**¿A qué hora abre/cierra?**	*a ke ora abreh/ s-yairra?*
May I pay with a credit card?	**¿Puedo pagar con tarjeta de crédito?**	*pwedo pagar kon tarheta deh kredeeto?*

SIGHTSEEING

avenue	**avenida**	*abeneeda*
beach	**playa**	*pla-ya*
castle, fortress	**castillo**	*kastee-yo*
cathedral	**catedral**	*katedral*
church	**iglesia**	*eegles-ya*

district	**barrio**	*barr-yo*
garden	**jardín**	*hardeen*
guide	**guía**	*gee-a*
house	**casa**	*kasa*
map	**mapa**	*mapa*
highway	**autopista**	*owtopeesta*
museum	**museo**	*mooseh-o*
park	**parque**	*parkeh*
road	**carretera**	*karretaira*
square	**plaza**	*plasa*
street	**calle, callejón**	*ka-yeh, ka-yehon*
town hall	**municipalidad**	*mooneeseepaleedad*
tourist bureau	**oficina de turismo**	*ofeeseena deh tooreesmo*

TRANSPORT

When does it leave?	**¿A qué hora sale?**	*a keh ora saleh?*
When does the next train/bus leave for...?	**¿A qué hora sale el próximo tren/bus a...?**	*a keh ora saleh el prokseemo tren/boos a...?*
Could you call a taxi for me?	**¿Me puede llamar un taxi?**	*meh pwedeh yamar oon taksee?*
airport	**aeropuerto**	*a-airopwairto*
railroad station	**estación de ferrocarriles**	*estas-yon deh fairrokarreeles*
bus station	**terminal de buses**	*tairmeenal deh booses*
customs	**aduana**	*adwana*
boarding pass	**tarjeta de embarque**	*tarheta deh embarkeh*
car hire	**alquiler de carros**	*alkeelair deh karros*
bicycle	**bicicleta**	*beeseekleta*
rate	**tarifa**	*tareefa*
insurance	**seguro**	*segooro*
fuel station	**estación de gasolina**	*estas-yon deh gasoleena*
garage	**garage**	*garaheh*
I have a flat tyre	**Se me pinchó una llanta**	*seh meh peencho oona yanta*

STAYING IN A HOTEL

I have a reservation	**Tengo una reserva**	*tengo oona rresairba*
Are there any rooms available?	**¿Tiene habitaciones disponibles?**	*t-yeneh abeetas-yones deesponeebles*
single/double room	**habitación sencilla/doble**	*abeetas-yon sensee-ya/dobleh*
twin room	**habitación con camas gemelas**	*abeetas-yon kon kamas hemelas*
shower	**ducha**	*doocha*
bath	**tina**	*teena*
balcony	**balcón**	*balkon*
I want to be woken up at...	**Necesito que me despierten a las...**	*neseseeto keh meh desp-yairten a las...*
warm/cold water	**agua caliente/fría**	*agwa kal-yenteh/free-a*
soap	**jabón**	*habon*
towel	**toalla**	*to-a-ya*
key	**llave**	*yabeh*

EATING OUT

I am a vegetarian	**Soy vegetariano**	*soy begetar-yano*
Can I see the menu, please?	**¿Me deja ver el menú, por favor?**	*me deha ber el menoo por fabor?*
fixed price	*precio fijo*	*pres-yo feeho*
What is there to eat?	**¿Qué hay para comer?**	*keh I para komair?*
The bill, please	**la cuenta, por favor**	*la kwenta por fabor*
glass	**vaso**	*baso*

cutlery	cubiertos	koob-yairtos
I would like some water	Quisiera un poco de agua	kees-yaira oon poko deh agwa
wine	vino	beeno
The beer is not cold enough	La cerveza no está bien fría	a sairbesa no esta b-lyen free-a
breakfast	desayuno	desa-yoono
lunch	almuerzo	almwairso
dinner	comida	komeeda
raw	crudo	kroodo
cooked	cocido	koseedo

MENU DECODER

aceite	asayteh	oil
agua mineral	agwa meenairal	mineral water
ajo	aho	garlic
anticucho	anteekoocho	kebab
arroz	arros	rice
asado	asado	roasted
atún	atoon	tuna
azúcar	asookar	sugar
bacalao	bakala-o	cod
betarraga	betarraga	beetroot
café	kafeh	coffee
camarones	kamarones	prawns
carne	karneh	meat
carne de chancho	karneh deh chancho	pork
causa	kowsa	potato salad
cerveza	sairbesa	beer
chancada	chankada	maize cake
chifa	cheefa	Chinese food
choro	choro	mussel
dulce	doolseh	sweet
ensalada	ensalada	salad
fruta	froota	fruit
guargüero	gwargwairo	sweet fritter filled with fudge
helado	elado	ice cream
huevo	webo	egg
jugo	hoogo	fruit juice
langosta	langosta	lobster
leche	lecheh	milk
mantequilla	mantekee-ya	butter
marisco	mareesko	seafood
mazamorra	masamorra	pudding made with corn starch, sugar and honey
pachamanca	pachamanka	meat barbecued between two hot stones
pallar	pa-yar	butter bean
palta	palta	avocado
pan	pan	bread
papas	papas	potatoes
pescado	peskado	fish
picante	peekanteh	spicy meat stew
pisco	peesko	eau-de-vie made from grapes
plátano	platano	banana
pollo	po-yo	chicken
postre	postreh	dessert
potaje	potaheh	soup
puerco	pwairko	pork
queque	kekeh	cake
queso	keso	cheese
refresco	refresko	drink
sal	sal	salt
salsa	salsa	sauce
sopa	sopa	soup
té	teh	tea
té de yuyos	teh deh yoo-yos	herbal tea
tuco	tooko	tomato sauce
vinagre	beenagreh	vinegar
zapallo	sapa-yo	pumpkin

TIME

minute	minuto	meenooto
hour	hora	ora
half an hour	media hora	med-ya ora
quarter of an hour	un cuarto	oon kwarto
week	semana	simana
next week	la próxima semana	la prosima simana
month	mes	mes
last month	el mes pasado	el mes pasadou
Monday	Lunes	loones
Tuesday	Martes	martes
Wednesday	Miércoles	m-yairkoles
Thursday	Jueves	hwebes
Friday	Viernes	b-yairnes
Saturday	Sábado	sabado
Sunday	Domingo	domeengo
January	Enero	enairo
February	Febrero	febrairo
March	Marzo	marso
April	Abril	abreel
May	Mayo	ma-yo
June	Junio	hoon-yo
July	Julio	hool-yo
August	Agosto	agosto
September	Setiembre	set-yembreh
October	Octubre	oktoobreh
November	Noviembre	nob-yembreh
December	Diciembre	dees-yembreh

NUMBERS

0	cero	sairo
1	uno	oono
2	dos	dos
3	tres	tres
4	cuatro	kwatro
5	cinco	seenko
6	seis	says
7	siete	s-yeteh
8	ocho	ocho
9	nueve	nwebeh
10	diez	d-yes
11	once	onseh
12	doce	doseh
13	trece	treseh
14	catorce	katorseh
15	quince	keenseh
16	dieciséis	d-yeseesays
17	diecisiete	d-yesees-yeteh
18	dieciocho	d-yes-yocho
19	diecinueve	d-yeseenwebeh
20	veinte	baynteh
30	treinta	traynta
40	cuarenta	kwarenta
50	cincuenta	seenkwenta
60	sesenta	sesenta
70	setenta	setenta
80	ochenta	ochenta
90	noventa	nobenta
100	cien	s-yen
500	quinientos	keen-yentos
1000	mil	meel
first	primero/a	preemairo/a
second	segundo/a	segoondo/a
third	tercero/a	tairsairo/a
fourth	cuarto/a	kwarto/a
fifth	quinto/a	keento/a
sixth	sexto/a	seksto/a
seventh	sétimo/a	seteemo/a
eight	octavo/a	oktabo/a
ninth	noveno/a	nobeno/a
tenth	décimo/a	deseemo/a